Creating Organizational Advanta

For Jill

Creating
Organizational
Advantage

Colin Egan

BUTTERWORTH
HEINEMANN

Butterworth-Heinemann
Linacre House, Jordan Hill, Oxford OX2 8DP
225 Wildwood Avenue, Woburn, MA 01801-2041
A division of Reed Educational and Professional Publishing Ltd

℞ A member of the Reed Elsevier plc group

OXFORD   BOSTON   JOHANNESBURG
MELBOURNE   NEW DELHI   SINGAPORE

First published 1995
Reprinted 1996, 1997, 1998

British Library Cataloguing in Publication Data
Egan, Colin
    Creating Organizational Advantage
    I. Title
    658.4012

ISBN 0 7506 1937 6

Typeset by Scribe Design, Gillingham, Kent
Printed and bound in Great Britain by
Biddles Ltd, Guildford and King's Lynn

Contents

Preface

This book emerged as a cure for my intellectual schizophrenia. After studying the sociology of organizations for three years I plunged into an intensive MBA programme where I majored in Business Policy. The contrast was stark. Moving from Burrel and Morgan's *Sociological Paradigms and Organisational Analysis* to Lipsey's *Positive Economics* is a stern test of one's academic endurance!

This formative experience is reflected in the conceptual foundations of *Creating Organizational Advantage*. The following pages draw heavily on the disciplines of industrial economics and organizational behaviour to develop the book's core theme, i.e. an examination of the artistry of strategic management in the context of organizational survival. Over the years theorists and researchers have endeavoured to maintain and reinforce the 'scientific credentials' of the strategic management discipline. In the process they have tended towards 'theoretical closure', a phenomenon described elsewhere by Michael Reed (1985) as a 'paradigmatic mentality'. The outcome of such blinkered thinking is obviously dangerous but certainly no more so than the core assumption which underpins it, i.e. that legitimacy in strategic management thought is a function of its successful imitation of 'pure' science. The comparison is flawed. As the social theorist Antony Giddens (1984) has noted, 'Both conceptually and practically, the social sciences seem distinctly inferior to the natural sciences. But if we accept that social science should no longer be some sort of replica of natural science and in some respects is a quite divergent enterprise, a very different view of their relative achievements and influence can be defended.'

In this book, then, researchers representing the view that management is science or that management is art will have their perspectives respectfully reviewed.

The ideas articulated in the following pages owe much to many people, not least the MBA students and business executives I have worked with over the past seven years. The intellectual environment at Bradford Management Centre and Warwick Business School (my previous employers) provided a stimulating context to develop ideas and, of course, to have them rigorously challenged! Particular gratitude is owed to Professor Peter McKiernan, a collaborator on previous writing projects and a continuous source of ideas and expertise. I have been extremely fortunate to have been mentored over the years by Professor David Shipley of Trinity College, Dublin. David's constant encouragement, support and enthusiasm have made many a difficult challenge much easier to handle. He will certainly recognize his own particular style in sections of this book although, as is always the case, I accept full responsibility for the material which follows.

On the administrative side, thanks are due to Jill Grinonneau for her rapid response, Just-in-Time, zero-defect typing skills, an extraordinary achievement given the manic state of my handwriting. At Butterworth-Heinemann Jonathan Glasspool has always provided encouragement and, on this project, tremendous patience.

Finally, I must express my appreciation to Jill Shepherd for an appropriate balance of critical appraisal, positive reinforcement and general endurance!

Colin Egan

The big picture

Introduction

A striking feature of modern capitalist economies is the ruthlessness with which floundering firms are allowed to expire. Fame and past glory spare none as a look in any country's corporate graveyard will reveal: in today's sink or swim business environment only the strongest survive. Even state-owned companies are being given their last rites along with their final subsidies as governments the world over are washing their hands of business, privatizing their firms and deregulating their markets with unprecedented passion and fervour. In this hectic and hostile world firms often appear to run around like headless chickens, madly seeking breakthrough business solutions but more often 'muddling through' in time-honoured fashion.

This book

This is a book about organizational survival. It is not a 'How to' book in the traditional sense although the serious-minded manager should gain many practical insights from the ideas expressed. The book integrates research streams from economics, strategic management, marketing, operations management and organizational behaviour. It takes a cross-functional and pragmatic perspective, all the while avoiding simple solutions and patronizing prescriptions.

The book is essentially written in two parts with Chapter 4 playing a pivotal role. The first three chapters provide the background to the whole series of complex issues associated with organizational success and failure. The nature of competition is examined alongside a detailed investigation of the essence of strategy and strategic management. By drawing insights from economics the role of marketing in organizational survival is evaluated with reference to how market structures are being redefined. The key driver in the latter process is identified as the globalization of the world economy and the internationalization of the firm. Two quotes demonstrate the nature and impact of this contemporary phenomenon. Firstly, the following statement by Eiji Toyoda, Chairman of the Toyota Motor Corporation (taken from a letter to the editor of the

Harvard Business Review) illustrates concisely the global context of economic activity:

> Today every national economy is an integral part of the world economy. We cannot consider the best interests of any nation as an issue separate from the economic good of the world as a whole.

Here Toyoda reflects a principle which underpins the economics of international business: free trade in goods and services between countries brings a range of benefits (over time) for all nations. While the economic arguments supporting free trade have changed little over time, the fundamental nature and dynamics of the world economy have altered beyond recognition. In this context many companies have attempted to internationalize their operations, in the process massively complicating the already difficult task of management. The catch-phrase 'Think Global – Act Local' and its many derivatives are often advanced as panaceas for managing the internationalization process although the harsh realities of the real world tend to expose its lack of substance. The second quote demonstrates this well. It is taken from an interview with Percy Barnevik, the President and Chief Executive Officer of ABB, a company widely regarded as one of the most successful global organizations (cited in Taylor, 1991):

> ABB is an organization with three internal contradictions. We want to be global and local, big and small, radically decentralized with centralized reporting and control. If we resolve those contradictions we create real organizational advantage.

Here Barnevik highlights the true substance of the internationalization task, noting its complexity but seeing within this an opportunity for creating genuine and sustainable competitive advantage. The key to success is to have a clear grasp of the dynamics of the business environment, to create effective strategies and to develop an organization which can implement its chosen strategic direction. As we shall see, the trickier task is to sustain performance over time. With this background the first three chapters explain why firms should constantly strive to secure organizational advantage in an era where market forces increasingly expose the weak corporation.

Breakthroughs and baubles

Chapter 4 presents a very critical perspective on fashions and fads in strategic management. So-called business solutions such as TQM and Business Process Re-Engineering (BPR) are put under the microscope in a rigorous search for substance. Of particular concern is to find out whether or not such solutions provide the 'breakthroughs' they claim to offer. BPR is examined in some depth, with a full account being given of what it actually is and what it claims to do. Numerous examples of BPR successes are given but it is ultimately identified as a reactive approach to business and far removed from strategic management. Its inherent weakness is similar to that exposed in most fashionable approaches to business malaise, i.e. quick-fix solutions will never solve long-term problems. In the second part of the book we move on to the behavioural aspects of organizational life which explain why change is so difficult to achieve within companies, particularly, as in the BPR case, when it is imposed without reference to organizational structure and culture.

Continuity and change

Organizational survival is a safer bet in periods of 'continuous change', i.e. where change is around but, on the whole, is predictable. In periods of 'discontinuous change', however, there is a premium on strategic direction and organizational flexibility. The transition from one type of change to another tends to expose the fallibility of even the most prestigious organizations (witness IBM's fall from grace), often to the point of bankruptcy (witness Wang's collapse). In Chapters 5 to 7 we offer a strategic perspective on managing change, a view which starts by recognizing change antecedents and develops to embrace the broad range of behavioural issues which will determine the success or failure of change programmes. Special attention is given to the important relationships which exist between organization structure and organizational culture. Through this lens an appraisal of concepts such as 'the learning organization' and 'human resource management' is presented with reference to how change programmes should be managed strategically. The emphasis is on *organization* as a more significant competitive variable than products or technological processes. As Stalk *et al.* (1992) have argued:

> Competition is now a war of movement in which success depends on anticipation of market trends and quick response to changing customer needs. Successful competitors move quickly in and out of products, markets, and sometimes even entire businesses – a process more akin to an interactive video game than to chess. In such an environment, the essence of strategy is not the structure of a company's products and markets, but the dynamics of its behaviour.

This emphasis on organizational factors in the strategic creation of competitive edge is emerging as a dominant theme in the research literature across all management disciplines. In this book an integrative and critical evaluation of contemporary issues surrounding the debate on organizational competitiveness is offered, a key aim being to distinguish fashion and fad from the more lasting contributions to the literature of recent years.

Competition and collaboration

A key theme encountered throughout the pages of this book relates to how the intensity and sophistication of competition in a context of the globalization of the world economy is forcing the strategic emphasis towards seeking organizational advantage. Despite this, a surprising corollary of more competition is more collaboration. Themes such as 'Collaborating to Compete' (Bleeke and Ernst, 1993) and 'Collaborate with your competitors – and win' (Hamel *et al.*, 1989) have proven to be seductive palliatives for executives struggling to cope on their own. Despite its reputation as a feature of contemporary business practice cooperative behaviour is not a new phenomenon. Consider the following quote from the Egyptian story-teller Aesop, writing in the 6th century BC:

> A man lying on his death bed called his three sons. To each of them he gave a single arrow and asked them to break the arrows. They did with ease. He then passed round a bundle of arrows tied together, again asking his sons to break the arrows. Not one of the sons could break the bundle of arrows. 'This is the advice I give you', said the man: 'Individually you are weak, but work together and you are strong.'

Despite the obvious attractions of collaboration, many joint ventures and strategic alliances fail. As an old Chinese proverb warns us, 'One bed, different dreams'. In this book the theory of interorganizational behaviour is outlined and, through an examination of the dependency dimension of joint ventures and strategic alliances, the reasons behind the fragility of such relationships are explored. On a positive note, evidence is presented which demonstrates that clear objectives and the bringing together of complementary assets and skills underpins strategic alliance success and can lead to sustainable competitive edge. An old Chinese idiom, *gu zhang nan ming*, suggests why this is so: a literal translation is, 'it is difficult to clap with only one hand'. More broadly, a free translation suggests that achieving anything single-handedly is difficult, a pooling of resources and efforts being more likely to lead to success.

Balanced solutions

In the final sections of the book the core themes are integrated and the role of organizations in society as we approach the year 2000 is considered. In presenting the notion of 'balanced solutions', an argument is advanced for a new contingency theory which accommodates both internal and external solutions to the problem of securing organizational survival. In the final analysis futuristic, 'megatrend' scenario analysis is avoided but it is contended that organizational life is becoming substantively different, the new realities having few historical precedents. This is a view which is consistent with the thoughts of Peter Drucker, one of the most enduring and eminently sensible management gurus (cited in Harris, 1993):

> Corporations once built to last like pyramids are now more like tents. Tomorrow they're gone or in turmoil. And this is true not only of companies in the headlines like Sears or GM or IBM. Technology is changing very

quickly, as are markets and structures. You can't design your life around a temporary organization.

In the long run, of course, nothing is temporary. But as the economist John Maynard Keynes once observed, 'In the long run we are all dead.'

How to get the most from this book

Any book is necessarily selective in the body of knowledge from which it assimilates and articulates its ideas. *Creating Organizational Advantage* is no exception. Its principal concern is to cover a broader range of subject areas than would normally be found in a single text, the intention being to provide a cross-functional, multidisciplinary perspective on the challenges of organizational life in a highly competitive business environment.

In a similar vein, any text must be highly selective in its coverage of articles or books reviewed. The problem here is interpretation, and there always lurks the danger that the author is misleading the reader about the intentions and meanings within the original source. Where there is any doubt in the reader's mind there is no substitute for seeking out the article in question and examining it in its entirety. This is one reason why a book like *Creating Organizational Advantage* is fully referenced. A more positive reason for full referencing is to allow the reader to take any particular topic of interest and follow it through to its broader domain. In this book, for example, you could follow the Jones and Hendry (1994) reference in Chapter 5 and very quickly have a detailed bibliography on the important topic of the 'Learning Organization'. Likewise, following a few references in Chapter 6 would give the reader a broad background in the conceptual and practical issues associated with joint ventures and strategic alliances. This approach of 'chasing the references' is the best way to obtain the most from any text but will be of particular benefit with *Creating Organizational Advantage*. While the following chapters are broad in scope the intention has been to develop a sharp focus on the strategic and organizational challenges faced by companies in a harsh and turbulent business environment. As we shall see, in the quest for organizational advantage there are many hurdles which must be cleared.

1
Competition and the art of strategic management

Introduction

In developing the core themes of this book we will encounter ambiguity, cynicism, positive thinking and, on occasion, despair. We shall examine simple and complex theories of strategic management and find them both wanting. Worse still, exciting tools for 'doing' strategy – business process engineering, benchmarking, TQM – will be discussed but will often be exposed as mere packaging, i.e. as constituting no more than the appellation of labels to age-old techniques for dealing with age-old problems. Indeed, it will be shown that many such tools – so-called business solutions – tend to become part of the larger management problem. As Senge (1990) has noted in a rigorous critique of the large majority of management fads, the solutions offered generally attack the symptoms of organizational sickness, not the causes, thus producing short-term benefits but inflicting longer term organizational malaise.

Throughout this book we will deal with the two most challenging phenomena facing organizations in capitalist society: competition and strategy. As in warfare the two are inextricably linked, the one driving the other in an iterative process and with wearisome persistence. The problem with understanding this dynamic is partly a function of the proliferation of books on the topic which have obscured rather than clarified the core issues. As Pettigrew and Whipp (1993) note, 'The concepts of competition and strategy have become diluted with familiarity. No positive correlation has emerged between understanding and the volume of print on these subjects'.

In the following chapters we try to make sense of this literature, cutting a swathe through the chaff to examine a number of core debates surrounding the 'subject' of marketing and strategic management. Prior to this, however, the book has to be 'placed' in the sense that any discussion of the discipline must make clear its conceptual foundations and philosophical perspective (Pettigrew and Whipp, 1993). This is best achieved by examining two key contributions to the literature which have challenged and classified theoretical approaches to the nature of strategy (Whittington, 1993) and competition (Pettigrew and Whipp, 1993). Each is considered in turn.

The strategy question: what is it, and does it matter?

In a provocatively titled book, *What is strategy – and does it matter?*, Whittington (1993) classifies four different approaches to the 'strategy question', profiling the assumptions upon which each is based and critically appraising the prescriptions they offer. The four-fold typology he proposes is shown in Figure 1.1 and each approach is now considered in more detail.

The *classical approach* is described by Whittington as the oldest and most influential of approaches to strategy. This particular perspective is heavily reliant on rational decision making and the logically-grounded structured planning techniques which dominate traditional textbooks on strategic management. The approach has three key features: (i) an attachment to rational analysis; (ii) the separation of a strategy's conception from its execution; (iii) a commitment of senior executives to profit maximization. Considered collectively, these distinguishing features can be traced to economic fundamentals (capital flows to the highest potential returns; supply and demand meet equilibrium through rational decision-making processes) and militaristic management techniques (command and control via hierarchy). The link between the concept and its management is leadership and, more specifically, the notion that strategy formation emanates from some 'heroic figure', the general or, in the business context, the CEO. This font of knowledge proposes strategic direction which, in turn, is seen to be readily implementable by disciplined and obedient front-line staff. According to Whittington (1993)

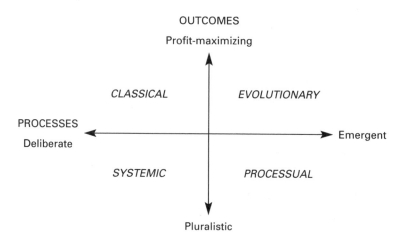

Figure 1.1 *Generic perspectives on strategy (Source: Whittington, R. (1993),* What is strategy – and does it matter? *London: Routledge)*

such iconoclastic romanticism explains the fundamental weakness of the approach but secures its popular appeal amongst practitioners: 'Flattered by the image of Olympian detachment, lured by the promise of technique-driven success, managers are seduced into the Classical fold.'

The *evolutionary approach* is a philosophy of strategy which is Darwinian in nature. It focuses on the twin propositions that the fittest will survive and that the market will be the arbiter of such natural selection. In this approach the emphasis shifts away from the executive as profit-maximizer towards the notion of 'the market' as disciplinarian. The latter is seen as being the adjudicator of strategic choice in any given competitive environment which, in its broadest sense, refers to the various markets for labour, management, capital, supplies and, where appropriate, shelf-space. The commercial organization finds itself fighting on a number of fronts and not just for customer patronage versus established and well-understood rivals. Regarding the latter market, survival depends on strategies of differentiation but this, in turn, requires deliberate choices and sustainable strategies. Evolutionary theorists doubt that this happens since organizations, as complex entities, are likely to adapt more slowly than their environments. Given the dynamism of competitive environments, strategy is a nonsense, a dangerous delusion, since the efficiency of markets will quickly erode short-term advantage gains. In this model strategizing is seen as an expensive extravagance and, since markets are unpredictable, firms should stick to basics, focus on constantly reducing transaction costs and seek to secure profit advantage through relative efficiency. Growth objectives should be driven by numerous small initiatives, giving full support to the successes while harshly culling the apparent failures. In this way firms regain some control over Darwinian forces. As Whittington notes, 'The Evolutionary advice, then, is that, in searching for the best strategy, it is best to let the environment do the selecting, not the managers.'

The *processual approach* sees both markets and organizations as fallible entities. Strategies are pragmatic outcomes which emerge incrementally from the imperfect interactions of companies and markets. This perspective poses a direct challenge to economic rationality. Its conceptual base is the behavioural theory of the firm and markets and it draws attention to the 'bounded rationality' of individuals (i.e. their cognitive limitations) and the 'political bargaining' which characterizes much decision making within organizations. Human nature constrains the ability of organizations to understand complex business environments, a problem offset to some extent by such environments being relatively tolerant of under-performance. This tolerance, in turn, allows firms to buffer the harsher realities of competition and strategic change through building organizational slack, a layer of inefficiency which is an outcome of taking satisfying rather than profit-maximizing decisions. Strategy, as such, is internally focused; it is 'crafted' incrementally from a company's core competences, emerging from 'what is' rather than the 'what should be' associated with rational analysis. Firms get by, they 'muddle through' using established heuristics to model and simplify an otherwise complex and chaotic world. Through a process of 'logical incrementalism' – trial and error, experimentation and learning – firms develop a universal 'strategic intent' which gives direction, flexibility and accommodates opportunistic behaviour. Markets are sticky, not perfect, and firms can leverage their distinctive competences to secure advantage (Whittington, 1993): 'Giving due attention to implementation, exploiting imperfect markets to build distinctive competences, cultivating flexibility for incremental adaptation – these are really the means to maximum performance.'

The *systemic approach* sees economic behaviour as embedded in networks of social relations, the means and ends of strategy closely intertwined with the cultural and political systems which provide their historical context. So, for example, Anglo-Saxon companies behave as they do – typically short-termist – as a result of a separation of ownership from control ('managerial capitalism'), liquid equity markets and a predominantly disloyal institutional investment community. The classical approach to strategy, which emerged from this context, provides a common language if nothing else. From the systemic perspective even the largest of multinational enterprises retains firm roots in its country of origin, transporting its behavioural patterns, strategic goals and strategy processes to its adopted environment. Japanese companies, for example, strive to dominate markets wherever they operate, sacrificing the short-term profits (a predominant feature of their classicist-inspired western rivals) for longer term market position.

In the systemic approach the role of the state in society has a major impact on strategic method. So, for example, the Japanese state body, MITI, has played a key role in 'advising' on strategic industries and markets, the South Korean government has nurtured the giant *chaebols* while the Taiwanese ruling class has fostered (and supported) entrepreneurial strategy. In contrast, Anglo-Saxon contexts are dominated by nineteenth-century liberalism, a free market philosophy which traces its roots firmly to the founding father of capitalism, Adam Smith. So, for example, when state-owned French utility companies took equity stakes in the recently privatized and deregulated UK water companies, the immediate reaction from market-minded Conservative politicians was that this represented 'nationalization by the back door'.

The systemic approach accommodates strategic thinking in the sense that it acknowledges that firms can (and do) plan for and achieve successful performance in complex environments. The point of departure from other perspectives is contextual. As Whittington (1993) notes, systemic approaches 'emphasize how strategic goals and processes reflect the social systems in which strategy is being made. Variations in market, class, state and cultural systems make a difference to corporate strategy'.

The important point to draw from the preceding discussion is that strategy is not a uni-dimensional construct. It has different connotations and characteristics depending on different points of view and disparate interpretations of points of fact. The power of Whittington's classification is that each approach appears plausible and, indeed, manageable. Despite this, and in many ways, the four different approaches are mutually exclusive when one examines their core conceptual foundations. While acknowledging the scope for movement and crossover on the dimensions presented in Figure 1.1, Whittington, a systemic theorist, argues that dominant theories have evolved over time as the geopolitical context has revealed its dynamic. In this sense, the key period for classical approaches to strategic management was the 1960s, for processual approaches the 1970s and for evolutionary approaches the 1980s. In the light of recent world events, however, Whittington makes clear his view of the dominant approach for the contemporary era:

> The Anglo-Saxon model is no longer the archetype, but just one of many variants in an increasingly complex competitive world. Competitive strategy in this complex environment will demand a systemic sensitivity to the diversity of economic practices.

Making sense of strategy

In this book we acknowledge the systemic approach. Indeed, its acceptance of geopolitical context is entirely consistent with a recurrent theme developed throughout the book, i.e. that the globalization of markets and the internationalization of the firm provide the fundamental dynamic of contemporary capitalism. We acknowledge the industrial economics which underpins both the evolutionary and the classical approaches to strategic management, arguing that, for the immediate future, national oligopolistic and monopolistic market structures are being shattered by the globalization phenomenon. Markets are being redefined; *ergo*, traditional, parochial measurements of market structure are themselves imperfect. We argue that strategic management is possible. Market dynamics, by definition, can be modelled, both quantitatively and qualitatively, and educated executives can take effective and efficient decisions given an appropriate organizational context. Finally, we accept organizational facts of life, i.e. that inertias, resource constraints and political processes combine to impede rational strategic analysis, strategy choice and implementation. The approach we take is Darwinian in the sense that it argues that turbulent, competitive environments – increasingly global in nature – have a deterministic impact on what firms must do if they are to survive in any independent sense. It departs from traditional Darwinism in timescale – firms can, and do, adapt to dynamic environments quicker than their genetically determined molecular counterparts. The key is competitiveness but, like strategy, the concept of competition is itself the subject of debate regarding its nature and impact. As Pettigrew and Whipp (1993) note, 'If the family of students of competition have a religion then it is surely housed in a broad church.' In the next section we move on from our broad discussion of strategy to address the central issues surrounding the competitiveness debate.

Understanding the nature of competition

Pettigrew and Whipp (1993) have identified five broad schools of thought relating to the nature and impact of competition. The first is founded on classical microeconomic theory. Its basic principles rest on a series of assumptions regarding market structure, factor (resource) conditions, information flows and rational, optimizing behaviour by all parties to all transactions. Although microeconomics accommodates some dynamism it is essentially concerned with the tendency in all markets towards equilibrium states of rest. Three dominant perspectives have emerged in this tradition. Firstly, the Chamberlinian view focuses on the ability of firms to create some uniqueness in their products and/or technologies. It is based on early theories of intermediate market structures which challenged the basic assumptions of perfect competition. In particular, this view argues that firms can use product differentiation to create a small degree of market power, thus contributing to a market structure characterised by monopolistic competition. Much of the marketing discipline rests on this principle, one notable example being the nature and role of branding activities in creating competitive edge (e.g. Egan and Guilding, 1994). Second in the microeconomic school is the Industrial Organization (IO) approach. This accepts the Chamberlinian perspective as context but sees industrial structure – the relationship between firm and industry – as a major determinant of profitability. Executives building their SWOT (strengths, weaknesses, opportunities, threats) charts are working within this framework in the sense that they are profiling their relative industrial position against market opportunity and challenges. One of the most influential developments of the IO perspective is Porter's (1980) concept of extended rivalry, the famous 'Five Forces' model. Porter saw a firm's success or failure as a function of industry rivalry but he also examined the pressures on industry profitability which came from new entrants to the market, technological substitutes, concentration (and power) among either or both of the supply base and customer targets. Porter integrates the IO model with the Chamberlinian perspective by classifying industries with reference to the development status of market structures, the principal types he identified being fragmented markets, emerging markets, mature markets, declining markets and global markets. A corollary of this analysis is that some industrial sectors are inherently more seductive than others in absolute terms, the defining characteristics of attractiveness being the dynamics of the competitive environment. Third in the microeconomic school is the Schumpeterian perspective, a model which departs from the previous two in characterizing competitive dynamics as unstable and uncertain, not stable and predictable. Schumpeter examined the role of innovations in economic development, focusing specifically on revolutionary technological and product market changes. His work was principally concerned with growth economics and the role of the entrepreneur in influencing economic cycles (Roll, 1992). Schumpeter's perspective corresponds most closely to Porter's emerging market model but suggests much greater levels of uncertainty and introduces the economically 'unsound' notion of luck.

The second school of thought identified by Pettigrew and Whipp (1993) is labelled 'The New Competition'. It highlights the fundamental failure of the microeconomic perspective to address international dimensions of competitiveness and it challenges the assumptions regarding the inevitability of maturity and decline which are a major feature of the IO models. Drawing attention to emerging Asian competitiveness in the world economy, researchers in this school revitalized the role of innovation and expanded it from a technology focus to embrace innovativeness in product, process and management systems. Indeed, management weaknesses were put forward as a major explanation of declining US competitiveness, particularly the short-termism and risk averseness engendered by an over-reliance on portfolio management concepts and financial controls which, taken together, created a 'cult of quantification'. The New Competition school saw a qualitatively different form of competition, particularly in the manufacturing and engineering sectors which they had investigated. Despite their narrow empirical base and, according to Pettigrew and Whipp, their over-emphasis on and uncritical approach to technological aspects of innovation, the New Competition writers have made a valuable contribution to the competitiveness debate, not least for the possibilities they bestow on the more qualitative dimensions of strategic management.

The third school of thought identified by Pettigrew and Whip is the perspective embraced by 'Institutional Economists'. Emanating from the mainstream of traditional economics, the 'institutionalists' nevertheless rebut its static analytical stance and its assumption of rational economic action. The institutionalists see competition as a continuous process, economic behaviour being shaped by experience and learning but constrained by, *inter alia*, legal frameworks, management-employee relations and government actions.

The fourth school of thought identified is embodied in 'The Economic Retardation Debate', a perspective which attempts to explain relative declines in national competitiveness. Explanations of the UK's relatively poor economic performance, for example, include reference to cultural factors, government macroeconomic policy, an inability to commercialize inventions, poor industrial relations, the high level and nature of state involvement in the economy and weak domestic demand. From a strategic management perspective this view of competitiveness has limited value. While it does provide a sound contextual framework it offers little explanation of how *individual* firms have prospered or struggled and therefore how strategic change processes have been affected by competition.

The fifth school of thought on competition is captured in the 'Excellence and Turnaround' literature. This school looks closely at organizational competitiveness and, as its label suggests, seeks to learn lessons from companies who excel or who have trawled the depths of economic performance, in the latter case stimulating a crisis and radical response. Pettigrew and Whipp (1993) argue that the distinguishing feature of this genre is the tendency of its output to be highly prescriptive. The excellence literature is discussed more fully in this book in the following chapter. From a competitiveness perspective, however, it tends to focus too much on the firm and managerial solutions rather than developing a systematic evaluation of the competitive environment and its dynamics. The fashionable status of the excellence literature has attracted many spurious texts which feed off, but contribute little to, the established academic debate on the true foundations of corporate success. As Pettigrew and Whipp (1993) note, 'The urge to prescribe sometimes seems to have overcome the need to show how the data were collected ... the impression is often left that successful management can be encapsulated in neat laundry lists.'

The strengths and weaknesses of established theory

Economics provides a common thread to these five schools of thought identified by Pettigrew and Whipp and there is explicit or implicit reference to organizational survival being a function of competitive forces. In particular, it is made clear that where companies are to some extent shielded from competition this is due to the market and/or industry entry barriers they have erected or the protection they are afforded by national boundaries and/or government interventions. Each approach offers valuable insights on the nature of competition but, separately, they only paint a partial picture. There are four key weaknesses within traditional explanations of competitiveness which must be addressed, each of which is elaborated in the following sections.

1   Conceptual weaknesses in the nature of the relationship between the firm and its environment, specifically, the patterns of interaction between competitive dynamics and organizational dynamics. Stacey (1993), for example, has argued that the vast bulk of the strategic management literature has produced only static frameworks and models, creating a dominant management paradigm which is based on simplistic assumptions about organizational dynamics. A key question relating to this is the nature of and extent to which organizations can systematically address competitive environments, and whether this process is a scientific or creative process. This conceptual gap is addressed in the next section and serves as a preface to the core themes explored throughout the book.
2   Established models of competition are essentially parochial in nature, particularly in their definitions of market structure as a national phenomenon. Within economics, international trade is typically treated as a macroeconomic construct, i.e. as falling within the remit of governments, not firms. Furthermore, as mentioned above, competition is typically modelled as a quantitative construct, thus precluding more qualitative and contextual interpretations of its nature and impact. A significant contribution to resolving this conceptual weakness is Porter's research into the competitive advantage of nations. Porter (1990) draws heavily on traditional economic explanations of trade and competition but considerably expands the horizons of his early work to propose an integrated and systematic perspective on international competitiveness. In doing so he fills many of the gaps emanating from the partial explanations offered by the five schools of thought profiled above. A more detailed analysis of Porter's framework is given in a later section of this chapter.

3   Traditional models of competition tend to take a 'one-world' view of capitalism, thus lending themselves to an accusation of self reference. While this critique is essentially robust, there does seem to be a convergence of political and economic systems within the global economy, a trend accentuated by the collapse of the Soviet Union and accelerated by the formation of the World Trade Organization, an institutional framework created to implement and police free trade between member nations. The 'end of history' debate which has emerged from such observations is discussed in more depth below.

4   A remarkable omission from the strategic management literature is a structured discussion of the customer role in the economic process. Bland assertions regarding their rational (or irrational) behaviour, coupled with a tendency to see customers as an aggregate phenomenon (for example, a 'market' or a demand curve) do little to consider the impact that consumer preference can and does have on company profitability. This issue will be addressed in the final sections of this chapter and will set the scene for a more detailed discussion of one of the most powerful paradigms of modern capitalist business: the marketing concept.

An integrated and dynamic perspective on competition and the firm

A consistent and significant finding of research undertaken within the Centre for Corporate Strategy and Change at the University of Warwick is that strategic management and competitive analysis are closely intertwined in the practice of management, despite the fact they are often treated as disparate units of analysis in management theory. Commenting on the realities of perpetual environment change, Pettigrew and Whipp (1993) point to the overwhelming evidence that, 'Competition and strategic change must be seen together as a compound process.' They argue that managers constantly encounter and shape the practical situation where knowledge, decisions and actions are inextricably interconnected. Furthermore, empirical evidence demonstrates that strategic thinking, strategic choice and strategy outcomes coexist and are readily observable at any point in time. Successful management of this complex, compound process delivers the ultimate strategic asset, i.e. the ability to handle the twin demands of continuity and change.

In addition to linking competition and strategic change the Warwick research has offset another conceptual weakness of the traditional approaches to competition. From this new perspective, competitive decisions and strategic processes are modelled at multiple levels across time, i.e. they are seen to advance within firm, industrial sector and national contexts. At the firm level competitive dynamics are driven by, *inter alia*, strategic choice, capabilities for change and selection of appropriate bases of competition. Regarding the latter, competitive strength will typically be a function of multiple layers of competence which will embrace internal factors such as distribution channels, supplier relationships and so on. At the sector level competitive dynamics are driven by, *inter alia,* commercial networks, industry life-cycle stage (e.g. growth, maturity, decline) and market structure. At the national level competitive dynamics are shaped by economic factors such as exchange rates and inflation levels, the relationship between finance and industry and the average industrial cost structure achieved within the boundaries of the nation state. The latter is principally a function of combinations of factor inputs (land, labour, capital, technology) which arise either by endowment or transfer.

This multilevel dynamic view of competition and strategic change is enhanced further by a recognition that these processes are 'structured by a trinity of forces' which embrace objective decision making, subjective learning and the political dimensions of organizational life. In modelling strategic change and competition in three dimensions, then, Pettigrew and Whipp (1993) have captured the process and dynamics of strategic management in a holistic fashion:

> In short, strategic change should be regarded as a continuous process which occurs in given contexts. We find it impossible to comprehend such changes as separate episodes divorced from the historical, organizational and economic circumstances from which they emerge.

The three-dimensional model proposed by Pettigrew and Whipp is shown in Figure 1.2. When combined with the dynamic and multilevel approach taken (firm, sector, national context) this model provides a unique perspective on competition and strategic change, offsetting many of the conceptual gaps referred to earlier. An empirical test of the model has identified that two qualities characterize the ability of firms to compete effectively in their business environment:

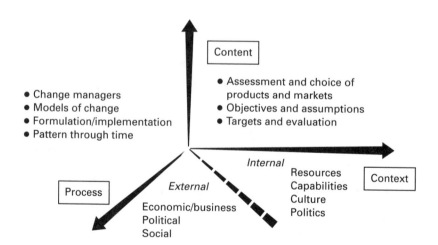

Figure 1.2   *Dimensions of strategic change (Source: Pettigrew, A. and Whipp, R. (1993),* Managing Change for Competitive Success, *Oxford: Blackwell)*

1   The capacity of the firm to identify and understand the competitive forces in play and how they change over time, linked to
2   The competence of a business to mobilize and manage the resources necessary for the chosen competitive response through time.

A more detailed discussion of the implications of these findings is given in Chapter 7 when we draw together the core themes of the book. In the next section we expand our horizons and consider the nature of competitiveness from a perspective which embraces an international dimension.

The competitive advantage of nations

Contemporary thinking on national competitiveness puts great stress on factor costs (especially labour), economies of scale, economies of scope and the impact of fluctuating interest and exchange rates. At the level of government, efforts have been made to manage exchange rates, relax anti-trust regulations and shelter particular national companies through protectionism and subsidy. At the corporate level, perceived gaps in international competitiveness have been 'filled' by an emphasis on cooperation through joint ventures and strategic alliances (a trend discussed in detail in Chapter 6).

In a strong critique of the explanatory power of the above Porter (1990) has argued that they are fundamentally flawed, noting that they do not address the real challenge of seeking out, securing and, of particular concern, rejuvenating a nation's true competitive advantage: 'Pursuing them, with all their short term appeal, will virtually guarantee that the United States – or any other advanced nation – never achieves real and substantial competitive advantage.'

Porter claims that such 'market distortions' support wide inter-nation cost/price differentials on similar goods (e.g. automobiles and telecommunications services) and create broad supply-side inefficiencies. He argues for a new paradigm of competitiveness, one which emanates from an analysis of internationally successful industries in a research process without regard for conventional wisdom. His is a normative approach of observing what works, why it works and understanding how it can be applied.

Porter embarked on a four-year study and examined ten major trading nations in detail: Denmark; Germany; Italy; Japan; Korea; Singapore; Sweden; Switzerland; United Kingdom; United States. Together these countries accounted for over 50 per cent of total world exports in 1985. The focus of the research was on documenting the process of gaining and sustaining competitive advantage in relatively sophisticated industries and industry segments; the key measure of competitiveness of a nation was taken to be high and rising productivity within such sectors. The nations selected for investigation gave a broad cross-sectional profile. Alongside the major industrial nations of the USA, Japan and Germany were other nations chosen to vary widely in size, government policy toward industry, social philosophy, geography and region.

The scope of Porter's research is one of its greatest strengths. There are many studies which focus on a single nation or provide comparative analyses of just two or three nations (often benchmarking Japan as a point of reference). Although such studies are useful they are limited in breadth and are often misleading. For example, bilateral comparisons of the UK or USA with Japan will frequently point to Japanese cooperative research projects as a key expanation of contrasting success rates. Calls for their repetition would be flawed. Nations have individual contexts and inherent asset clusters. Countries like Germany and Switzerland, for example, sustain competitive advantages in many industries without cooperative projects but they continue to excel by virtue of other intrinsic strengths. Moreover, when a third or fourth nation is brought into the sample for comparison or control purposes the results tend to lack consistency and attempts to generalize across nations begin to fall down.

Porter was assisted by over thirty researchers, most of whom were native to the countries under study. In each country support was received from national institutions; for example MITI (Japan) and Deutsche Bank (Germany) provided infrastructure, access and local help. A common methodology consisting of two broad parts was applied in each nation:

(i) *Mapping successful industries in national economies* This process involved collating data on those industries or segments (from both manufacturing and service sectors) in which the nation was represented by demonstrably successful international companies. International success was defined as being when an industry possessed a competitive advantage relative to the best worldwide competitors and was measured by: (a) the presence of substantial and sustained exports to a wide array of nations; and/or (b) significant outbound foreign investment based on skills and assets created in the home country. It is important to note that these measures incorporate competitive dimensions of foreign trade and investment, thus allowing Porter to claim that the resultant theory is holistic, combining explanations of trade, investment and innovation. The study created a profile of all the industries in which each nation was internationally successful at three points in time: 1971, 1978 and 1985. The pattern of successful industries in each nation was then mapped utilizing a 'cluster chart', with particular emphasis being placed on the interconnectedness between the industries and how this changed and was shaped over time.

(ii) *Profiling the histories of the successful industries* It is common practice among strategy researchers (e.g. Pettigrew 1985, 1990) to adopt a processual approach to their work. To understand an organization and its culture it is crucial to have a grasp of its history – i.e. to document *how* it got to where it is. Porter utilized this approach to understand the dynamic processes of industries at the national level. More than a hundred key industries in the ten nations he studied were subjected to a thorough appraisal over time. Industries were chosen to represent the most important groupings within the nation. The period covered by the research varied with each industry; for example, centuries for German cutlery and Italian fabrics but only decades for US software and Japanese robotics. The historical process was studied to identify the changing nature of competitive advantage in each sector, i.e. how it was gained, sustained or lost. By taking a global perspective it was possible to identify the most significant competitors in the industry from different nations and to identify their distinct advantages over time. In addition, the broad scope of the sector studies allowed the researchers to identify how nations had lost previously powerful positions in some sectors and to offer explanations as to how nations had failed to gain positions in others. There is little doubt, then, that this methodology is one of the most comprehensive yet employed in the field of international business and one of the few which proffers strategic management insights in the context of macroeconomic issues and trends. In the next section we profile the model which emerged from the research.

Determinants of national competitive advantage

The fundamental question raised by Porter was why a specific nation achieved international success in a particular industry. In seeking a comprehensive explanation he proposed a 'diamond system' of four attributes which shape the national context in helping to promote or impede the creation of competitive advantage. The system is shown in Figure 1.3.

The diamond represents a mutually reinforcing system of individual components. Each factor is essential for real competitive advantage yet, without the 'glue' provided by the interactive system, strength in individual constituents will not guarantee success. In this schema, the effect of one determinant is contingent on the state of the others.

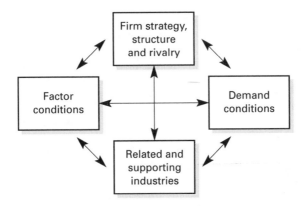

Figure 1.3 *Determinants of international competitive advantage (Source: Porter, M. (1990),* The Competitive Advantage of Nations, *London: Macmillan)*

Favourable demand conditions will not lead to advantages unless the state of rivalry is sufficient to trigger a corporate response to them. Similarly, while reliance on one or two determinants may be sufficient in a natural-resource-dependent industry which has low technology levels it is clearly not a *sustainable* advantage. It is the complex interplay of the whole system which provides the unique context for international competitive advantage and which is extremely difficult for other nations to copy. Once in place the system tends to be self-reinforcing.

The 'diamond system' is influenced by two additional factors: chance and government. Chance events create discontinuities which significantly and radically change industry structure. Examples include wars, technological breakthroughs and changes in political regimes. Government can create and foster or impede the development of an appropriate dynamic within the diamond system. Overt interference, protectionism, shelter strategies, slack anti-trust regimes and the 'narcotic' of subsidies impede a nation's industries from developing real and sustainable advantages. Conversely, careful stimulus through the four attributes of the diamond can inject dynamism and innovation within the system. For example, investments in training and education fundamentally and lastingly affect factor conditions although the positive results are only visible in the medium or long term. The role of government and the nature and intensity of the impact of its intervention provide a powerful context for effective operation of the diamond system. The significance of government should not be underestimated. As Porter (1990) comments, 'Policies implemented without consideration of the entire system of determinants are as likely to undermine national advantage as enhance it.'

A look at the four attributes of the diamond will facilitate a closer analysis of Porter's new paradigm.

1 Factor conditions

This component refers to the mix of factors of production which are necessary to compete in a specific industry. These include human, physical, knowledge and capital resources together with the delivery infrastructure of transportation, communications, mail, financial services, health care and so on. According to classical international trade theory such factor conditions are the key (and sole) determinants of trade flows. In modern times this eighteenth-century doctrine is, according to Porter, 'at best incomplete and at worst incorrect'. It remains the case that nations inherit resources and that this initial endowment plays a role in their ability to trade. The rapid growth of manufacturing in low-wage economies such as Hong Kong, Taiwan and, more recently, Thailand confirms this basic proposition. But factors play a more complex role than classical theory has traditionally acknowledged. The initial endowment is a low-level gift, despite its abundance and fertility. It is the higher level, advanced and specialist factors which nations create and develop that give true and sustainable competitive advantage. So, while a nation *inherits* its natural resources and climate it *develops* higher level

educational skills and it *acquires* technologies in laser physics or semicon-
ductors. Significantly, these are created by individuals, organizations or
institutions in a dynamic system of continuous upgrading through
innovation. There should be no standing still with regard to the initial
factor endowments a country inherits – a criticism that Porter, in a
separate study, levelled at the Canadian economy in 1991. He claimed
that Canada's focus on primary industrial sectors and its relative failure
to move down the value-added chain in industry or commerce had
fundamentally weakened its international competitive position.

The stock of factors in a nation at any time is not as important as the
rate at which they are created and upgraded. Furthermore, rising world
standards make it essential that nations continually reinvest and enhance
their core factor advantages. Despite this, factor disadvantage need not
necessarily be an impediment to competitiveness since, where there is a
threat, there is often an opportunity. For instance, Japan is an island
nation and its limited natural resources has encouraged it to make
competitive innovations in product and process technology. Such
circumvention of factor disadvantages can lead individual sectors to
greater and more sustainable competitive advantage and can accelerate
faster upgrading of international competitiveness (although favourable
conditions must be present elsewhere in the 'diamond system' to facilitate the progress of the advantage formation).

2 Demand conditions

This component relates to the nature of home demand for industry
output. Porter claims that this element may be the most powerful single
influence since it shapes the character and the rate of improvement and
innovation of a nation's firms. Three broad attributes of home demand
are important: (a) its composition; (b) the size and pattern of its growth;
(c) the mechanisms by which domestic preferences are transmitted to
foreign markets. The significance of the latter two is contingent upon the
first. It is the *quality* of home demand – not its quantity – that determines
competitive advantage. Nations gain advantage where the composition
of home demand is so sensitive, strong, discerning and critical that the
resultant competitive dynamism continuously challenges the way in
which supplying companies think regarding quality, range of options
offered, rate of innovations and general but continuous improvements.
This, in turn, requires access to buyers, open communication, the
presence of top technical and managerial staff in the home market and
a closeness to buyers' circumstances. It is easier to tackle less discerning
foreign customers after providing successfully for the choosy local buyer.
Three elements of demand composition are important:

1   *The number and size of segments*   These enable local firms to gain
    knowledge, skills and superior positions against intense local
    competitors and thus facilitate their transfer to foreign markets.
2   *The sophistication and discerning nature of buyers*   These pressurize
    local firms to meet high standards in terms of product quality,

features and service support. For example, America's vast road network meant that truck buyers placed exceptional value on reliability and performance, thus forcing Cummings, Caterpillar and Detroit Diesel into strong internationally competitive positions. Japanese consumers in small tightly packed homes must contend with hot humid summers and high electricity costs. In response, Japanese companies have pioneered compact, quiet air-conditioning units powered by energy saving rotary compressors. National passions and cultural phenomena give a good clue as to where buyers are sophisticated, often with regard to quite specific product categories; for example, the British love their gardening and so British firms are world class in garden tools; Italians love fashion, food and fast cars – areas in which Italian firms excel.

3   *Anticipatory buyer needs*   Firms can gain advantages if the needs of home buyers act as a barometer for world consumer trends. For instance, Sweden's political and social values have given it an advantage in the caring trades (e.g. handicapped people). The American desire for convenience has underpinned the international success of its companies in fast food (e.g. McDonald's) and credit cards (e.g. American Express, Visa, Diners Club, Mastercard).

Considering demand size and patterns of growth, there has long been debate as to whether or not the size of home demand is a significant variable in a nation's competitiveness. The limited domestic markets of Switzerland, Sweden and, to a lesser extent, Korea have hardly inhibited the international success of some of their leading companies. The most important gains of size are in industries with economies of scale, heavy research and development requirements, large step leaps in technology and high levels of uncertainty. In such industries, investment decisions are underwritten by large domestic markets. Perhaps more important than the absolute size of the market is the number of discriminating independent buyers within it and, more generally, the rate of growth of home demand. Both stimulate market entry and external investment which trigger competition, change and innovation, i.e. they add the dynamic components to demand. Global success is also driven by an early, anticipatory home demand that allows local firms to gain advantage on foreign rivals and an early home market saturation that forces them to innovate and internationalize their operations.

While the composition of home demand is at the root of national advantage, its size and pattern of growth can increase that advantage through its differential impact on investment behaviour, timing and motivation. A third factor, the internationalization of domestic demand, can effectively 'pull' a nation's products or services into foreign markets. It has two distinct components: (a) the pressure of mobile or multinational local buyers (giving an early opportunity for internationalization); (b) influence on foreign needs, where national trading of foreigners, for example airline pilots, introduces them to a nation's products/services and, naturally, they may insist on this on their return home. As an extension, ex-colonial powers such as Britain and France can influence such transfers by the provision of foreign aid to former colonies.

3 Related and supporting industries

The supporting presence of internationally competitive suppliers or related industries is the third broad determinant of national advantage in Porter's diamond system. It is usual for nations who succeed in an industry to also be successful in its supplier industries. For example, Denmark has an edge in dairy products and brewing but is also successful in industrial enzymes; Japan is strong in cameras and is also successful in photocopiers; the UK is strong in engines and is also successful in lubricants and anti-knock preparations.

The presence of internationally competitive suppliers creates rapid downstream advantages through giving access to cost-effective inputs and quality of service. Moreover, perhaps the most important advantage lies in close working relationships between world-class suppliers and their customers. An inherent feature of such value chain linkages is the transfer of innovative new methods and technologies in a two-way process which has synergistic benefits for both parties. The joint problem solving they undertake leads to faster, more efficient solutions, thus speeding up the general rate of innovation. If local suppliers are international, their competitive edge will be so much sharper. This should inspire them to upgrade consistently, to predict demand pattern shifts, to latch on fast to new technologies and, consequently, to inspire domestic producers to act similarly. Furthermore, the presence of international competitors in the value chain means that they can share intelligence, technology development, manufacturing or marketing services. This duality is fired by the motive that international success in one industry can act to 'pull' through demand for a nation's complementary products and services, a strong example being US computer peripherals and software. Once again, any benefits from duality clearly hinge upon the presence of other advantages in the 'diamond system': without active domestic demand or advanced or specialist factor inputs, the presence and/or effectiveness of duality will be limited.

4 Firm strategy, structure and rivalry

The context in which firms are created alongside the way in which they are organized, are managed and the intensity with which they compete forms the final part of the diamond system. In this component the emphasis is on matching observations of strategy and goals to the individual national context. Competitiveness results from a confluence of management practice and organizational modes which are favoured in particular national business cultures. For example, Italian companies are world leaders in lighting, furniture, footwear and woollen fabrics. Their companies are family-owned, small and medium size enterprises (SMEs) which have an emphasis on focused strategies and niche marketing. They are able to undertake rapid change and they demonstrate a 'breathtaking' flexibility which fits both the dynamism of the industry and the character of the Italian management system. German success is much rarer in such consumer goods – the character doesn't fit. Their hierarchical management systems work well in technical or engineering orientated industries such as optics, chemicals and complex precision machinery where a strong discipline is needed in technical development and after-sales service.

An integral part of strategy is a firm's goals, a measure of their commitment to achieving them and their 'fit' with a national context. These goals generally reflect corporate governance factors such as the structure of national capital markets and management compensation packages. Where banks are typically shareholders (e.g. Germany, Switzerland, Sweden and Japan) there tends to be relatively little share trading, thus laying a solid platform for long-term ventures. In this context companies succeed in mature industries where ongoing investments are needed in research and development but where immediate returns are moderate. So called 'short-termism', the hallmark of the US and UK economies which have highly liquid equity markets, tend to induce shorter investment horizons. Despite this, indigenous companies may do well in relatively new industries such as software and biotechnology. Countries in which shareholders and employees are strongly committed to their companies and industrial sectors often demonstrate strong and lasting competitive advantages. This may be a function of ploughing back significant profits into product development, quality improvement and enhanced customer service despite the risks which such investment incurs. It is interesting to note that where a nation's corporations choose unrelated diversification as a strategy option the outcomes are usually unsuccessful. This, in turn, is a statement about the commitment of corporate governance to the development, enhancement and continuous rejuvenation of the core business. The fundamental question to ask is, if the latter is the source of a company's competitive advantage, why dilute it?

A final aspect of the fourth diamond component is the strong association Porter found between vigorous domestic rivalry and the creation and sustenance of significant competitive advantages. This is in contrast to policies which aim to promote economies of scale between a few national champions. Nations with leading world positions in global industries often have strong local rivals, examples being Switzerland in pharmaceuticals, Germany in chemicals, Sweden in cars and trucks, the US in computers and software, and the UK in biscuits. Surprisingly, nowhere is this rivalry greater than in Japan, as Figure 1.4 demonstrates.

Such intense rivalry creates pressure on firms to innovate, to drive down costs, to improve quality and service and to introduce new products and processes. Sharpened by such advantages, domestic companies can take on global competitors with more confidence. In a Darwinian sense such rivalry will inevitably create casualties but the surviving companies will be fitter and thereby prosper. Furthermore, rivalry is important in continuously upgrading a sector's advantages to a higher order, thus making them become better protected by the entry

Air conditioners	13
Personal computers	16
Audio equipment	25
Semiconductors	34
Automobiles	9
Sewing machines	20
Cameras	15
Shipbuilding	33
Copiers	14
TV sets	15
Facsimile machines	10
Typewriters	14
Machine tools	112
VCRs	10

Figure 1.4   *Estimates of numbers of Japanese competitors in selected industries (1987) (Source: Porter, M. (1990),* The Competitive Advantage of Nations, *London: Macmillan)*

barriers they have created. These benefits are all reinforced by a tight geographical concentration of rivals which makes it very difficult for foreign companies to tap into this process.

The complete system

As mentioned above, both chance and government influence each of the four attributes of the 'diamond system'. The point to note, though, is that chance events are fruitless without existing national advantages elsewhere in the diamond to make rapid use of the discontinuities created. Government has a significant role to play in stimulating this national advantage by influencing each of the four attributes, for example factor conditions (policies towards education, capital markets, regions, etc.) and demand conditions (local product standards or regulations). To reiterate, government is a true influencer of the national diamond either as a stimulator or destroyer. However, as Porter consistently emphasizes, the effect of government policy should only be partial and is highly unlikely to be the sole source of a nation's advantage.

Any system is only as good as the sum of its parts and this is clearly true of the 'diamond system' introduced by Porter. Each contributing attribute must feed off and stimulate the others in a self-reinforcing manner. Moreover, advantages are not static to any attribute since they can move around the diamond as environments change. The challenge is to keep the system 'positive' since a slip into a negative spiral will be reinforcing and difficult to stem. There are a number of key reasons why sectors lose their traditional advantages and thus initiate a downward spiral of decline: (a) local needs are no longer a good predictor of global demand, thus throwing national firms off the international trail; (b) domestic buyers become less demanding than foreign customers; (c) basic factor conditions deteriorate, thus causing relative increases in factor costs; (d) technological change leapfrogs any endowed factor advantages, in the process causing supply industries to become uncom-

---

The slide of Britain
- Weaknesses in human resources
  - poor education system
  - poor investment in training
  - loss of key people
- Lack of domestic rivalry
- Ineffective R&D
  - high public sector percentage in defence
  - relatively low private sector R&D
- Firms target less-sophisticated customers
- Competition on price
- Poor infrastructure (road, rail, ports)
- Dominance of institutional investors
- Widespread state ownership
- Poor labour relations

(a)

The rise of Japan
- Intense domestic competitive pressure
- Obsessive collection and use of information
- Sophisticated domestic market
- Early adoption of flexible manufacturing
- Drive for market share
- Push-driven international outlook
- Knowledge creation through company training
- High, non-defence R&D expenditure
- Unique ability for functional coordination
- Extreme emphasis on product quality
- Pursue internal, related diversification

(b)

Figure 1.5 *International competitiveness: (a) the UK, (b) Japan (Source: Porter, M. (1990),* The Competitive Advantage of Nations, *London: Macmillan)*

petitive; (e) short-term goals limit long-run investment; (f) domestic rivalry becomes soft and placid, arguably one of the most fatal and common causes of lost cost advantage. Though the effects of this latter condition may be initially invisible, the negative spiral it initiates can spread rapidly through the entire 'diamond system' as innovation slows and complacency dominates.

Such events can have a knock-on effect in clusters of industries: if one or two firms go (perhaps leading suppliers) the remainder can quickly deteriorate, a good example being the Swedish and British shipbuilding sectors. There can be no substitute for personal study of Porter's book to understand fully its contribution to explaining a system as complex as the global economy. Figures 1.5 (a) and (b) present a summary of

Porter's application of the diamond thesis to understanding the relative fortunes of the UK and Japan in the post-war era. The comprehensiveness of his coverage is readily apparent.

In the next section we examine the effectiveness of the 'diamond system' in describing national competitive advantage and disadvantage. We also consider the timeliness of Porter's contribution given the lack of consistency and coherence in the strategic management literature when confronted by such a fundamental phenomenon as the internationalization of the world economy.

Evaluating Porter's model of international competitiveness

There is little doubt that Porter's new paradigm is timely, well researched and well founded. It provides a powerful portrayal of competitive advantage in key industrial sectors of nations and it grows, quite naturally, out of his early work on corporate strategy (1980) and competitive advantage (1985). Indeed, there are a number of core themes which are shared with his previous publications, not least the role of government as a sixth force in both the diamond and the five-force industry analysis, the role of powerful buyers and suppliers in a supply chain context, the role of economies of scale and scope in raising entry barriers, the impact of intensity of industry rivalry, the influence of firm strategy and structures and so on. The language is common and this raises a significant question: is the new paradigm a vertical extension into a theory of international trade and investment, as Porter claims, or merely a lateral – and convenient – explanation of sector competitive advantage applied to nations in the hope that it will stick? There are a number of alleged criticisms:

1   It is an explanatory framework rather than a deterministic theory. Sam Britton of the *Financial Times* (1990) likened it to Arnold Toynbee's doctrine of challenge and response – its meaning emerges from what it contradicts.
2   The book's theme (and title) is flawed in two regards. Firstly, it deals primarily with the competitive advantage of firms and sectors and only, by dubious extension, that of nations. The links from the former to the latter are not always clearly made. Secondly, 'competitiveness' can be applied to firms and sectors but is limited in its extension to nations. It suggests that international economic activity is a zero-sum game in which one country only gains what another loses.
3   The measurement of a competitive nation based solely on productivity is questionable. There are alternative and competing measures that would provide a different league table from the one which Porter offers. For example, economists use a concept of 'rent per unit output' where rent equates to value added less wage and capital

costs (almost like gross profits). Though Porter found the UK to be a laggard during the 1970s and 1980s based on productivity measures, Haskel and Kay (1990) found it to be a star on rent measures, rising a full 12 percentage points in efficiency between 1979 and 1986.

4 Purist methodologists may question the process by which Porter's 'diamond system' evolved. Traditional method would develop theory and confront it with data. Porter seems to have used observation from data to develop the theory which is then tested on the same data.

5 In his attack on classical theory, Porter may have missed the key point, i.e. that a country can trade advantageously even if it is more efficient (or even less efficient) than its partners in every product.

6 In a world of regional trading blocs (ASEAN, EU, NAFTA), the role of the individual nation may be less pronounced as national factor and demand conditions move towards equality across nations in the blocs.

7 Much of the observation on local competitive rivalry is time dependent. True, there are many rivals in specific Japanese sectors as Figure 1.4 demonstrated. But sectors can evolve in dynamic patterns over life-cycles that involve considerable 'shake-outs'. Future tables may show less rivalry as more markets mature and overcapacity is shed. The principle of rivalry and the effect of its intensity is not questioned; where it may emerge from in the future is the more pertinent question.

8 Some criticism has focused on the diamond's inability to explain all national economic wealth, a key example being the impact of unique but rich factor endowments such as oil and natural gas.

9 Though Porter stresses the importance of the system as a whole, there are overlapping categories within it. The function of his thesis is broad-based yet the individual impact of each factor on the other and each on national competitive performance could benefit from greater explanation.

Porter has offered a mammoth 855-page volume as a new paradigm to explain world trade, investment and innovation. Many of the criticisms alluded to above are misplaced or locked within the closed paradigms of their proponents. Others simply require further elaboration, a natural feature of scientific enquiry. Two key factors emerge from a close reading of Porter's research. Firstly, there appears to be a convergence of economic systems around the classical microeconomic models first proposed by Adam Smith and David Ricardo, particularly with regard to the structure of markets and the Darwinian impact of competitive forces. Secondly, the advent of sophisticated consumers as a key force in the economic process appears to be emerging as a profound driver of international competitiveness. In the following sections these two themes are considered as features of modern capitalism in a fashion which considers their historical antecedents and contemporary consequences.

The internationalization of the world economy

The following quote taken from a letter to the Editor of the *Harvard Business Review* (published in the July–August edition, 1991) is illustrative of the global context of economic activity:

> Today every national economy is an integral part of the world economy. We cannot consider the best interests of any nation as an issue separate from the economic good of the world as a whole.

This statement by Eiji Toyoda, Chairman of the Toyota Motor Corporation, reflects a principle which underpins the economics of international business: free trade in goods and services between countries brings a range of benefits (over time) for all nations. Conversely, a climate which fosters protectionism and raises barriers to trade damages world economic growth. It is widely accepted, for example, that a major determinant of both the depth and length of the Great Depression of the early 1930s was the protectionist trade policies pursued by the major industrial countries throughout the period and it is generally acknowledged that the lessons learned as a consequence still underpin government policies around the world (see, for example, Galbraith, 1994).

The economic arguments supporting free trade have changed little over time but the fundamental nature and dynamics of the world economy have altered beyond recognition. A number of factors are driving what can be described as the internationalization of the world economy. By this we refer to the economic dependence which countries (or groups of countries) have on each other. Such interdependence was clearly illustrated with the equities market crash of October 1987 when stock exchanges around the world collapsed in a simultaneous sequence interrupted only by international time zones. The old cliché that 'when America sneezes the world catches a cold' was never illustrated better. Five years on, the collapse of the Japanese Nikkei index and the concern regarding its potential impact on world trade and global competition is a further demonstration of the internationalization of the world economy. Such concern is also a strong indicator of Japan's emergence as a world economic superpower, with many commentators now talking of a group of three countries – America, Germany and Japan – dominating the world economy in years to come.

It is important to note that the factors which have led to the internationalization of the world economy are not purely economic. In the next section we describe the important contextual issue of political economy and analyse the convergence of previously disparate forms of economic structure and political organization.

The end of history?

Whatever view one takes regarding the stability or otherwise of business environments one thing is certain: the world is a changed and rapidly changing place. Many people nowadays talk about a 'new world order' although what this actually is and the nature of its antecedents are intensely debated. One contemporary event, however, has acted as a milestone for the creation of a general awareness that the course of world history has taken a distinctly different direction. The destruction of the Berlin wall was both a symbolic and tangible event which signalled the end of communist-inspired industrial and social organization and marked the return of market-based economies to the former COMECON trading nations. As these momentous events were taking place an article called 'The End of History' was published by Francis Fukuyama, an unknown US State Department official, in an equally obscure American journal called the *National Interest*. The thesis presented was powerful: it suggested that a new world order had emerged and it argued that this would be the final output of a long historical process of continuity and radical change. The main arguments concern the apparent convergence of economic systems and modes of political organization around the world. The original article has subsequently been developed into a book which defends and expands the thesis and accommodates developments (such as the collapse of the former USSR) since its original publication. The following quote captures the essence of the thesis (Fukuyama, 1992):

> If we are now at a point where we cannot imagine a world substantially different from our own, in which there is no apparent or obvious way in which the future will represent a fundamental improvement over our current order, then we must also take into consideration that history itself might be at an end.

Fukuyama's thesis demands evaluation against a rigorous analysis of comparative models of political and economic organization and their dynamics, a task beyond the scope of this book (see Schnitzer, 1994, for a thorough and contemporary assessment). Suffice to say, he saw nothing less than a new world order. From his observations of political and economic developments Fukuyama argues that there appears to be a fundamental and sustained trend towards a dominant role for liberal democracy in the world geopolitical system, as even the most totalitarian of political regimes moves towards enfranchisement of the populace and a general freeing up of markets. It is this 'new world order' – based on the political and economic freedom of the individual – which marks what Fukuyama describes as The End of History: 'liberal democracy remains the only coherent political aspiration that spans different regions and cultures across the globe'. The alleged collapse of the previous status quo in models of political economy (*in extremis*, capitalism versus communism) is often viewed as a late twentieth century phenomenon driven by Thatcherism, Reaganism and/or the principles of *perestroika* and *glasnost* developed by Gorbachev. In reality, however, the process has much deeper historical roots although, even here, there is debate regarding the genesis of liberal democracy. Fukuyama, for example, states that 'the growth of liberal democracy, together with its

	1790	1848	1900	1919	1940	1960	1975	1990
United States	X	X	X	X	X	X	X	X
Canada		X	X	X	X	X	X	X
Switzerland	X	X	X	X	X	X	X	X
Great Britain		X	X	X	X	X	X	X
France	X		X	X		X	X	X
Belgium		X	X	X		X	X	X
Netherlands		X	X	X		X	X	X
Denmark			X	X		X	X	X
Piedmont/Italy			X	X		X	X	
Spain								X
Portugal								X
Sweden			X	X	X	X	X	X
Norway				X		X	X	X
Greece			X			X		X
Austria				X		X	X	X
Germany, West				X		X	X	X
Germany, East				X				X
Poland				X				X
Czechoslovakia				X				X
Hungary								X
Bulgaria								X
Romania								X
Turkey						X	X	X
Latvia								X
Lithuania								X
Estonia				X				X
Finland				X	X	X	X	X
Ireland					X	X	X	X
Australia				X	X	X	X	X
New Zealand				X	X	X	X	X
Chile			X	X		X		X
Argentina			X	X				X
Brazil						X		X
Uruguay				X	X	X		X
Paraguay								X
Mexico					X	X	X	X
Colombia				X	X	X	X	X
Costa Rica			X		X	X	X	X
Bolivia						X		X
Venezuela						X	X	X
Peru						X		X
Ecuador						X		X
El Salvador						X		X
Nicaragua								X
Honduras								X
Jamaica							X	X
Dominican Republic								X
Trinidad							X	X
Japan						X	X	X
India						X	X	X
Sri Lanka						X	X	X
Singapore							X	X
South Korea								X
Thailand								X
Philippines						X		X
Mauritius								X
Senegal							X	X
Botswana								X
Namibia								X
Papua New Guinea								X
Israel						X	X	X
Lebanon						X		
TOTALS	3	5	13	25	13	36	30	61

Figure 1.6 *Liberal democracies worldwide (Source: Fukuyama, F. (1992),* The End of History and the Last Man, *London: Hamish Hamilton)*

companion, economic liberalism, has been the most remarkable macropolitical phenomenon of the last four hundred years.'

Figure 1.6 lists the countries which Fukuyama claims demonstrate the 'worldwide liberal revolution' and marks the year by which they had achieved membership.

It should be noted here that the conceptual and empirical foundations of Fukuyama's thesis are fiercely debated. Despite this, the heavy emphasis it places on liberalism as the dominant economic paradigm has significant implications for strategic management, particularly in the light of our previous critique of traditional models of competition.

In the liberal model, economic resources are allocated through the interaction of supply and demand factors. Consumers have free choice as to what to buy and firms have free choice as to what to produce. This is the essence of liberalism, a philosophy based on the twin principles of consumer sovereignty (freedom to choose) and self-interest (rational choice). The market mechanism determines prices and, consequently, output. It is the profit motive which ultimately drives firms to produce efficiently and consumers to maximize their satisfaction. The founding father of political economy and the greatest proponent of liberalism, Adam Smith (1776), described the process as follows:

> Every man, as long as he does not violate the laws of justice, is left perfectly free to pursue his own interests in his own way, and to bring both his industry and capital into competition with those of any other man, or order of men.

The fundamental principle underpinning this liberal form of economic organization is free competition and a market mechanism which links individual decisions to aggregate output. As Smith famously noted, every individual 'intends only his own gain and is in this as in many other cases led by an invisible hand to promote an end which was no part of his intention.'

In a liberal form of economic organization, the government's role is primarily to set an institutional framework which facilitates rather than obstructs free choice. In developing his thesis on the wealth of nations, Smith integrates these two themes of government and economy as follows:

> In the midst of all the exactions of government ... capital has been silently accumulated by the private frugality and good conduct of individuals, by their universal, continual, and uninterrupted effort to better their own condition. It is this effort, protected by law and allowed by liberty to exert itself in the manner which is most advantageous, which has maintained the progress of England towards opulence and improvement in almost all former times, and which, it is to be hoped, will do so in all future times.

The significance of this quote two centuries after its composition and its implications for the future direction of the world economy in the next millenium will be elaborated upon later. In a political economy context, meanwhile, it can be generally stated that governments deliver policies which involve a greater or lesser degree of state ownership and a greater or lesser degree of intervention in directing the way in which economic decision making is practised (e.g. through taxes, anti-trust, tariffs, etc.). In autocratic political organizations opposition to a dominant political party is either forbidden or heavily controlled. Decision making is highly centralized and normally restricted to very few individuals (e.g. a polit-buro) or, in the extreme case, to one person (a dictator). In complex autocratic societies heavy use is made of a military force to administer such decision making and individuals' freedom of movement and political choice is tightly constrained. Where voting is allowed, it is seldom 'free' in the sense described below.

Democratic political organization is based on the principles of equality, freedom of choice and the participation of all individuals in the decision-making processes which develop and maintain society. In complex democratic societies, individuals are represented by members of political parties who are free to organize without constraint and who develop policies which they are mandated to implement if elected by a majority of voters. Terms in office are limited and the whole system is regulated by 'checks and balances' through independence of the executive (government) and legislature (legal system). It is this form of political organization which, coupled with economic freedoms, has led to capitalism as a dominant paradigm and has underpinned the internationalization of the world economy.

That the world has changed substantively and in an unprecedented manner over the last few years is beyond question. While the nature and direction of world economics and geopolitics is uncertain the antecedents of the current situation are better understood although, of course, still intensely debated. The collapse of communism and the emergence of a new form of world political and economic organization has its roots in the small village of Bretton Woods in New Hampshire, USA. In 1944, on the brink of victory in the Second World War, Britain, America and their allies met to establish, among other things, the foundations of the post-war economic order. As Crook (1991) notes: 'Their goal was extraordinarily ambitious ... what was needed was nothing less than a new beginning – by design – for the global economy.'

The principal means of achieving this goal was through the promotion of international trade. The twin pillars of the proposed system were the International Monetary Fund (IMF) and the World Bank. Described by *The Economist* (Crook, 1991) as being among the world's most powerful institutions, there are growing question marks about the roles they perform and, at the extreme spectrum of the debate, whether they should even exist. Despite this, it is clear that the two organizations have a phenomenal impact on the conduct of world economics. As Crook (1991) notes:

> As lenders in their own right, they directly control billions of dollars each year; indirectly, tens of billions more. They sit in judgement on governments, using their financial clout to influence economic policy in scores of developing countries. The fate of hundreds of millions of people turns on the decisions these institutions make.

The creation of the new world order has itself led to a new agenda of priorities which, in turn, require the type of global financial infrastructure already embodied in the IMF and the World Bank. This is strikingly illustrated by the institutions' role in facilitating the transition of the former USSR into a market-based rather than planned economy. In the summer of 1992 the IMF arranged $24 billion dollars of Western aid for Russia and made $1 billion immediately available to replenish her foreign exchange reserves. The deal was made on now familiar IMF terms and conditions (*The Economist*, 1992a): a currency system would be created over which Russia would have full control; the country's budget deficit would be cut from 17 per cent of GDP to 5 per cent by the end of 1992; targets for the monthly inflation rate were set for the achievement of single figures within the same period.

Such policy conditions tied to loans and/or development aid have created the framework of a new economic orthodoxy, a consensus on macroeconomic policy which is being adopted around the world. As *The Economist* notes (1991a), 'The most dramatic and unexpected shift has come in Eastern Europe. But in Latin America, Africa and Asia a change in thinking almost as profound is also well under way.'

Whether or not we have reached the 'end of history' remains open to debate. The strongest critique levelled at Fukuyama is the deterministic nature of his 'End of History' thesis. He is not the first thinker to claim directional and finite characteristics for historical processes. The German philosopher Hegel wrote of a 'higher synthesis', what he described as the outcome of a process which incorporates rational components while rejecting the irrational. Hegel's process is grounded in logical argument but is applicable to historical progression. For Hegel the 'end of history' was the liberal state. Perhaps the most famous producer of an 'end of history' thesis was Karl Marx who, through his studies of politics, economics and society, saw capitalism as one stage of a historical process, a precursor to socialism *en route* to a truly communist society.

The critiques levelled at Hegel and Marx can equally be directed at Fukuyama. The future is always shrouded in a cloudy present. History helps but only in the sense that it provides a benchmark which may or may not provide some causal explanation of future events. Furthermore, from a managerial perspective, it must be acknowledged that business does not operate in a vacuum. It acts upon and is shaped by the environment in which it operates. As Tsoukas argued in a critique of Fukuyama published in the *Independent* newspaper ('History and an uncertain future', 3 March 1992): 'in open social systems myriads of unintended or unforseen interactions conspire to vitiate any attempt at foretelling the precise shape of future events'. The more we understand the nature and dynamics of such systems the greater will be our chance of creating the future we desire.

At the level of the firm, the ability of individual companies to determine their own future remains one of the fiercest areas of debate within the strategic management literature, as we shall see. This debate readily cascades into broader areas of social theory, particularly the literature which examines the sociology of organizations (e.g. Morgan, 1990) and their impact on state and society. Although we explore some such points of contention the broader level of analysis required is beyond the scope of this book. In the next section, however, we pick up on a general point raised in earlier sections of this chapter: the powerful role of customer preference as a driving force in the economic process.

An added dimension: the sovereign customer

The strategic management literature leaves a yawning gap in its discussion of markets by virtue of the lip service it pays to the role of consumer preference. As we shall see in the next chapter, the consumer role is a powerful one, a power base greatly enhanced in an environment characterized by unfettered international trade and its consequences: globalization and excess supply. A point which must be grasped is that, given choice, customers will exercise it.

Industrial buyers are becoming far more sophisticated, radically reducing their supply base and demanding 'partnership sourcing' arrangements, a sharp contrast to the transaction-based relationships of the past. In this sector purchasing is taking on a much more strategic role (Cammish and Keough, 1991), thus placing business process demands on suppliers which we evaluate more fully in Chapter 4.

In the service sector consumers – enjoying a broader and deeper choice than at any time in the past – are becoming more demanding, punishing those suppliers who fail to meet consistent and ever-higher standards by taking their custom elsewhere. As customer satisfaction has been raised so have their expectations. As Vandermerwe (1993) notes:

> On the threshold of the third millenium, despite earlier fears that standardization and globalization would 'massify' the human race still further, the individual has triumphed to become more significant.

In consumer goods, too, expectations of quality – functional and aesthetic – are at an all-time high (McKenna, 1991), a demand which is being met and reinforced by the ever-increasing power of the retail groups who serve them. Customers are choosy and their time has come. Though treated as a macro-economic concept, the chronic trade deficits of advanced industrial economies such as the USA and the UK have more mundane roots in the High Street, i.e. they are an immediate reflection of consumers purchasing imported rather than domestically-produced goods.

The Change Management literature is dismissive or, at best, ignorant of the customer role in providing the rationale for their subject. Programmes such as TQM, JIT, 'continuous improvement', quality circles, time to market and so on are all, one way or another, focused on improving the performance of the business by adding more value to the customer. When examining strategic change, then, it is essential to factor in the fundamental impact of the customer role as an antecedent to the whole process.

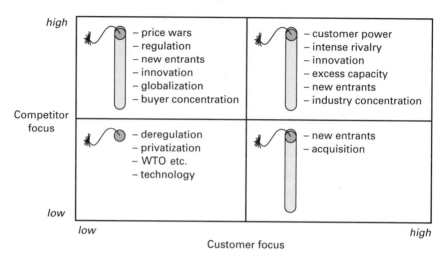

Figure 1.7   *Market orientations and equilibrium threats*

Kotler (1991) has noted that companies must strive to seek balance between customer and competitor orientations in contemporary marketing environments. He offers a simple matrix and argues that – over time – companies have shifted from a product orientation, when they cared little for anyone other than themselves, through development of a customer orientation, then a competitor orientation and, finally, a market orientation.

While this is a gross simplification and over-generalization, the idea that we should analyse the customer–competitor dynamic as a major influence on the change dimension of strategic management is a powerful one. In particular, if market structures are applied to the Kotler framework then valuable insights can be gained from an examination of the economic processes which underpin the management of strategy and strategic change. A matrix of customer focus and competitor focus with market equilibrium threats is shown in Figure 1.7.

In Cell 1, low customer focus–low competitor focus, the only sustainable market structure is monopoly. In practice monopolies rarely exist, although very dominant firms may demonstrate monopolistic behaviour. The ability of monopolists to control output gives them tremendous scope to extract high prices and to sustain gross inefficiencies in operations. In market-based industrial economies (the USA being a major exception) the tendency has been for government to assume ownership of 'natural monopolies', i.e. those market structures where the minimum efficient scale of output is so high that the industry can only support one supplier (very common in utilities such as gas, electric, water and telecommunications). While nominally in the consumer interest, the reality of natural monopoly is somewhat different. Governments have systematically exploited the monopoly power they own, using sole supplier status to charge monopoly prices, an indirect tax indiscriminately charged on rich and poor alike. They have also tended to starve the industries of appropriate levels of capital investment, compromising customer service levels and laying the foundations for chronic infrastructure problems and the erosion of national competitiveness. There have been undoubted benefits to society from nationalized industries, the most notable being the ability of such sectors to support very high levels of employment. In sector after sector, country after country, though, the status quo which has existed is being shattered. The twin forces of privatization and deregulation are forcing competition into previously protected markets. The dynamic is being shaped and accelerated by a growing intolerance within the world trading institutions of the heavy subsidies such industries attract from their governments. The granting of massive subsidies to Air France, for example, has met universal condemnation from its rivals and otherwise impartial observers.

Another major pressure on this market structure is technological innovation which, as we shall see in the next chapter, can have a dramatic impact on cost structure and revenue earning potential. The UK telecommunications sector provides a clear example of the mythical nature of the concept of natural monopoly in today's hi-tech environment. Privatized in 1984, British Telecom has faced an increasingly deregulated market. The first phase of deregulation was the imposition of direct competition, the regulatory authorities allowing the Cable and Wireless subsidiary, Mercury Communications, to form a duopoly alongside BT. The second phase of deregulation has allowed the emergence of a type of competition which is less direct but more threatening. Cable TV operators are rapidly 'hard wiring' major cities in the UK and are exploiting their assets to the full by offering telephone services. Power transmission companies are also attacking BT, diversifying into telephony through exploiting their established overland cabling infrastructure to become a low-cost operator on profitable long-distance routes. The third phase of deregulation is allowing a new stream of generic and direct competition to materialize as the UK and, to a lesser extent, the European market is liberalized further. Wireless communication innovations such as digital cellular technology are being marketed to a much broader base of customers. On a grander scale, AT&T, the giant US telecommunications corporation, is actively building market presence in Europe, as is its Canadian neighbour Northern Telecom. Worse still for BT, the sector itself is being redefined as digital technology is forcing a convergence of the previously disparate telecommunications and computer industries. AT&T, with its wholly owned computer subsidiary NCR, is arguably in a much stronger position to survive and exploit this trend than BT.

Even the most rigid of market structures – government-owned monopoly – is cracking under multiple pressure points. With few exceptions, and these only partial and/or transient, governments of the large industrial democracies are washing their hands of business management, a philosophy being rapidly adopted by the ex-communist countries of the Soviet bloc and the once highly interventionist states of South America.

In Cell 2, low customer focus–high competitor focus, the only sustainable market structure is oligopoly, i.e. where the majority of total market share is owned by a few firms. In a typical oligopolistic market structure, for example, five firms might account for 70 per cent of total output. A tendency towards oligopoly is a characteristic feature of capitalism, particularly where benefits of scale are readily apparent and the merger and acquisition of assets is unfettered by regulation and/or is facilitated by liquid equity markets. Although it is an economic concept, oligopoly can also be explained by reference to behavioural theories of the firm (March and Simon, 1958, 1992; Cyert and March, 1963) and the typical feature of modern capitalism whereby ownership and management of the firm are divorced (Berle and Means, 1967). Regarding the former, it has been convincingly argued that senior managers do not pursue the corporate profit maximizing behaviour suggested by economic theory. On the contrary, they are more likely to pursue self-interest, a condition typically fulfilled, both financially and psychologically, by expanding their realm of control through acquisitive strategies.

Oligopoly, then, is characterized by industry concentration. This, in turn, leads to a high level of interdependence between the main firms in the industry. Typically, the firms become very competitor-oriented, forever wary of their next moves and/or reactions. Strategies tend to be reactive or 'follower' in nature. On the whole, the output of such market structures tends to be of 'me-too' type products, market position being secured by ownership of distribution, heavy advertising expenditure, high capital intensity of production and a range of additional 'entry barriers' peculiar to any particular sector. While the theory of oligopoly accommodates product differentiation, in practice any advantage gained is short-lived since it will be readily matched by eagle-eyed rivals. New service supports are immediately copied, new product concepts imitated or bettered.

The combination of follower strategies and me-too products is bound to create a price-sensitive customer base since price is the only value signal available within the individual consumer's choice set. When industry concentration reaches its natural or legal limit individual producers will be strongly tempted to win share through price, particularly if the industry is mature and carrying excess capacity. In practice, however, firms are fully aware (or strongly perceive) that price cuts will be instantly matched, thus damaging industry profitability. In oligopolistic market structures, then, there is an inherent tendency towards a 'cartel culture', whereby firms avoid price cuts through a variety of mechanisms ranging from simple price leadership by a dominant supplier through to tacit or overt collusion. Oligopolistic behaviour is the dominant *modus operandi* of modern capitalism, but it is inherently unstable. As Figure 1.7 demonstrates, its fragile structure is subject to bombardment on a number of pressure points. The most obvious is regularity constraint, enacted through ongoing observation of industry behaviour and the vetting of mergers and acquisitions which are judged to have anti-competitive implications. In practice the vetting role is easier though, arguably, more politically sensitive. In contrast, observations of persistent anti-competitive behaviour are extremely difficult to prove, as many famous cases have demonstrated: if all firms are charging the same price, or moving price points in tandem, this can be explained both by competitive or anti-competitive behaviour!

The principal concern of anti-trust is the consumer interest. As Adam Smith once noted, 'people of the same trade seldom meet together, even for the merriment and diversion, but the conversation ends in a conspiracy against the public, or in some contrivance to raise prices.' Despite the policing difficulties there is growing evidence that the anti-trust question is being taken far more seriously by the regulatory authorities, increasingly within the auspices or under the watchful eye of international trading conventions.

A distinctive characteristic of oligopoly is the chronic inefficiencies this type of market structure accommodates. This factor leaves tremendous scope for rival firms to penetrate the market and such attacks normally come from two different sources. Firstly, new entrants, attracted by the high prices attainable and often enjoying lower cost structures, will penetrate the market, often radically changing the economics of the industry in the process. Secondly, innovations in product and process technologies will radically enhance economic utility and thus reconfigure the nature and structure of demand. These twin forces have been rapidly accelerated by the globalization of competition, most notably the 'new competition' emanating from Asia.

A further pressure point on this market structure, particularly in the consumer goods industry, arises from the growing concentration of retailers. Galbraith (1967) long ago drew attention to the theory of countervailing power to explain what he describes as 'the paradox of the unexercised power of the large corporation'. The theory is founded on the following proposition:

> ... private economic power is held in check by the countervailing power of those who are subject to it. The first begets the second. The long trend toward concentration in industrial enterprise in the hands of a relatively few firms has brought into existence not only strong sellers ... but also strong buyers ... The two developed together, not in precise step but in such a manner that there can be no doubt that the one is in response to the other.

He sees this as an inevitable process and concludes that, in general, most positions of market power in the manufacture of consumer goods will be covered by positions of countervailing power. In some cases, however, firms have protected themselves from the exercising of this power by integrating their distribution through to the consumer which, he argues, reflects 'a strategy which attests the importance of the use of countervailing power by retailers.'

Market power, then, and its use and effectiveness must be viewed in context. Perhaps the most significant aspect of power is the reaction of those who are affected by it and, in particular, their tendency to resist it where the achievement of their own goals is being threatened.

Cell 3, high customer focus–high competitor focus, seems to characterize perceptions and realities of contemporary competitive environments. Customers have power, they are increasingly exercising it and a focus on their needs and preferences seems essential. Competitors are many, they are global, they are sophisticated and they are aggressive. A focus on their strategic orientation, competitive bases and market responsiveness is essential. If pushed, economists might label this cell 'monopolistic competition', a type of market structure which is characterized by excess capacity, a large number of independently-minded suppliers and buyers, relatively free market entry and market exit and a heavy emphasis on product differentiation. Any tardiness to accept this definition will probably relate to the conceptual requirement of low entry barriers, arguably a weakness rooted in the static definitions associated with general theories of intermediate market structures. In our examination of global competitive positions in the next chapter we aim to address this problem. Indeed, the discussion presented there has Cell 3 as its context, as does the book in its overall discussion.

It is highly predictable that, beyond the year 2000, the global economy will have a market structure which demonstrates oligopolistic characteristics (a few giant firms dominating global industries). This contention is mere cold comfort for companies struggling to come to terms with the contemporary environment they must cope with. The market dynamics within Cell 3 of Figure 1.7 most closely approximate the efficient market hypothesis, a general theory which, *inter alia*, argues that any surplus value a company creates will be eroded by sophisticated consumers and/or efficient and effective rivals. Product life-cycles will be short, technological advantage rapidly transferred and diffused and there will be a premium on speed to market. Pressure points on this cell include the ubiquitous new entrants, technological substitutes and, spanning both these forces, 'breakthroughs' in process technologies as all market players will constantly strive for efficiency gains. There will be a tendency towards industry consolidation through mergers and acquisition as companies seek comfort (and market power) through scale. Similarly, a sharp focus on transaction costs and a desire to control opportunistic behaviour by supply chain members will lead some firms towards vertical integration (Williamson, 1975, 1985). An interim solution to the challenges of the market dynamics in Cell 3 will be the creation of joint ventures and strategic alliances as firms fail to cope alone, particularly as the market structure will tend more and more to be defined globally. Within this cell a strategic orientation is essential, a theme neatly captured in Ohmae's (1982) three Cs of corporation, customer and competitors. This three-pronged conceptual approach to the study of strategy was echoed in Anderson's (1982) seminal article linking marketing with strategic planning and a new theory of the firm wherein he identified a threefold role for marketing: to identify strategic positions that will ensure customer support; to generate strategies to achieve those positions by developing competitive advantages over firms with similar positioning aspirations; to negotiate with management and other functional areas to obtain the resources with which to pursue the strategies. Focusing specifically on the business orientation essential for survival in Cell 3, Narver and Slater (1990) concluded that there was a significant positive impact of a marketing orientation on profitability for both commodity and non-commodity businesses. The three constituent elements of marketing orientation in their study were customer orientation, competitor orientation and interfunctional coordination. An underlying theme of these three contributions to the strategy and marketing literature is that they provide universally applicable heuristics for all organizations, a theme developed in the next two chapters. To summarize here, though, the predominant thesis of contemporary marketing wisdom appears to be that successful organizations, whether service- or product-based, whether large, medium or small in size, need to plan strategically, need to understand their competitors and need to adjust their market position in accordance with the desired matching of corporate resources, customer needs and competitor stance.

Cell 4, high customer focus–low competitor focus, rests uneasily in the scheme of things as we are presenting them here. This theoretical difficulty is offset to some extent by the practical reality that few markets demonstrate this structural condition or that long-term (independent) survival is tenable. While a monopolist company could occupy a position where competition was meaningless, history suggests that such an organization is more likely to appropriate surplus value than distribute it to customers. Likewise, basic economics suggests that any company earning high returns from having a sharp customer focus will very quickly find itself in competition with rivals seeking a piece of the action. The essential dynamic of this cell, then, is towards Cell 3 as new entrants challenge the incumbent firms.

Concluding remarks

In this chapter we have set the scene and the theme for the rest of the book. Our context has also been outlined. Industries are taking on a global character, in the process shattering traditional and parochial definitions of market structure. Capitalism has emerged as the dominant mode of economic organization but, in the process, has brought with it many discontinuities and the range of challenges this poses for organizational survival is formidable.

Throughout this book this context and the challenges it presents are discussed in greater depth. In the next chapter we develop our discussion of 'marketing orientation' and introduce the 'marketing concept' as a way of doing business which is intuitively appealing but extraordinarily difficult to adopt.

2
Marketing strategy and the science of survival

Introduction

As he roamed the world seeking inspiration and support for his theory of evolution, Charles Darwin had to suffer the ignominy of squalor and a variety of diseases, only to be branded a heretic on his return. This was poor payback for honourable endeavour. Those of us interested in the natural selection of successful commercial organizations are luckier than Darwin. We need only to relax at our desks with the *Financial Times* or the *Wall Street Journal* to see the 'survival of the fittest' in action. These newspapers provide a communication channel between the chief executive officers (CEOs) of public companies and their sponsors, the investment community. Read one at random and witness corporate evolution in real time.

Explanations of poor business performance

Over the last few years the annual reporting season has been an embarrassing time for many CEOs. Explaining away poor business performance, low growth and reduced dividends they seek solace in factors which they claim are beyond their control, a trusty ragbag of what economists would describe as exogeneous factors. Figure 2.1 gives a sample.

Interestingly, what we don't hear the CEOs saying to their investors is, 'Oh, and by the way, we're poor at marketing'! The reasons are obvious but so are the implications. The factors listed in Figure 2.1 are not explanations. They are excuses for poor performance and 'explain' nothing other than managerial incompetence. Consider the first excuse, general economic recession. Recessions are an economic fact of life and have a history which comfortably predates the industrial era. Every recession which there has ever been has had a variety of antecedents and consequences. One factor alone has been a constant: they all end! It is the companies that are well-managed throughout the recession which go on to thrive in the upturn. In the US recession of the early 1980s, for example,

We've had a bad year ...
• General economic recession
• Cost inflation
• Exchange rates
• Sluggish demand
• Fierce competition
... but it's not our fault

Figure 2.1 *Explanations of poor business performance*

many Japanese companies established a platform which underpinned their success for the rest of the decade. Their American counterparts were busily reducing investment decisions to discretionary expenditures, thus 'justifying' wholesale reductions in areas such as advertising, training, distribution and new product development. Taking a longer term view, the Japanese did exactly the reverse, in the process creating a springboard for sustained commercial success to the present day.

Marketing (as we shall describe it) explains strong business performance while the factors listed in Figure 2.1 reflect the excuses of weak management. In the next section we introduce the notion of the marketing concept, one of the most persuasive management models available to explain superior business performance in the era of contemporary capitalism (Doyle, 1993).

The marketing concept

In this section we define marketing. We examine the misconceptions regarding its nature and explore why it has emerged as a major force in contemporary business theory. We then go on to describe the difficulties which firms encounter when trying to 'do' marketing and thus establish the focus for the rest of the book.

Marketing in its broadest sense is best understood as a business philosophy, i.e. marketing is not about image creation, advertisements, selling, direct mail, publicity, public relations and so on. Lee Iacocca, then Chairman of Chrysler, made the distinction between marketing as function and form in his reflections on the dire commercial situation which his company experienced in the late 1970s (cited in Brown, 1993):

> I thought we were doing marketing. We have a corporate Vice-President for marketing, a top-notch salesforce, a skilled advertising department and elaborate marketing planning procedures. These fooled us. When the crunch came, I realized that we were not producing the cars that people wanted. We were not responding to new needs. Our marketing operation was nothing more than a glorified sales department.

Iacocca is describing a common characteristic of many commercial organizations. The situation he found was a company doing 'marketing things' not marketing in the sense in which we describe it here. As Drucker (1974)

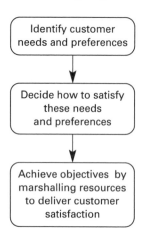

Figure 2.2   *The marketing concept*

has stated, marketing 'is the whole business seen from the point of view of its final result, that is, from the customer's point of view. Concern and responsibility for marketing must permeate all areas of the enterprise.'

The notion of shared responsibility for marketing is a powerful one and those firms who have embraced it have been rewarded with business success. Marketing as a business philosophy is encapsulated in the notion of the marketing concept, illustrated in Figure 2.2.

Few people argue with the fundamental principle of the marketing concept, i.e. that primacy of customer needs and recognition of customer preferences should drive an organization's strategic focus. Some executives point out that customers do not always have readily identifiable needs but, while this is often the case, a starting point of being 'close to the customer' facilitates the innovative solutions such a situation demands (Doyle, 1993).

The problem with the marketing concept is not so much the principle itself or its economic and behavioural foundations. The practice of marketing, i.e. the implementation of the philosophy, is where the real difficulties lie. For most established firms, adoption of the marketing concept requires a transition from 'doing what we've always done' to 'doing what we need to do to succeed'. The suggestion here of essential change and its potential clash with organizational inertia immediately draws our attention to the core problem with the marketing concept. This is compounded when the timing of the transition is taken into account. As Drucker notes (1974):

> Most managements, if they ask the question at all, ask, 'What is our business?' when the company is in trouble. Of course, then it must be asked ... But to wait until a business – or an industry – is in trouble is playing Russian roulette. It is irresponsible management.

The organizational challenges such change requirements impose on management will be addressed in a later section of this chapter and they provide the focus of this book.

Having established what marketing is, we must establish a case for why it matters. This is a relatively uncontentious task and can be handled with brevity. Given a number of suppliers, freedom of choice and the ability to pay, consumers invariably select the value package which best suits their needs. They certainly honour the supplier of this package with repeat business, one of the prime determinants of sustainable competitive success. Consequently, the company which delivers the greatest customer satisfaction enjoys purchase loyalty and, *ceteris paribus*, strong profits which drive a virtuous cycle of investment and return (Drucker, 1974).

A more controversial question is to ask *when* marketing matters, not least because it suggests that 'marketing' is a contemporary phenomenon. While this is certainly not the case (consider the eighteenth century 'brand' Chippendale, for example), a historical context is essential to reinforce our subsequent argument for the urgency of organizational solutions to 'marketing' problems.

Within the marketing literature (e.g. Kotler, 1991) the external face a company presents to its markets is commonly referred to in terms of its orientation. Such classification of company orientations is a grouping of the views that various authors have expressed in the literature over a period of time. They are outlined below in approximately chronological order, thus demonstrating how they reflect contemporary developments in market dynamics and structures.

Production orientation   This concept suggests that customers will favour products that are widely available at low cost. The appropriate strategy involves concentrating on achieving high production efficiencies and wide distribution coverage. The orientation's deficiency lies in the intrinsic force which drives all organizational energy towards efficiency, in the process neglecting the value of effectiveness, i.e. its predominant focus is on 'doing things right' rather than developing a sharp focus on 'doing the right things' (Drucker, 1974).

Product orientation   This approach maintains that customers will favour those products which offer superior quality or best performance. The driving force becomes one of constant product improvement and innovation. A forceful critique of this orientation was provided by Levitt (1960) in 'Marketing Myopia', where it was argued that customers buy solutions to their needs, not products. A typical example is that a consumer buys a quarter-inch hole, not a quarter-inch drill: a better solution, for example laser technology, creating the hole quicker, cheaper, more safely and more accurately than the traditional drill will rapidly capture the market.

Selling orientation   The principle underpinning this orientation is the notion that, left alone, customers will not buy enough of the company's products, thus obliging the organization to promote and sell its products aggressively in an attempt to increase sales (Kotler, 1991). The selling concept is particularly prevalent among firms which operate in industries with overcapacity, this latter state being a common feature where products are manufactured for consumption in mature and/or declining markets.

Marketing orientation   In stating that 'the aim of marketing is to make selling superfluous', Drucker (1974) captures the force behind this orientation. The fundamental premise is that companies should make what customers need rather than directing their attention towards selling what the organization is able to make. The guiding principles of such an approach are embodied in the marketing concept, which holds that organizational goals should be achieved through determining the needs and wants of target markets and delivering the desired satisfactions more effectively and efficiently than competitors (Kotler, 1991). The difference between the marketing concept and the selling concept is that the former seeks earnings from customer satisfaction and, more specifically, it attempts to achieve such profits by way of an integrated marketing effort as opposed to a heavy and expensive focus on selling and promotion.

Kotler (1991) has demonstrated that many industries have failed to adopt the marketing concept as a set of guiding principles to compete successfully in the markets they serve. He argues that many companies think they have 'marketing' because they have marketing executives and advertising budgets. However, they 'fail to see the big picture' and do not adapt to changes in consumer demand and changing competition; rather, they are driven to the marketing concept by particular circumstances, examples of which are: sales decline; slow growth; changing buying patterns; increasing competition; increasing marketing expenditures just to maintain sales.

In a classic exposition of the marketing concept Levitt (1960) argued that in every case where growth is slowed or stopped the problem lies in a failure of management and not because the market is saturated. The article is addressed to those industries which it is suggested are endangering their futures through improperly defining their purposes, or which are failing to seek and exploit growth markets 'even after the obvious opportunities have been exhausted.' The contrast between marketing and selling is concisely summarized by Levitt thus:

> Selling is preoccupied with the seller's need to convert his product into cash, marketing with the idea of satisfying the needs of the customer by means of the product and the whole cluster of things associated with creating, delivering, and finally consuming it.

It should be noted here that an important approach to the problem of mature markets and concentrated industry structures (hence few merger possibilities) is for companies to pursue diversification strategies. However, diversification should not be considered a surrogate for implementing appropriate marketing strategies in the core business, although this latter process will often be made difficult because of the inertias which have built up around the traditional values and business practices which permeate most business organizations. Levitt (1960) has convincingly argued that such inertias are a major contributory factor in the development within companies of the phenomenon of 'marketing myopia':

> The reason that the customer (and the satisfaction of his deepest needs) is not considered as being 'the problem' is not because there is any certain belief that no such problem exists, but because an organizational lifetime has conditioned management to look in the opposite direction.

More than three decades after their publication the original propositions laid down by Levitt have taken on a much sharper focus, growing massively in significance as international competitors have systematically eroded the market positions of indigenous corporations.

Marketing in the era of global competition

In this section we simplify the previously outlined structure of competitive orientations and examine two primary business approaches within a post-war historical context. Figure 2.3 presents the 'selling orientation' and the 'marketing orientation' as contrasting approaches to doing business.

For argument's sake, we will examine a fifty-year period from the end of the Second World War, i.e. 1945 to 1995, and take an arbitrary cut-off point of 25 years: 1970. In the years prior to 1970 the majority of firms could be classified as having a 'selling orientation', i.e. they established or, more likely, inherited a business capability, did 'marketing things' (e.g. selling, advertising) and expected customers to be grateful recipients of the goods or services they offered. On the whole they were fortunate since this was a period during which, in most sectors, demand exceeded supply. Moving beyond 1970, however, the world economic situation was changing dramatically, fuelled by technological innovation, technology

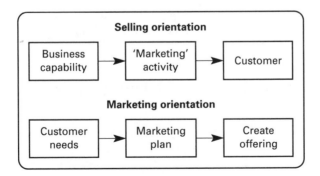

Figure 2.3 *Selling versus marketing orientation*

transfer, the reconstruction of the Japanese and German economies, a dramatic reduction of trade barriers and, *inter alia*, a widespread freeing of capital movement. Crucially, supply now exceeded demand which, coupled with an increasingly sophisticated and demanding customer base, forced companies to adopt, or approach, the marketing orientation.

Government-sponsored advertising such as the 'Buy British' campaign of the 1970s floundered on the British public's desire to secure the best value package they could obtain, regardless of county of origin. More generally, international competitiveness has become a substantial geopolitical issue, culminating in the debate surrounding the chronic trade surpluses of Japan throughout the 1980s and into the early 1990s, particularly with the USA.

Leaving the politics of international business aside, we can return to the commercial organization and restate our question, 'When does marketing matter?' Addressing this question in its broader strategic context, Day (1990) criticizes the implicit but fundamental assumption of the production concept, i.e. that an organization can adapt faster than the business environment is changing. He profiles the dynamic nature of competitive markets and identifies the following key drivers: (a) markets are fragmenting, and traditional market boundaries are blurring; (b) previously self-contained national markets are being transformed into linked global markets; (c) competitive advantages are harder to sustain as product life-cycles shorten and global competitors contest more markets; (d) supply gluts further intensify competitive pressures by giving customers more bargaining power; (e) buyer–seller relationships are changing as customers reduce the number of suppliers they deal with and information technologies permit closer supply chain links; (f) new market opportunities are being created from demographic and life-style changes, technological changes and rising environmental concerns; (g) old organization arrangements are suffering at the hands of more agile, entrepreneurial specialists.

Day (1990) clearly identifies the globalization of business and the growing sophistication of demand as key factors driving companies towards a marketing orientation. He also suggests that the spoils of world markets are going to newcomers, entrepreneurial companies who, through sharp strategic focus, are successfully challenging 'old organization arrangements'. In the next section we examine such arrangements and attempt to explain why they are not appropriate for the 'marketing orientation' era.

Market analysis and organizational process

The relationship between market analysis and organizational process is problematic. One point of view posits organizational activity as a dependent variable, a series of responses to external, uncontrollable and random events. An alternative (Marxist) perspective sees networks of organizations shaping the environment (now the dependent variable) in a process of reproducing the capitalist basis of power (Morgan, 1990).

'Marketing' rests uneasily here. Of course, in explaining the 'marketing discipline' we must focus on the customer and, in particular, the complex rational and psychological decision-making processes manifested in their purchase behaviour when choosing one supplier over another. Beyond this level of analysis, however, we must beg the question of what marketing means to the individual firm. Here, as suggested in Chapter 1, we are guided by the disciplines of industrial economics and organizational analysis. Economists guide us towards the market imperfections we should create for competitive edge while organizational analysts document the behavioural factors constraining such rational behaviour. In this sense, economics tells us what we should do while organizational behaviour tells us why we can't do it!

In this vein, Kotler (1991) posits three hurdles to successful implementation of the marketing concept: slow learning; fast forgetting; organized resistance. The first two can be proxied as lack of sensitivity to the need for change, while the last describes the inertias which prevent organizations from 'doing the right things', even when 'correct' market signals have been picked up. Consequently – if the marketing concept is a valid construct – true competitive advantage is organizational. The recent inclusion of the verb 'implementation' in Kotler's textbook title and general developments in the strategy literature (for example, Kanter, 1983, 1989; Ansoff, 1987; Ansoff and McDonnell, 1990; Pascale, 1990; Mintzberg and Quinn, 1991) suggest an emerging recognition of this fact. In rethinking 'marketing', then, we should first and foremost be rethinking 'organization'.

The organizational challenge

As organizations grow they inevitably become more complex. Companies have pursued growth strategies of innovation, market development and diversification via a combination of organic development

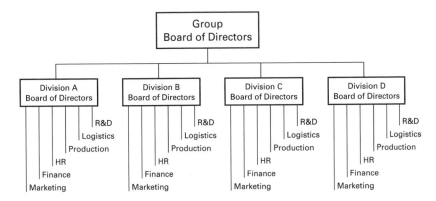

Figure 2.4 *The multidivisional firm*

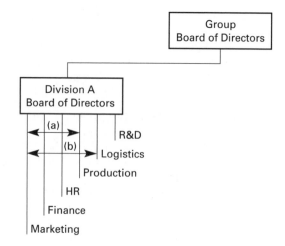

Figure 2.5   *The functional division*

and acquisition. In the process, the multidivisional organization structure has become the norm. A simple representation of such organizational form is illustrated in Figure 2.4.

Of course there are many variations of this structure and we will examine some of these in subsequent chapters. Despite this, from the organization theory literature the organizational form represented in Figure 2.4 is a very familiar construct. To examine the problems with such a structure for adoption of the marketing concept we will first explore *intra*divisional tensions. Figure 2.5 examines Division A of the multidivisional firm in more detail.

The functional structure illustrated in Figure 2.5 is common to many companies. We will now consider the characteristics of the fundamental tensions which exist between the functional components of Division A. Line (a) represents the relationship between marketing and production while line (b) represents that between finance and logistics.

When asked to describe the characteristics of these interfunctional relationships, executive course delegates, MBA students and, indeed, most managers with reasonable experience of organizational life offer adjectives such as adversarial, tense, strained and so on. As a proxy, we will examine the most often cited description of these relationships: conflictual.

Explaining interfunctional conflict

Figure 2.6 examines relationship (a) – marketing and production – and presents this as a 'management trade-off'.

The pivot symbolically represents the delicate nature of the relationship. The marketing department, by definition, is close to the market,

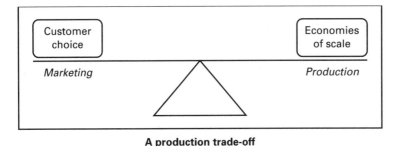

A production trade-off

Figure 2.6 *Management trade-off decisions (1): a production trade-off*

both conceptually (through research) and physically (via the sales team). Markets which are characterized by competition and innovation fragment, creating clusters of customers which form discrete market segments and subsegments, each of which demonstrates an exclusive set of needs and preferences. From Figure 2.6, then, we can see that the marketer's task is to meet customer choice criteria through the provision of variety in product offerings. The production department, by contrast, has a different agenda. Figure 2.7 shows a typical output schedule of a manufacturing organization. We acknowledge the variety of production process choices available to manufacturing organizations (e.g. Hill, 1985) but focus here on those typically associated with long production runs of products created for mass markets.

We now need to examine two key components of Figure 2.7 in more detail.

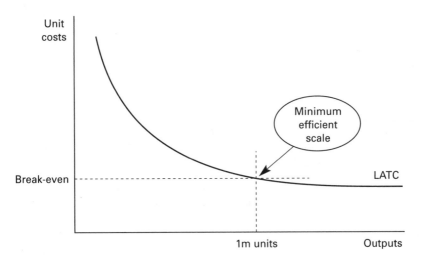

Figure 2.7 *The production function*

1   *Unit costs*   The curve in Figure 2.7 is the Long-run Average Total
    Cost (LATC) function of the company. This includes the cost of all
    factor inputs (natural resources, labour, capital) within an existing
    technological framework. When output increases unit costs fall as a
    result of economies of scale. Eventually the cost curve levels off,
    producing the characteristic L-shaped LATC curve.
2   *Minimum efficient scale (MES)*   At this point constant returns to scale
    set in so that extra output does not give additional cost advantage
    (economies of *experience* notwithstanding). In Figure 2.7 we have
    added a hypothetical MES of 1 million units.

From this discussion we can see the source of the dilemma depicted in
Figure 2.6. While the marketer wishes to offer variety, the production
manager, driven by economic efficiency criteria, generally desires long
production runs of the same product. Morgan (1986) has identified such
basic conflicts of interest, among others, as being a pathological characteristic of most organizations:

> Conflict may be personal, interpersonal, or between rival groups or coali-
> tions. It may be built into organizational structures, roles, attitudes, and
> stereotypes, or arise over a scarcity of resources. It may be explicit or covert.
> Whatever the reason, and whatever the form it takes, its source rests in
> some perceived or real divergence of interests.

In the case of the production trade-off illustrated in Figure 2.6 we have
identified a fundamental and very real tension between the conflicting
desires for 'variety' and 'sameness'. The marketing manager's career
progression, financial remuneration and status within the organization
will be a function of his or her ability to meet sales targets which, in
turn, will depend on meeting customers' needs better than rival companies. The production manager, in contrast, will have a career progression, financial package and status driven by measures of economic
efficiency, i.e. getting the maximum output from the minimum input of
production factors. If this requires a production run of one million units,
so be it.

Understanding the conflict process

A seminal contribution to the understanding of organizational conflict is
'Organizational Conflict: Concepts and Models' by Louis Pondy (1967).
Pondy's major insight is the fundamental notion that conflict is processual, i.e. it is a dynamic process of conflict episodes, each of which leaves
an aftermath which is an antecedent to its successor. He succinctly
describes the process by analogy to the decision-making process:

> In the same sense that a decision can be thought of as a process of gradual
> commitment to a course of action, a conflict episode can be thought of as a
> gradual escalation to a state of disorder. If choice is the climax of a decision,
> then by analogy, open war or aggression is the climax of a conflict episode.

That war or open aggression is not the norm in intra- or interorganizational conduct is an indication that the conflict construct has dimensions of *intensity* and *frequency*, and these will be variable for different conflict episodes. Furthermore, the requirement of a degree of stability and cooperation for organizational success illustrates the need for appropriate conflict management mechanisms.

Pondy identifies five dimensions of a conflict episode:

1 *Latent conflict* The underlying sources of organizational conflict.
2 *Perceived conflict* Conflict is perceived but no latent conflict conditions are present.
3 *Felt conflict* An important distinction from perceived conflict. Tension and anxiety are introduced and dissaffection emerges. Conflict is now personalized.
4 *Manifest conflict* This describes conscious behaviour by one party to frustrate one or more other parties' goal attainment. With reference to how conflict might be managed, Pondy makes the following observation: 'The interface between perceived conflict and manifest conflict and the interface between felt conflict and manifest conflict are the pressure points where most conflict resolution programs are applied.'
5 *Conflict aftermath* The legacy of a conflict episode which may feature genuinely successful resolution or, alternatively, mere suppression. In the latter case the latent conditions persist and may subsequently be aggravated, perhaps beyond resolution.

Given the systems perspective of this book, it is important to note that environmental factors can play an important role in aggravating or reducing the intensity of any of these conflict stages. Pondy (1967) provides a valuable insight into the debate which addresses the question of whether conflict is functional or dysfunctional for organizational performance. He derides the 'fashionable' nature of the debate and challenges those who seek uniformly to abolish conflict, although the argument is 'not so much with their *a priori* assertion that conflict is undesirable, [but rather] with their failure to make explicit the value system on which their assertion rests.' He describes such organizational values as productivity, stability and adaptability, and he argues that conflict should be discussed as functional or dysfunctional only with reference to its inhibitive or facilitative impact on these values.

It is immediately apparent that these values could themselves clash. For example, if stability is sought then organizations may fail to pursue the adaptive behaviour required in a changing environment. Thus conflict must be viewed as a situational construct (Pondy, 1967):

> ... a given conflict episode or relationship may have beneficial or deleterious effects on productivity, stability or adaptability. Since these values are incompatible, conflict may be simultaneously functional or dysfunctional for the organization.

In more recent research Pascale (1990) has provided support for the argument that, in certain business environments, conflict can be functional. He examined the shaping of the organization in response to environmental forces and argued that, when the latter are discontinuous, then the effective management of conflict is necessary to foster organizational change and survival. Pascale's contribution is discussed in more detail in Chapter 3.

With these thoughts in mind we return to the dilemma presented in Figure 2.6. To deal with the inherent conflict of such situations trade-off or suboptimal solutions have become the norm. Thus firms offer some variety but not too much. After all, organizational life must go on and conflicts must be managed. Rationally, of course, companies *should* seek a 'better solution'. The realities of organizational life, however, tend to constrain such an approach.

Organizational life and the 'satisfactory solution'

In a seminal text first published in 1958 James March and Herbert Simon (1992) laid down the foundations of the behavioural theory of the firm. They examined the human constraints on rational choice and outlined the tendency of managers to 'satisfice', i.e. to take satisfactory rather than optimal decisions:

> Most human decision making, whether individual or organizational, is concerned with the discovery and selection of satisfactory alternatives; only in exceptional cases is it concerned with the discovery and selection of optimal alternatives.

The trade-off situation in Figure 2.6 is a clear example of a satisficing solution to a management problem. While organizations can manage in this way for extended periods they will always be vulnerable to rivals who find an optimal solution to the core problem. In this example a better solution is the adoption of flexible manufacturing systems (FMS) and robotics technology to remove or reduce the need for a trade-off decision.

Figure 2.8 reproduces the previous figure and demonstrates the impact of the introduction of FMS on the LATC function. Cost schedule (ii) is enjoyed by a hypothetical rival, Company B. In this simple example we see that Company B has an MES of only 250,000 units which, in practical marketing terms, means it can offer four products for every one produced by Company A.

More satisficing: a financial trade-off

Referring back to Figure 2.5 and considering line (b), we will now explore the satisficing characteristics of the finance and logistics relationship within Division A. We examine its core tension and identify an optimal (or better) solution to the problem. Figure 2.9 illustrates the distinctive characteristics of the financial trade-off.

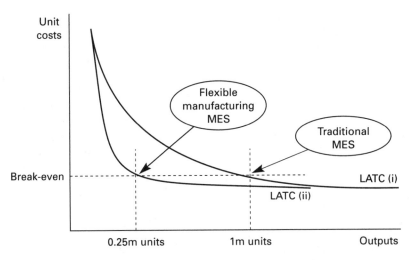

Figure 2.8 *The economic impact of flexible manufacturing systems*

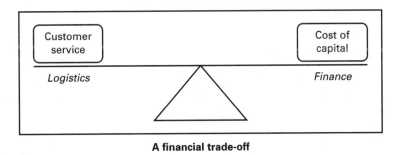

A financial trade-off

Figure 2.9 *Management trade-off decisions (2): a financial trade-off*

A principal role of logistics is to maximize customer service and ensure that the right product is delivered on time, every time. There is an empirically-based adage in logistics that 95 per cent of customers faced with a 'stock out' will buy from a rival supplier. To meet his or her objectives, then, the logistics manager will want to maximize availability. The individual's career progression, remuneration package, status (internally and externally) and pride in the job will be driven by the provision of 100 per cent customer service levels. By contrast, the key motivation of managers in the finance function is ultimately to reduce the company's cost of capital. Let us assume that this averages 10 per cent and then examine the financial manager's view of the £10m of inventory and warehousing the logistics manager requires to provide 100 per cent customer service.

The £10m customer service provision incurs a £1m interest cost to the company (assuming it would have to incur a debt to finance it).

Furthermore, the opportunity cost of the £10m is £1m foregone on a risk-free investment. A trade-off looms, in this case reduced stock levels and fewer warehouses but, inevitably, reduced customer service performance.

The trade-off is the satisfactory solution, the management of the inherent tension associated with another very real divergence of interests. The optimal (or better) solution to the core problem is Just-in-Time (JIT) inventory management systems, where stocks travel through the supply chain based on 'demand-pull' rather than 'supply-push' principles. JIT is based on the Japanese *Kanban* system, a philosophy underpinned by Japanese abhorrence of waste which, when combined with scarce physical and natural resources, drives companies to achieve what one Japanese manufacturing executive described as 'squeezing the last fart from the ferret'! Christopher (1992) describes the philosophy of Kanban and JIT as follows:

> The Kanban philosophy essentially seeks to achieve a balanced supply chain with minimal inventory at any stage and where the process and transit quantities of materials and stock are reduced to the lowest possible amount. The ultimate aim, say the Japanese, should be the 'economic batch quantity' of 1!

Pursuing an optimal solution has once again given sustainable advantage to companies prepared to 'break the mould' of organizational norms. Furthermore, advantages over and above simple cost reductions have accrued to those firms seeking better solutions and making the appropriate capital investments. A corollary of JIT adoption is zero-defect quality, since the cost of downtime in continuous process manufacturing systems will far outweigh the cost of inventory. Firms employing JIT processes reduce complexity and error potential through using far fewer suppliers who, in turn, are given partnership status and longer term contracts. When combined with the adoption of flexible manufacturing systems to solve the production trade-off, the implementation of JIT inventory systems and their associated quality enhancements provide formidably competitive commercial organizations. In discussing the 'manufacturing advantage' accruing to such companies Slack (1991) illustrates the combined impact of the 'better' solutions outlined above:

> Those companies who have attempted the difficult task of separating the benefits which come directly from investment in technology and those which come from methodology and better managerial understanding, have reported some surprising results. Paradoxically, capital investment often makes it necessary to consider the organization of the operation as a whole, which in turn prompts improvement which is independent of the technology for which it is preparing the way.

Consequently, organizational advantage begets organizational advantage. Phase one is a willingness to do something different, to seek better solutions which, as a corollary, triggers phase two, an organizational learning process. The concept of 'organizational learning' is a powerful one (which we return to in later chapters), particularly if we accept that

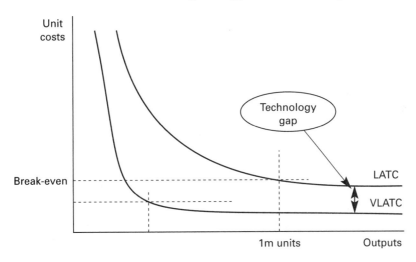

Figure 2.10   *Cost benefits of the 'better solution'*

the Darwinian doctrine of natural selection applies to organizational life.

We now combine the benefits of the 'better solution' to the organizational problems depicted in Figures 2.6 and 2.9 and gain an insight into a fundamental source of organizational advantage: innovation. Using hypothetical cost curves, we return again to economics in Figure 2.10.

Figure 2.10 has one major distinguishing feature from Figure 2.8. The *technology gap* is a function of a technology efficiency gain giving a cost function which economists, with their usual candour, describe as the Very Long-run Average Total Cost (VLATC) curve. The key difference here is the removal of the technological boundary constraint of the LATC curve, thus giving a broader base of factor inputs (now natural resources, labour, capital and technology) to the supplying firm. The shape of the curve has changed and moved to the left, thus giving a much reduced MES and lower unit costs at every level of output. This, in turn, has allowed companies to offer what has been described as 'mass customization' (Pine, 1993), i.e. the ability to produce high levels of variety while maintaining a strongly competitive cost base. We return to the strategic implications of such technological breakthroughs in the next section.

The combination of shape and shift movement in the production function demonstrated in Figure 2.10 has had a dramatic impact on late twentieth century capitalism, ranging from the factors underpinning German Mittlestand (smaller firm) success to the emergence of Japan as a true economic superpower and creditor to the world. In the next section we focus on international competitiveness at the level of the firm. In particular, we evaluate the implications of our discussion of 'the better solution' for strategy formulation and organizational design in the era of global competition. We begin with an examination of the seminal contribution of Harvard Business School Professor, Michael Porter, to the understanding of industry analysis and strategic choice.

Rethinking strategy

Michael Porter (1980) has published what has become one of the most widely disseminated books on competitive strategy. In this text he argued that in any particular industry there were three potentially successful generic strategies which could lead to superior business performance. These were: (i) overall cost leadership; (ii) differentiation; (iii) focus.

Porter has been heavily criticized for presenting these as mutually exclusive options, although the critique itself is often flawed. Porter's principal concern in isolating the three approaches was to warn of the dangers of 'strategic sloppiness', whereby firms achieved neither differentiation nor cost leadership and so ended up being 'stuck in the middle'. Nonetheless, Porter is pretty unambiguous on exclusivity of generic strategic approach: 'Sometimes the firm can successfully pursue more than one approach as its primary target, though this is rarely possible.'

Given our previous discussion we can readily see the problem with Porter's contention. In Figure 2.10, the combination of technological breakthrough and management learning has allowed firms to achieve the 'holy grail' of being able to offer higher value at lower cost, an irresistible combination for the well-informed buyer.

Porter's analysis drew heavily on American case studies and, in particular, examined market share and its cost relationships principally in the US market context. If we consider world market share as the key cost driver in the era of global competition a very different picture emerges. In the next section we examine the developing structure of global industries in the 1990s and, in particular, we profile the emerging 'super-league' of innovative global companies.

Profiling the super-league: competitive positioning in the era of global competition

The wholesale restructuring of international business has generated a general hypothesis that, by the end of the century, most industrial sectors will be dominated by relatively few global companies. In Figure 2.11 we examine current and projected global competitive positions and, in the process, question the validity of Porter's generic strategies for the contemporary business environment.

For illustration purposes, imagine that Figure 2.11 depicts one global industry with nine firms competing for industry profits. Firm 1 is the Market Ruler. It is enjoying the greatest profitability through a combination of higher revenues and lowest delivered costs. Firm 2, a Thriver, enjoys similar regard among buying groups but operates from a higher cost base than Firm 1. Its strategic intent is driven by process innovation and it constantly strives to dislodge Firm 1 from its coveted position by driving costs lower without compromising customer value. Firm 3 is also

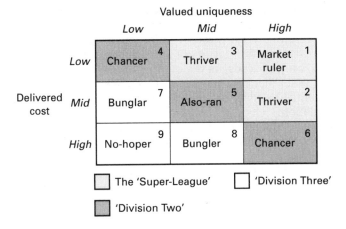

Figure 2.11   *Global competitive positions*

a Thriver. While it does not deliver the highest perceived value it does operate from a relatively low cost base, thus enjoying high margins. This company's strategic intent will be marketing mix innovation, i.e, enhancement of product, distribution, communication and customer service offerings to dislodge Firm 1 from its market ruling position. This constant jockeying for position through process and product innovation leads to the emergence of a 'Super-League', a group of companies who develop an apparently impenetrable competitive position and enjoy strong profits to defend it. An output of their constant innovations is that they raise entry barriers, for example through raising the capital intensity of production, securing the best distribution channels, attracting the best human resource, building large sales forces, enhancing customer service levels and committing to heavy advertising expenditures. Stalk (1988) has demonstrated that many Japanese manufacturing companies have progressed through capital intensiveness, focused factories and flexible manufacturing in a constant search for improved productivity and lower costs, a corollary of this process being zero defect quality levels and enhanced speed to market.

Firms 4, 5 and 6 are in the 'Second Division'. Firm 4 is a Chancer. Its competitive position is clearly Porter's original cost leader, i.e. the lowest cost producer in the industry or, more likely, it is a company among a group of low cost suppliers. This stance is risky because of the lower margins the company will earn and, more significantly, because of the fragility of this market position. Firstly, it will have to compete on price (because of its low perceived value) while, over time, all markets buy on value, i.e. consumers maximize their economic utility (Doyle, 1993). There can be only one cost leader in an industry whereas the scope for differentiation is as broad as managerial imagination. Secondly, other firms in the industry will constantly strive to drive down cost, thus removing Firm 4's flimsy advantage. Porter's original 'danger list' associated with the cost leader position remains applicable today: technological change that nullifies past investments or learning; low-cost learning by industry newcomers or followers, through imitation or through their ability to invest in state-of-the-art facilities; inability to see required product or marketing changes because of the organizational attention placed on cost; inflation in costs that narrow the firm's ability to maintain enough of a price differential to offset competitors' brand images or other approaches to differentiation.

Firm 6 we also describe as a Chancer. It does have high perceived value but its wafer-thin margins threaten the stability of its position, with other firms constantly striving to raise their own perceived value. The danger for Firm 6 is of drifting into the Bungler box or, in the worst case, becoming a No-Hoper. Firm 6's approach is similar to Porter's Differentiation Strategy and the potential pitfalls he identified for them remain valid today: the cost differentiation between low-cost competitors and the differentiated firm becomes too great for differentiation to hold brand loyalty. In this case buyers sacrifice some of the features, services, or image possessed by the differentiated firm for large cost savings; furthermore, buyers' need for the differentiating factor falls, a common occurrence as buyers become more sophisticated; finally, imitation narrows perceived differentiation, a common occurrence as industries mature.

Firm 5 is quite clearly 'stuck in the middle' in Porter's original sense:

> The firm lacks the market share, capital investment, and resolve to play the low-cost game, the industrywide differentiation necessary to obviate the need for a low-cost position, or the focus to create differentiation or a low-cost position in a more limited sphere.

Firms 7, 8 and 9 form the rump of our industry, a Third Division who are extremely vulnerable to takeover or extinction.

The above scenario is becoming a distinguishing characteristic of global industries. In an extensive examination of the world automobile industry, Womack *et al.* (1990) have identified 'lean production' as a new industrial paradigm to replace traditional mass manufacturing modes of operation. Lean production combines the talents of multiskilled workers with highly automated machinery and, though developed initially by Japanese automoblie manufacturers, it is an applicable approach for all companies in all sectors. As the authors note:

> Lean production is 'lean' because it uses less of everything compared with mass production – half the human effort in the factory, half the manufacturing space, half the investment in tools, half the engineering hours to develop a new product in half the time. Also, it requires keeping far less than half the needed inventory on site, results in many fewer defects, and produces a greater and ever growing variety of products.

As the quote suggests, a corollary of lean production in terms of output is higher quality, greater variety and lower costs, a combination of product characteristics which has proven irresistible to European and

North American consumers and which has underpinned the success of many Japanese companies in world markets.

In a comprehensive benchmarking study Jones (1993) has demonstrated a vast quality and productivity gap between Japanese companies and their British counterparts. He is not referring to the well-known companies such as Toyota, Nissan or Sony, but rather to the companies which supply them. These are the component manufacturers, makers of products such as wiring harnesses, brakes, seats and exhausts. Jones found that such 'world-class' companies produced greater variety at lower cost, achieved faster throughput, higher first-time quality, reduced rework levels, kept minimal stocks and demonstrated more stable work schedules. Such achievements were only partly explained by technology, with highly progressive employment practices ensuring that 'world-class' plants met their full potential. Employees were intensively involved in problem solving and there were identical conditions of employment and performance appraisal for all employees (including management). In 'world-class' plants teams were pivotal, with team leaders being responsible for developing the skills of team members and taking charge of quality and management issues. 'World-class' operations also had excellent external relationships throughout the supply chain, a 'partnership' relationship which recognized the 'shared destiny' of each channel member, characterized by a mutual understanding of each other's needs, fair rewards and shared learning. The following list summarizes the main findings from Jones's comprehensive research:

- Some plants (the 'world-class plants') are simultaneously able to achieve outstanding levels of productivity and quality.
- All the world-class plants are Japanese but not all Japanese plants are world class. Some UK plants have either high quality or high productivity, but none have both.
- The world-class plants show a 2:1 productivity differential and a superiority in quality of 100:1.
- This superior performance was achieved despite high product variety and a rapidly changing line-up of products.
- The world-class plants were more automated than the others, and had higher production volumes, but together these factors are estimated to account for less than 20 per cent of the performance gap.
- The world-class plants engage in only one-third of the amount of rework and carry one-seventh of the amount of inventory compared with the other plants.
- The world-class plants have much more active structures for shopfloor problem solving and improvement; production team leaders play a particularly significant role in these plants.
- The supply chain in which the world-class plants are embedded differs markedly from that of the other plants.
- The world-class plants carry one-quarter of the stock of finished goods compared with other plants. They serve customers who

operate active clubs for their suppliers and the variability of their schedules from their customer is low.
• The world-class plants keep 75 per cent less stock of incoming parts, run clubs for their suppliers, and receive far fewer defective items from their suppliers – a 50:1 differential with the other plants.

We can examine this 'total integrity' approach more closely by considering the foundations of Nissan Motor Company's manufacturing success. Describing the company's total quality manufacturing philosophy, Keith Jones, Director of Quality Assurance, gives the following insights (cited in Preston, 1993):

> [total quality] ... means that we plan to do things correctly to ensure that quality is considered at every stage of the design and manufacture of our products. It also means that we ensure everything at the plant is done in the most effective way in respect of quality. We set quality standards and targets, and then we monitor the plant's performance against these. We feed back the results of the monitoring process and use them to help improve individual processes from what we have learned. We also ensure that we get the maximum amount of customer feedback and comments, and again this is incorporated into the way in which we do things at the plant.

The following quote illustrates concisely the Japanese philosophy of close relationships throughout the supply chain and demonstrates the competitive edge this gives them in the ongoing management of their business (cited in Preston, 1993):

> Nissan has been able to accelerate its location programme as a result of positive improvements in quality standards achieved by our suppliers. Our increasing international manufacturing presence put those companies who can demonstrate an ability to meet our standards in a very good position. In the coming years, Nissan is going to be spending a great deal more money in Europe and we are currently working on developing worldwide standards for component and material suppliers, incorporating a common evaluation standard that will allow both Nissan and its suppliers to clearly understand what is required, in terms of cost, design and engineering facilities and product quality.

This comment by Peter Hill, Nissan's Purchase Director, is illustrative of Japanese companies' drive to internationalize their management philosophy, in this case the 'soft systems' approach to supply chain management. Here, the principal objective is to create win–win situations between Nissan and its principal suppliers, a supply chain focus which is in sharp contrast to the adversarial zero-sum attitude of many traditional (western) interorganizational relationships.

Time, then, has taken its toll on Porter's generic strategies, relegating them to a division two of good ideas. The Super-League will dominate the global industry and create a virtuous cycle of investment and return. Occasionally a Second Division player will make a product or process breakthrough and enter the realms of the Super-League, but in doing so they will have to raise the stakes and, as in sport, the odds are stacked against their survival chances. Instant relegation beckons.

Linking competitive strategy to corporate strategy: another organizational challenge

The unit of analysis of the previous sections was Division A of the organization introduced in Figure 2.4. This is appropriate since competitive advantage arises at the product/market (customer) interface and must be separated from corporate strategy, which is more concerned with the portfolio of businesses the organization wishes to compete in.

In Figure 2.12 we re-present our organization and add a 'relationship line' between Division A and Division C. When asked to describe the relationship between Division A and Division C the overwhelming majority of executives say, and with some passion, 'competitive'. The reason is simple. An organization, like any entity, has finite resources, a scarcity which requires some form of zero-sum allocation exercise. Thus Division A and Division C feel they are competing against each other for resources, a perception which, on the whole, is very true. Many organizations deliberately create a 'flat' organization similar to that shown in Figure 2.12. The logic is fine, the objective being to empower the division with the decision-making autonomy which is essential given their closeness to the market. In practice, however, the management of such structures has been problematic. Consider portfolio management, for example. These theories guide firms to balance cash generative businesses (normally in mature markets) with 'Tomorrow's Breadwinners', i.e. those businesses which consume cash now but will deliver strong earnings in the future (normally in growing markets). Such schemes are deceptively simple and, therefore, potentially flawed

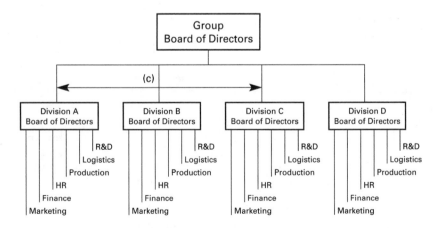

Figure 2.12 *Internal competition in the multidivisional firm*

(McKiernan, 1992). Consider the following scenario. Division A is positioning itself for a rapidly growing market sector in the Pacific Rim. Division C, meanwhile, has share leadership in a European market which is large but declining slowly, a sector which has not seen any mainstream innovation for many years. Division C executives anticipate European market entry from a major Japanese firm which has revolutionized the process technology in this industry, driving down production costs and adding more value to the product. Division C desperately needs investment funds to improve its technical efficiency yet is refused them since the parent company's scarce resources are targeted elsewhere. The Dog Box looms, the dreaded scenario of low growth and low market share and, ultimately, divestment or closure.

This portfolio management approach to business management is very common but, as Porter (1987) has argued, 'is no way to conduct corporate strategy'. He also points out that in the creation of such business portfolios strong claims are regularly made by managers of potential synergies between the collection of businesses, i.e. that the whole is greater than the sum of the parts (often expressed as 2 + 2 = 5). Describing such linkages as 'paper synergies', Porter is dismissive of their potential manifestation:

> Such corporate relatedness is an *ex post facto* rationalization of a diversification undertaken for other reasons. Even synergy that is clearly defined often fails to materialize. Instead of co-operating, business units often compete.

Porter's critique has emerged from a synthesis of his earlier observations on corporate strategy (1980) and competitive advantage (1985) and he makes a useful distinction between the two streams of thought. Corporate strategy, he argues, 'concerns two different questions: what business the corporation should be in and how the corporate office should manage the array of business units.' Competitive strategy, on the other hand, 'concerns how to create competitive advantage in each of the businesses in which a company operates.'

It seems clear that performance levels in achieving competitive advantages through implementing competitive strategies will have their limiting factors determined by strategic decisions made by senior management regarding corporate strategy. Indeed, in profiling the distinctive characteristics of competitive and corporate strategy Porter found that the latter presented the most serious cause for concern.

Porter studied the diversification histories of 33 large diversified US companies (chosen at random from broad sectors of the economy) between 1950 and 1986. He found that the majority of these companies had divested more acquisitions than they had kept and that the corporate strategies of most of the companies had dissipated rather than created shareholder value. He was particularly critical of portfolio management as a corporate strategy concept, a substantive critique since he also identified it as the one which most companies operated. He argues that the sheer complexity of the management task has defeated even the best portfolio managers as they found it increasingly difficult to find good but undervalued companies. Rather than being cheap, acquisitions were generally becoming more expensive: 'In the face of increasingly well developed capital markets, attractive companies with good managements show up on everyone's computer screen and attract top dollar in terms of acquisition premium.'

Porter also criticizes the portfolio management model for its failure to create economic value, reasoning that shareholders should be allowed to diversify their own portfolios to suit their individual preference and risk profiles. Finally, he argues that there is an increasing need for companies to develop a strong corporate identity and that this should be built around a strong corporate mission statement and an incentive system which rewards more that just business unit results. Porter then, is demanding a reassessment of strategy and he is highly critical of companies for their slavish adherence to strategic concepts no longer appropriate to today's business environment: 'The need to rethink corporate strategy could hardly be more urgent.'

We can now reconsider what Drucker (1974) has described as the sole purpose of an organization: a customer. Given that the organization is riddled with internecine conflicts within and between business divisions, who perceive themselves to be in intense competition with each other as they muddle through with their satisficing decisions, it is readily apparent that the customer hardly gets a look in. It is clear to see, then, why the world's best-selling textbook on marketing, Kotler's *Marketing Management*, describes 'organized resistance' as a major hurdle to the implementation of the marketing concept.

In subsequent chapters we draw on a broad range of management insights into potential resolutions of these organizational problems. These are essential to address given the growing supremacy of consumer sovereignty and the high intensity of sophisticated competition. The scale of the task, however, should not be underestimated. As Morgan (1986) notes, 'The potential complexity of organizational politics is mind-boggling, even before we take account of the personalities and personality clashes that usually bring roles and their conflicts to life.'

Even when there is a recognition of the need for change within a company, and even if that company has all the management tools at its disposal to implement change, the task is a daunting one. Morgan again: 'Many organizational conflicts often become institutionalized in the shape of attitudes, stereotypes, values, beliefs, rituals, and other aspects of organizational culture. In this socialized form, the underlying conflicts can be extremely difficult to identify and break down.'

In the next section we acknowledge the scale of the task of organizational change but drive home the point of its urgency. We are in an age of discontinuity and, if we accept the Darwinian evolutionary doctrine, it is at such times that natural selection takes place.

Whatever happened to the excellent companies?

One of the most common pursuits of management theorists during the 1980s was the search for 'best practice' and an understanding of what constitutes organizational competitiveness. A trigger for this pursuit was the publication of *In Search of Excellence* by Tom Peters and Robert Waterman in 1982. They studied 43 companies and modelled a framework of excellence based on 'fit' between strategy, structure, systems, skill, staff, style and superordinate goals. The 'Seven S' framework was well received by both academics and practitioners and certainly seemed to make a valuable contribution to the understanding of organizational performance. Despite this, within five years more than half of the companies examined were in some difficulty and, according to Pascale (1990), only 14 of the original 43 could still be described as excellent. Peters (1987) himself has stated in a subsequent text that 'There are no excellent companies.'

It is generally accepted that *In Search of Excellence* was not necessarily 'wrong' in its claims (see Chapter 5 for a broad critique); the failure of the 'excellent companies' is more a function of their inability to change their 'corporate recipes' in the context of an increasingly turbulent business environment. Even a revisionist author such as Pascale – an original member of the McKinsey team involved in the development of the Seven S framework – has been caught out in his pursuit of excellent companies. Unfortunately for Pascale (1990), he builds his own thesis on the survival capacities of IBM, one of the remaining 'excellent' companies he identified but an organization which, in the mid-1990s, is on the verge of commercial, if not financial, collapse. According to Pascale (1990):

> IBM's managerial approach somehow embraces the conflicting demands of fit (emphasis on uniform values, coherence of systems and strategy), split (rivalry among divisions, and the creation of independent business units), and an abundance of contention (customer versus cost, valuing employee dignity versus disciplined approaches to the business and demands of employee sacrifice).

We will return to Pascale's thesis of 'fit', 'split' and 'contend' in Chapter 3 since it provides powerful insights into a broad range of organizational paradoxes. The question we must address here, though, is not 'who' are the excellent companies but, rather, 'what' are the excellent companies?

What are the excellent companies?

This question is the title of a paper published by Doyle (1992) who, in charting the preoccupation with excellent companies back to the late nineteenth century, makes the following observation: 'Excellence has become a popular exhortation and aspiration among managers, but it is a dangerous concept.'

Doyle draws attention to the typical treatment of excellence as a unidimensional measure. He calls for a recognition of a much broader range of stakeholder interests, including those of shareholders, managers, customers, employees, creditors, governments, suppliers, minority

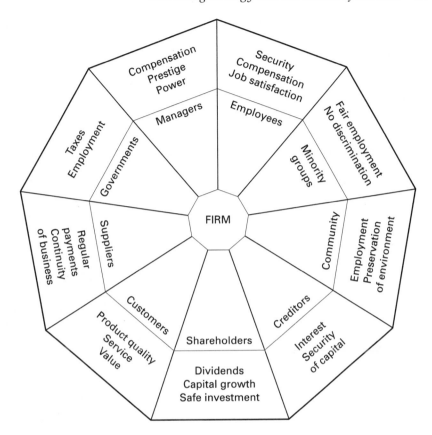

Figure 2.13   *The tolerance zone of stakeholder expectations (Source: Doyle, P. (1992), 'What are the excellent companies?' Journal of Marketing Management, 8, 2, 101–116)*

groups and local communities. Managing the multiple and often conflicting expectations of these interest groups is a key factor in ensuring organizational survival:

> Managers should therefore not seek to excel on any single goal, but rather to look for a balanced performance over time on a set of goals. They should seek to operate in the tolerance zone which gives all stakeholder groups a satisfactory level of achievement.

This 'tolerance zone' of stakeholders and their expectations is shown in Figure 2.13.

The true measure of success, according to Doyle, is organizational survival and this, in turn, is a function of 'achieving a satisfactory level of performance across a multiple competing set of criteria.'

In the final section of this chapter we examine the survival issue in more depth, identifying why it is that so many companies seem to become victims of their own success.

Nothing fails like success!

Implicit in our discussion in this chapter has been the notion of a dependency relationship between a firm and its business environment, the output of this being a function of the managerial actions company executives and employees undertake. As Tushman *et al.* (1986) have argued:

> A snug fit of external opportunity, company strategy, and internal structure is a hallmark of successful companies. The real test of executive leadership, however, is in maintaining this alignment in the face of changing competitive conditions.

This simple dynamic has been represented by Miller and Freisen (1984) as a triangle of environment, strategy and organization, with equilibrium being achieved when there is 'fit' among each of the three components. In Figure 2.14 we define the environment–strategy–organization relationship as a *nexus*, a word which describes the bonding of a linked group. The aim is to underline the dependency dimension which exists between the triangle's three components.

A common feature of all models of organizational competitiveness is the premise that it is the interaction among the components rather than their consideration in isolation which fundamentally explains performance, i.e. the whole is greater than the sum of its parts. This is also the basic premise of open systems theory and, indeed, underpins the substance of this book. Firms must ensure that the bonds between environment, strategy and organization remain intact, i.e. they must create and maintain a strong degree of 'fit' along each axis of the triangle in Figure 2.14.

What is clear, however, is that the nexus of environment, strategy and organization constitutes a complex range of interdependent variables which must be maintained in a state of dynamic equilibrium regardless of the rate of change in any of the three components. If imbalance emerges and remains there is likely to be corporate failure. As Pascale (1990) and others before him have noted, 'nothing fails like success':

> Winning organizations – whether the Israeli Army, the US Olympic Committee in its heyday, expanding young enterprises or established global corporations – are locked in the embrace of a potentially deadly paradox. This is because great strengths are inevitably the root of weakness.

One of the most remarkable commercial failure and recovery case histories is that of the Swiss watch industry. Swiss watch companies arrogantly underestimated emerging Japanese rivals and were dismissive of the notion of changing customer needs. The industry collapsed,

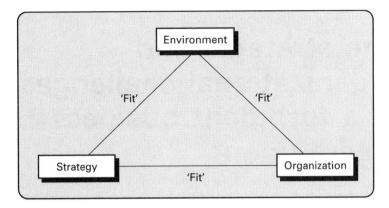

Figure 2.14 *The environment–strategy–organization nexus*

seriously damaging the Swiss economy. A remarkable recovery was made, with industry consolidation and product innovation (including the 'Swatch' phenomenon) restoring Swiss fortunes. The man responsible for the turnaround, Nicolas Hayek, aims to ensure that the industry does not repeat past blunders. Speaking to shareholders in June 1992, Hayek gave the following warning:

> The seeds of failure lie in success itself. We must be energetic and tireless, and every day fight against the beginnings of arrogance towards our customers. We must also be energetic and tireless against any tendency to become presumptuous, to rest on our laurels or fall back into old habits. This would be deadly for the enterprise.

In making this observation Hayek is warning against complacency, a poison which permeates many successful companies and precipitates their demise.

Concluding remarks

In this chapter we have tried to emphasize the fundamental dilemma facing many companies in the current era of discontinuity. Theory suggests that, in Figure 2.14, companies should take environmental analysis as their starting point, develop competitive strategies driven by customer focus and create an appropriate organizational form for their effective implementation. In practice, however, companies tend to do exactly the reverse. In the next chapter we examine why this is the case and the problems it causes. We examine each component of the 'strategic triangle' and explore the dynamics of the axes of 'fit' between them.

3

The strategic and organizational challenges of a turbulent business environment

Introduction

Economists and writers on strategic management draw attention to different levels and dynamics of change in the business environment in which firms operate. In periods of relative stability the factors which characterized previous years' business conditions are good predictors of future developments and the process of planning and managing the business can draw heavily on past experience. By contrast, when the business environment demonstrates 'discontinuous change' the management task becomes far more complex. Under these conditions independent environmental factors are changing in an unprecedented manner and, worse still, the dynamics between the factors are changing at the same time.

Environmental turbulence, complexity and change

The environment of any large organization encompasses an elaborate set of dynamic interactions, including economic, legal/political, competitive, technological, geographic, social/cultural and demographic variables, each of which will vary in importance and impact for individual firms and industries and will take on more or less significance at different periods of time. The business environment can be usefully subdivided into macro and micro variables to assist analysis, although it should be acknowledged that the influence, intensity and impact of such sub-environment forces will tend to be interdependent rather than independent. Figure 3.1 shows a typical representation of the business environment.

The key point to note is that a firm has very little control over those environmental variables external to it. So, for example, it has no influence over economic, legal, political, social and cultural factors. In its micro environment a company has little control over competitors,

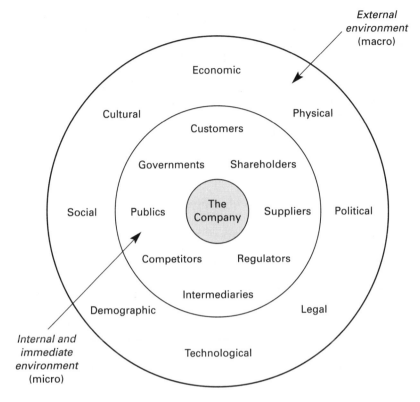

Figure 3.1   *The business environment*

suppliers, intermediaries or regulators. The immediate conclusion to draw from this is that a firm's success will depend upon its ability to maximize the effectiveness of those factors over which it has full control, i.e. its strategic choices and management processes. An equally immediate concern for companies is that such decisions and how it implements them will have a context riddled with risk and uncertainty.

Explaining risk and uncertainty

Risk and uncertainty permeate all functional aspects of corporate activities and they share a direct relationship with the dynamic nature of the business environment. The developing pace of such environmental change accompanied with the increasing size and complexity of the modern firm has given a high profile to the importance of accounting for risk among senior management, particularly in the strategic area of corporate planning. Here it has been recognized that large, diversified (or diversifying) companies have to understand the complexities involved in securing 'strategic fit', i.e. the particular relationship between the firm and its environment which facilitates the successful achievement of corporate objectives.

As the causes and effects of risk and uncertainty have become more significant to basic corporate objectives such as sales and profitability, so more and more complex models have been advanced for their analysis. Many such models have proved hopelessly inadequate, especially as their sophisticated mathematics have been found to be difficult to apply in practice (Mintzberg, 1994). Despite this, the challenge of knowledge acquisition remains one of fundamental importance if sensible strategies are to be formed and implemented.

Uncertainty, risk and the strategy challenge

Ansoff (1987) describes conditions of risk as the situation where alternatives are known and so are their probabilities; in contrast, conditions of uncertainty are those situations where alternatives are known but not their probabilities. Under conditions of risk and uncertainty, then, 'the consequences of different alternatives can be analysed in advance and decisions made contingent on their occurrence'. The means to achieving these contingent decisions is strategy, a process he describes as 'a rule for making decisions'. In this sense, strategies involve, at the most senior level, decisions regarding diversification and internationalization of operations. Before such major decisions are taken other sophisticated analysis might take place within a company, often based on the forecasting of future events and the delineation of corporate activities.

In analysing the impact of risk and uncertainty, then, firms should consider a variety of possible outcomes and then take a view as to the relative likelihood of their occurrence. Such a process would have as its starting point an overview of factors influencing the company at the present time and a consideration of key environmental trends. At the most senior levels of management within an organization risk is dealt with by decisions which are taken in the direction of corporate strategy (though note the definitional problems discussed in Chapter 2). The full complexities of risk analysis at this level are beyond the scope of this section but it is worth mentioning Ansoff's assessment of risk relating to corporate decisions to diversify or internationalize their business, a common strategic move among large organizations and one we assess more fully in Chapter 6. He sees two key problems within the practice of risk assessment: (i) there is a need to recognize at the outset that the ability to see the future in any detail is limited to only certain foreseeable events; (ii) there is every reason to expect that other events, unforeseeable at present, have a high likelihood of occurring. These factors, in turn, will affect the expectations derived from diversification or internationalization strategies, whose prospects will be dependent upon three sources of uncertainty: (i) uncertainties in the estimation of results; (ii) uncertainties in projecting the environment; (iii) uncertainties in anticipating competitive reaction.

Ansoff has usefully drawn together the implications of risk and uncertainty for decision making at the strategic level, indicating the importance of forecasting the variables which affect the business environment as well as highlighting the inherent difficulties of such predictive techniques. Of particular relevance here is to understand what he describes as the 'degree of changeability' in the business environment which, he argues, can be understood as levels of environmental turbulence. In attempting to quantify such turbulence, Ansoff (1987) has identified the following key factors which determine its force and impact: (a) the changeability of the market environment; (b) the speed of such change; (c) the intensity of competition; (d) the fertility of technology; (e) the level of discrimination by customers; (f) pressures from governments and influence groups.

In earlier work, Ansoff (1979) charted the history of environmental turbulence throughout the twentieth century and located its progressive increase among four key trends: (a) a growth in the novelty of change, whereby past experience becomes less useful; (b) a growth in the intensity of the environment, so that responsiveness to it absorbs a growing proportion of managerial resources; (c) an increase in the speed of environmental change, a major driving force being the speed of technological innovation; (d) the growing complexities of the business environment more generally.

Taken together, these key trends had led to a model of the business environment which Ansoff argued was characterized more by discontinuous change than the static and evolutionary nature of most environmental models in the available literature at that time. The recognition of revolutionary rather than evolutionary change was not a new phenomenon. In the broader context of the emerging post-industrial period, Peter Drucker (1969) had characterized the modern era as the 'Age of Discontinuity' and set in motion a theme which continued throughout the 1970s and 1980s. Kanter (1983) sums this up in the (American) managerial context:

American corporations are at a critical watershed because they face a transforming economic and social environment which has emerged since the 1960s. This new context ... makes past responses less effective; it changes the task for management at all levels.

She continued her study of environmental turbulence and the process of organizational change throughout the 1980s, concluding that the idea of change and acceptance of it was rapidly beginning a new corporate orthodoxy (Kanter, 1989). Further support for the ubiquitous nature of change drivers and processes in an international context was provided in a large survey of corporations around the world. The research was funded by the *Harvard Business Review* and coordinated by Kanter (1991). A truly global management perspective on change was sought and the background to the research was the identification of the following 'triggers' which were forcing radical corporate restructuring: (a) globalizing markets; (b) instantaneous communications; (c) travel at the speed of sound; (d) political realignments; (e) changing demographics; (f) technological transformations in both products and production processes; (g) a growing number of corporate alliances; (h) a flattening of organizations. Strong empirical evidence (from 11,678 responses) for both the ubiquitous nature of major organizational change and the continuing globalization of firms was presented, with 70 per cent of large companies reporting major restructuring programmes and 45 per cent undertaking international expansion.

The importance of such environmental change and turbulence is not its existence *per se*; rather, it is the ability of organizations to make appropriate responses. As Handy (1989) notes, 'discontinuous change requires discontinuous upside-down thinking to deal with it, even if both thinkers and thought appear absurd at first sight.' Discontinuity is similar in its meaning to Mitchell Waldrop's (1992) complexity construct, a concept developed from the emerging science of chaos theory. Providing a scientific perspective, Mitchell Waldrop, a physicist, took as the driving force behind his thinking the trend in scientific investigation towards holistic views as a challenge to the orthodoxy of deconstructing science into smaller and smaller parts of the whole. His notion of complexity is founded upon the following questions:

> Why is it that simple particles obeying simple rules will sometimes engage in the most astonishing, unpredictable behaviour? And why is it that simple particles will spontaneously organize themselves like stars, galaxies, snowflakes, and hurricanes – almost as if they were obeying a hidden yearning for organization and order?

Mitchell Waldrop (1992) has applied the complexity construct to economics. In a challenge to the equilibrium constructs of theoretical economists, he argues that such theories have shunned the reality of instability and change in the modern economy. Crystallizing his ideas within the notion of increasing returns, he argues that the complexity construct could help to 'understand the messiness, the upheaval, and the spontaneous self-organization of the world.' The concept of complexity embraces a flexible hierarchy controlled by the phenomena of evolution, adaptation and creativity. Emergence is seen as a behavioural construct in which, holistically, 'groups of agents transcend themselves and become more.' The construct develops the concept of co-evolution, in which survival strategies and fitness are seen to be dependent on context and interdependency, a notion developed in subsequent sections of this chapter and presented as the environment–strategy–organization nexus.

Understanding business environment dynamics

Ansoff and McDonnell (1990) have proposed a framework to interpret the implications of environmental turbulence for corporate survival. They offer a systematic approach which indicates the strategic and organizational changes necessary to assure a company's continued success in its future environment. The starting point, though, is to understand the dynamics of the business environment. Environmental turbulence is constructed from a joint measure of changeability and predictability and is defined by four attributes as follows:

1   Changeability:
  (i) Complexity of the firm's environment
  (ii) Relative novelty of the successive challenges which the firm encounters in the environment
2   Predictability:
  (iii) Rapidity of change, i.e. the ratio of the speed with which challenges evolve in the environment to the speed of the firm's response
  (iv) Visibility of the future which assesses the adequacy and the timeliness of information about the future.

Building from this analysis, Ansoff and McDonnell (1990) argue that a firm's performance potential is optimum when the following three conditions are met: (a) the aggressiveness of the firm's strategic behaviour matches the turbulence of its environment; (b) the responsiveness of the firm's capability matches the aggressiveness of its strategy; (c) the components of a firm's capability are supportive of one another.

From this synthesis of changeability and predictability a layered scale of turbulence is formulated which has five discrete levels of environmental turbulence: repetitive; expanding; changing; discontinuous; surprising. Figure 3.2 presents the Ansoff and McDonnell environmental analysis framework.

Different industrial sectors and companies from different countries will obviously be positioned at different points on the turbulence scale at any particular point in time. Despite this, in multisector, multicountry research Ansoff and McDonnell (1990) found that approximately 80 per cent of managers anticipated turbulence levels of 4 and above. Describing this phenomenon as a 'convergence toward the post-industrial predicament', the authors consider the implications of discontinuous or surprising environments for the strategic focus of commercial organizations. They propose a 'strategic success hypothesis' which matches 'the strategic aggressiveness' of the firm to the turbulence level of the business environment. This is demonstrated in Figure 3.3.

The implications are clear. Discontinuous or surprising business environments require radical departure from past strategic behaviour. This is fine in theory but extraordinarily difficult to achieve in practice. As Pascale (1990) notes:

Organizations have a tendency to do what they best know how to do. They are, if you will, the ultimate conservatives. The golden adage 'stick to your knitting' becomes an epitaph. This is because our fixation on 'what is' obscures that other aggravating necessity of worrying about 'what isn't' and 'what might be'.

Environmental turbulence	Repetitive	Expanding	Changing	Discontinuous	Surprising
Complexity Economic	National	+ Technological	Regional	+ Socio-political	Global
Familiarity of events	Familiar	Extrapolable		Discontinuous Familiar	Discontinuous Novel
Rapidity of change	Slower than response		Comparable to response		faster than response
Visibility of future	Recurring	Forecastable	Predictable	Partially predictable	Unpredictable surprises
Turbulence level	1	2	3	4	5

Changeability

Predictability

Turbulence scale

Figure 3.2 *A framework for environmental analysis (Source: Ansoff, I. and McDonnell, E. (1990), Implanting Strategic Management, Englewood Cliffs, NJ: Prentice-Hall)*

	Repetitive	Expanding	Changing	Discontinuous	Suprising
Environmental turbulence	Repetitive	Slow Incremental	Fast Incremental	Discontinuous Predictable	Discontinuous Unpredictable
	Stable	*Reactive*	*Anticipatory*	*Entrepreneurial*	*Creative*
Strategic aggressiveness	Based on precedents	Incremental Based on experience	Incremental Based on extrapolation	Discontinuous Based on expected futures	Discontinuous Based on creativity
Turbulence level	1	2	3	4	5

Figure 3.3 *Environmental turbulence and strategic response (Source: Ansoff, I. and McDonnell, E. (1990), Implanting Strategic Management, Englewood Cliffs, NJ: Prentice-Hall)*

Clearly, then, there is a strong dependency relationship between the environment of an organization, the appropriateness of its strategic posture towards this environment and the constraints on this strategic stance imposed by its organizational capabilities. This was modelled in Figure 2.14 as a triangle of 'fit', the suggestion being that an equilibrium be maintained among the three components. In the following sections each axis of the environment–strategy–organization framework is considered in more depth, the intention being to categorize key contributions from the literature and to capture the complexity behind what, on the surface, appears to be a relatively simple construct.

The environment–organization axis

Organization structure has been the subject of intense scrutiny by social scientists, ranging from the business historian to the social anthropologist. For our purposes the textbook definition given by Wilson and Rosenfeld (1990) is useful:

> the established pattern of relationships between the component parts of an organization, outlining both communication, control and authority patterns. Structure distinguishes the parts of an organization and delineates the relationship between them.

A key development in organizational analysis emerged in the 1960s with a recognition by researchers of a dynamic link between organization structure and a number of identifiable variables such as environmental stability, technology and firm size (e.g. Burns and Stalker, 1961; Woodward, 1965; Lawrence and Lorsch, 1967). In this perspective organizational structure is described as being 'contingent' upon a number of internal and external factors and the general proposition is that there can be no 'ideal type' of organizational form. Despite this, seminal research by Burns and Stalker (1961) in the UK, subsequently supported in the US context by Lawrence and Lorsch (1967), demonstrated that the most appropriate organizational structure is one which has a close 'fit' with its immediate environment. The Burns and Stalker research placed strong emphasis on the dynamic dimension of environmental analysis. It argued that stable environments were well served by *mechanistic* structures while turbulent and more difficult environments required the flexibility of an *organic* structure.

In a similar vein, Van de Ven (1988) has argued that the level of turbulence within an organization 'mirrors' that of its immediate environment. Where the degree of turbulence is high, an organic, flexible, organizational form is most appropriate, not only for immediate survival but also for the longer term benefits of organizational learning. Much of the work examining the environment–organization axis has focused on the role of technology as a determinant of structure. Significantly, the rate of change in technology development and how far this is predictable has also been proposed as a key factor explaining appropriate organizational form (Perrow, 1967).

Mintzberg (1979) has earned a reputation as an analyst of 'what is' rather than what 'should be' and as such has heavily criticized most studies of organizational form, being particularly vicious in his attacks on the prescriptive proposals so often advanced by researchers and consultants. Needless to say, he has developed his own perspective on appropriate organizational form and strategic processes. In arguing that the contingency school of thought has a number of limitations he proposes an advancement on their core principles:

> Spans of control, types of formalization and decentralization, planning systems, and matrix structures should not be picked and chosen independently, the way a shopper picks vegetables at the market. Rather, these and other elements of organizational design should logically configure into internally consistent groupings.

Mintzberg (1991) has developed his work further and now posits the notion of a 'floating' organizational form, one which demonstrates movements within a pentagon of organizational constraints (the nodes of which are developed from his earlier propositions regarding configuration). This movement can be described as the resultant vector of the action and interaction of five different forces: direction; efficiency; proficiency (knowledge and skill); concentration (market focus); innovation (learning and adaptation). The degree of movement is also regarded by Mintzberg as being a function of the organization's culture and political processes, i.e. as being heavily influenced and constrained by history and ingrained ideas as to what change is appropriate for the organization, *not* the environment in which it operates.

What is clear from the literature on organizational form is that a large number of possibilities exist to the creator of organizational structure and that many new forms are constantly emerging. From the complexity of Mintzberg's configured floating forms to the simple 'inverted pyramid' of Carlzon (1987), it is clear that the dynamic between the firm and its environment has a direct impact on organizational structure.

Just as organizational structure proves difficult to define with any precision, so does the notion of the environment of organization. Andrews (1991) describes the environment of organization as 'the pattern of all external conditions and influences that affect its life and development', a definition rooted in the theory of open systems. This latter school of thought recognizes the interdependence of influence between one entity and another, in this case the firm and its environment. As Pfeffer (1976) notes:

> Organizations are open social systems, engaged in constant and important transactions with other organizations in their environment ... As an open system ... the firm does not have control over many of the important factors that affect its operations. Because organizations are open they are affected by events outside their boundaries.

A recognition of the dependency dimension between a firm and its environment and an acknowledgement of the constraints imposed on an organization's will by external and uncontrollable variables has led to a plethora of tools and techniques for environmental analysis. The notion that, for continued success, the organization must establish appropriate 'fit' between itself and its environment is a powerful one and is empirically grounded in the work of the contingency theorists discussed above. To establish such fit it is clearly essential that the firm first of all understands environmental dynamics and, secondly, is responsive to them.

Some of the most influential approaches to environmental analysis have been published by Michael Porter (1980, 1985, 1990). The multifactor analytical approach to international competitiveness he developed (discussed in Chapter 1) is useful in explaining key global drivers and understanding how firms respond to them. While presenting an essentially historical perspective, Porter (1990) has highlighted the globalization of competition as a key characteristic of contemporary capitalism and as a major challenge to corporate orthodoxy. An examination of his findings explaining comparative international performance indicates that many of the fundamental success determinants of international competitiveness at the firm level are organizational in character.

Another seminal contribution from Porter (1980) was his notion of 'extended rivalry', whereby the determinants of an industry's profitability are broadened from the traditional market structure framework to embrace the threat of new entrants to the industry, the potential of technological substitutes to undermine an industry's established entry barriers and the profit impact of the bargaining power of buyers and suppliers. The threat of new entrants to an industry is frequently seen as a challenge to an established status quo and as such is often rigorously resisted, not only by industry incumbents at the point of attack but also by other members of the supply chain. The extreme hostility towards potential entrants to the UK brewing industry is a good example of how a supply chain's relentless pursuit of the status quo can raise powerful barriers to entry. In this case a concentrated supply base and a highly fragmented but wholly dependent distribution network have successfully fended off challenges from outsiders over a time frame spanning decades (Shipley and Egan, 1992).

When industrial structures are stable over time the organizational inertias which have developed tend to act as a major hurdle to innovation. Under these circumstances the 'substitute' in Porter's framework will often have to by-pass not just the established industry but the supply chain as a whole. A good example of this is the way that Dell Computer Company by-passed the traditional supply chain in the personal computer business to achieve rapid market penetration against companies such as Compaq with their established (and expensive) value-added dealer networks (*The Economist*, 1991b). Compaq have since applied this by-pass principle to rapidly penetrate the Japanese market, as have Toys-R-Us, the American toy retailer (*The Economist*, 1992b, 1992c).

An example which embraces both threat of new entrants and innovative substitutes is the Royal Bank of Scotland's entry into the UK insurance business through their Direct Line subsidiary. Once again the established and expensive intermediary network (brokers and agents) was by-passed, with the use of database marketing systems and effective advertising campaigns working to reassure customers of the superior service/lower price positioning of the offer. Initial attempts by traditional insurers to offset this competitive threat by underwriting insurance directly for car manufacturers (who offered 'free' insurance to their customers) were met with fierce resistance by insurance intermediaries. This is a good illustration of the environment–strategy–organization dependency nexus. Changes in the business environment of the large composite insurers (entrepreneurial and innovative market entry) forces a reformulation of strategy (direct sales to motor manufacturers) which, in turn, elicits a furious backlash from the established organizational form (insurance intermediaries) (*The Economist*, 1992d).

Markets or hierarchies?

One of the most influential writers on the relationship between organizational form and business environment has been Oliver Williamson (1975, 1985). Although it is firmly rooted within the discipline of institutional economics Williamson's approach is far more eclectic than is commonly recognized. It develops microeconomic theory to the level of transaction-specific issues, thus accommodating a behavioural dimension commonly ignored in economics discourse. The disciplines Willamson draws most heavily upon are economics and organizational theory (1975). He grounds these in a broad institutional context, placing particular emphasis on regulatory concerns (especially anti-trust) and the enforceability (and riskiness) of long-term contracts when confronted by unanticipated events.

Williamson's perspective constituted an attack on efficient market theory and embodied a recognition of the cognitive limitations (bounded rationality) found within organizations. The link between the two 'failure frameworks' (markets and organizations) is uncertainty and the related tendency of individuals to demonstrate opportunistic behaviour, i.e. to act in a self-interested manner but to do so with guile: 'Economic man, assessed with respect to his transactional characteristics, is thus a more subtle and devious creature than the usual self-interest seeking assumption reveals.' Given uncertainty, opportunism and the high costs of contingent planning (which in any case is constrained by knowledge and language limitations) both long-term and short-term contracting is fraught with peril. In these circumstances, 'the firm may decide to bypass the market and resort to hierarchical modes of organization. Transactions that might otherwise be handled in the market are thus performed internally, governed by administrative processes, instead.'

This, then, is what has become known as the 'markets and hierarchies' approach to organizational analysis. The basic premise is that firms will tend to absorb uncertainty by integrating its source inside their boundaries and within their control rather than expose themselves to bloody battle in the marketplace. This leads to two types of integration: (i) vertical – reflecting 'failures' in intermediate product markets; (ii) horizontal – the creation of multidivisional conglomerate organizations reflecting 'failures' in capital markets.

Valuable insights regarding the benefits, challenges and drawbacks of vertical integration have emerged within the strategy and marketing literature and these will be considered briefly here. In broad terms, 'marketing channels' constitute sets of interdependent organizations with generally independent objectives, but which are involved in essentially the same task. This task can be defined as 'the process of making a product or service available for consumption' (Stern and El-Ansary, 1988). Organizations in a channel system operate in a structured manner to undertake a set of distribution tasks, i.e. they exist to perform certain marketing functions. Stern and El-Ansary (1988) propose three important principles concerning structure in marketing channels: (i) one can eliminate or substitute institutions in the channel arrangements; (ii) however, the functions these institutions perform cannot be eliminated; (iii) when institutions are eliminated, their functions are shifted either forward or backward in the channel and, therefore, are assumed by other members. Thus, a set of marketing functions will need to be undertaken no matter who carries them out. The use of intermediaries in a marketing channel to perform such functions stems from two basic concepts: (i) specialization and division of labour; and (ii) contractual efficiency. The relationship between the two is concisely summarized by Stern and El-Ansary (1988): 'Marketing intermediaries, through their experience, their contacts, and their scale, offer other channel members more than they can usually achieve on their own.'

The theory of functional spin-off (Mallen, 1973) maintains that marketing channel members will perform only those tasks for which they have cost advantages and will delegate those tasks which other channel members can perform more cheaply. Cost is also a major consideration in deciding where inventory should reside in the channel. If a manufacturer is to be competitive, channel efficiency needs to be a consideration as well as channel effectiveness. The number of layers in a channel is often determined by the total number of potential final customers and the number of customers (either end-customers or intermediaries) that any one channel member can deal with effectively (Powers, 1989).

The implications for both efficiency and effectiveness need to be considered when any change to channel structure is proposed. The physical distribution/exchange side of the process (inventory, transport, order management) needs to be evaluated alongside the transaction-creating dimensions (negotiation, selling, post-transaction support). Marketing and physical distribution are often functionally separate in an organization, making integrated analysis difficult.

In corporate vertical marketing systems firms own and operate organizations at other levels in their distribution channel. This is the hierarchical basis of transactions as proposed by Williamson (1975). For example, a distribution channel is forwardly integrated where a manufacturer owns its own wholesale and/or retail outlets. Rosenbloom (1987) offers four broad reasons why manufacturers or other firms decide to develop a vertically integrated channel:

1   *Competition from competing systems*   This acknowledges the fact that the distribution channel itself can be considered as the unit of competition. A non-integrated manufacturer will be at a competitive disadvantage if its major competitors are vertically integrated or have formed tightly integrated contractual systems.
2   *Changes in market conditions*   Manufacturers might need to vertically integrate to give them the flexibility and control needed to adapt to changing market conditions.
3   *Scale economies*   For example, merger of formally independent units into a vertical channel allows them to operate at a level of production output and/or distribution capacity that is greater than they could have achieved on their own. Where demand is stagnant or declining, manufacturers might require a minimum level of secured outlets for its output to cover its long run average total costs.
4   *Channel conflict*   There is a conflictual tendency inherent in all interorganizational systems and the manufacturer may take the decision not to dedicate resources to managing the problem such conflictual relationships foster. This is a behavioural dimension of the market–hierarchy decision closely akin to the threat of opportunistic behaviour discussed by Williamson.

As previously mentioned, if a supplying firm removes a marketing intermediary from the supply chain the functions the latter performed have to be brought within the organization, i.e. the firm must undertake vertical integration (Stern and El-Ansary, 1988). Such decisions have a variety of market and financial implications. Regarding the latter, Lambert (1966) has argued that selling direct not only requires expenditure on the additional key distribution functions but that it also starves alternative projects of the capital involved.

More generally, the marketing and strategy literature has provided extensive coverage of the debate regarding the virtues or otherwise of vertical integration and its counterpart, disaggregation (e.g. Aspinwall, 1967; Bhasin and Stern, 1982; Buzzell, 1983; Clarke, 1987; Clarke and Gall, 1987; Coyne and Wright, 1985; Harrigan and Porter, 1983; Porter, 1980, 1987; Williamson, 1975).

Aspinwall (1967), for example, argued that patterns of distribution are a function of the characteristics of the goods being moved, prime determinants being replacement rate, profit margin, level of adjustment, searching time and consumption time. For industrial goods, Lilien (1979) demonstrated that the degree of vertical integration a firm employs is a function of firm size, average order size, purchase complexity (particularly technological issues), product life-cycle stage, the degree of product standardization and the level of purchase frequency. Porter (1980), meanwhile, sees vertical integration in the context of competitive analysis, whereby rivals would integrate to gain advantage of economies of scale, technology procurement, security of supply and, more generally, as part of a process of raising entry barriers.

There are, then, strong arguments supporting vertical integration. In a 'strategic' sense, manufacturers will have more control over exploiting new markets or dropping others. They will have more control over product sales (through carefully monitored promotional programmes) and pricing, as well as a greater ability to protect both the company and product reputation (Rosenbloom, 1987). There are also many arguments against, most commonly relating to the efficiency problems caused by increased bureaucracy and also diseconomies in management's ability to absorb and process information.

The factors favouring vertical integration appear to be on the wane and there is a growing awareness among researchers and practitioners of fundamental changes in traditional organization structures. Clearly defined roles and relationships both within and between organizations are breaking down and, in particular, there are fundamental changes in business relationships at the external boundaries of many organizations. Lorenz (1990) provides a useful summary of such developments:

> More and more activities which [organizations] used to carry out, in the cause (if not the name) of vertical integration, are being hived off to suppliers, alliance partners and so forth – not just cleaning and other peripheral functions, but ones which always used to be considered 'core', including production and distribution.

Among the most publicized discussions of these developments has been Handy's (1989) concept of 'The Shamrock Organization' although, like many writers, he has failed to address fully the issue of implementation. As Lorenz (1990) further argues, 'vertical disaggregation in favour of networking does not necessarily free an organization from unwanted tasks – it may simply make them more complicated, sensitive and difficult to manage.'

Despite such difficulties the general trend towards contracting out rather than integrating within seems inexorable. Hutt and Speh (1988), for example, report a survey which found that 67 per cent of purchasing executives were buying many more services than they were five years previously. Reasons for this included: the complexity of economic organization and the need to obtain economies from the division and specialization of labour; technological developments, e.g. computer information transmission, data collection and manufacturing systems; the need to remain flexible – capital commitment can be controlled by hiring services that provide 'use' without 'ownership'; time pressures (long lead-time to develop in-house expertise) and lack of available/appropriate internal resources.

A second general development in organizational relationships relates closely to the one discussed above. In order to remain competitive on costs firms are increasingly adopting Just-in-Time production methods which make more efficient use of capital, materials and physical space (O'Neal, 1987, 1989). An outcome of this development is the 'professionalization' of the purchasing function within organizations and the emergence of a more systematic approach to procurement (Cammish and Keough, 1991). A corollary of this has been that purchasing firms make heavier demands on their suppliers. JIT requires that suppliers ensure 100 per cent quality of the goods delivered and, of equal import, it demands close coordination in the physical distribution of materials.

It seems clear that the greater demands on suppliers as a result of the adoption of JIT needs to be matched by suitable inducements for the extra contributions to the relationship which they must make. In practice this has led to firms using fewer suppliers but offering assurances of long-term business relationships to companies which participate in 'partnership sourcing'. This parallels and to some extent complements the development in organization structure discussed above, particularly with regard to the changing nature of business relationships on the external boundaries of organizations.

From a systems perspective, the emergence of more and closer inter-organizational relationships suggested by the developments discussed above illustrates a general trend. Of particular note is that the closer reliance of organizations on each other greatly increases the internal dependency dimension between them. A literature base under the broad heading of network theory has rapidly emerged to observe and explain these developments; we discuss this more fully in Chapter 6.

Contemporary business environments, then, seem to be pushing companies more towards 'soft' integration, examples being partnership sourcing, relationship marketing, key account management, trade marketing and symbiotic marketing. A systemic perspective (Whittington, 1993) on strategy helps explain this phenomenon, particularly when considered alongside the economic and competitive dynamics which are driving the process. Regarding the latter, specialization and division of labour and the general strategic trend towards leveraging core competencies are driving the pace of disaggregation as firms seek to maximize the return on their assets by 'doing what they do best' as effectively as possible (Prahalad and Hamel, 1990). It should not be too surprising that Japanese companies are better placed to exploit the trend. The opportunistic behaviour described by Williamson is strongly associated with Western (and especially Anglo-Saxon) societies and is far less a feature of Asian culture. In this sense, Williamson's heavy emphasis on the legal dimension of transactions is more a function of the litigious character of American society than an explanation of competitive advantage (Kay, 1993a).

Willamson's contribution was seminal in its bringing together the behavioural and economic dimensions of organizational life and he did provide a very powerful tool (transaction cost analysis) to observe, prescribe and regulate corporate behaviour. Like any significant theory it emerged from a quite proscribed context. Williamson was heavily influenced by the business historian Alfred Chandler and was particularly impressed by the what he described as the 'organization innovation' of the 'M' form (multidivisional) organizational structure. While acknowledging some of its weaknesses Williamson was convinced that this particular organizational design provided the perfect facilitative mechanism for the hierarchical solution to risky and costly transactions. Despite this, Williamson's was a contingent approach, an observation neglected by many of his critics. Summing up his markets and hierarchies theory, Williamson drew the following note of caution:

> ... whichever way the assignment of transactions to firm or market is made initially, the choice ought not to be regarded as fixed. Both firms and markets change over time in ways that may render inappropriate an initial assignment of transactions to firm or market ... Thus we ought periodically to reassess the efficacy of completing transactions by one mode rather than another

Implicit in this statement is the suggestion that organizational form is readily manipulated to meet particular circumstances, i.e. that the decision to integrate or 'buy in' is an essentially rational choice. So, while suggesting a contingent approach we can also argue that Williamson is in fact showing his true colours. As he himself notes (1975), 'Scratch an economist and you find a deeply committed rationalist.' In the following sections we address this issue directly and examine the tremendous difficulties organizations have in changing from 'doing what we've always done' to 'doing what we need to do to succeed'.

The strategy–organization axis

The seminal research on the strategy–organizational structure dimension is that of the business historian Alfred Chandler. In an in-depth study of four large American corporations Chandler (1962) argued that the structure of an organization is heavily bound to the strategy it pursues and that, over time, successful firms adapt structure to 'fit' their strategic approach. In this sense, structure follows strategy, since 'growth without structural adjustment can only lead to economic inefficiency'.

The structure–strategy dimension is the subject of intense debate. Chandler's findings are empirically based and his prescriptions are accordingly normative: structure should follow strategy. In reality, however, organizations are bound by a complex array of inertias, not least of which is intense internal resistance to any change, let alone that required for new strategic direction. In particular, then, the reverse flow is often apparent. i.e. where strategy emerges from the existing organizational structure. As Tom Peters (1984) has noted:

> Strategy follows structure. Distinctive organizational performance ... is almost entirely a function of deeply ingrained repertoires. The organization, within its market place, is the way it acts from moment to moment – not the way it thinks it might act or ought to act.

Similarly, Rumelt (1991) has argued that a strict limitation on strategic choice is imposed by the extent to which individual and organizational capabilities are ingrained in the organization. The structure–strategy dimension encapsulates the clash between rational industrial economics and organizational behaviour, i.e. the conflict between what must be done for competitive success and the resistance to necessary change which is so common in large organizations. This friction and its survival implications are succinctly elaborated by Miller (1989):

> There are only a rather limited number of possible strategies and structures feasible in any type of environment. A few strategies and structures cause the organizations pursuing them to thrive at the expense of competing organizations. Competitors must therefore either begin to move toward the superior strategies, or perish. In either event the repertoire of viable strategic and structural configurations is reduced.

The structure–strategy dimension also embraces the implementation aspect of the marketing concept, which holds that a company should marshal its organizational resources to meet customer needs fully and better than rivals (Kotler, 1991). Keith (1960) has argued that companies pass through business orientations during their development in the same chronological order as the concepts themselves, i.e. production, product, selling and marketing. This suggests a degree of organizational latitude and temporal scope which is arguably untenable in the modern context. Contemporary reality is more accurately represented by a situation in which different functional teams within an organization absorb more of one philosophy than others, resulting in internal trade-offs in accordance with the notion that marketing should not be a function but a company mission. This view is shared by Achrol (1991), who argues that 'marketing's strategy concepts remain rooted in the historical evolution of functional approaches to a customer orientation.'

Such organizational barriers offer insights into the common scepticism which surrounds mission statements and their lack of success in uniting companies behind a common front. In operational terms this parallels a definition of 'quality' which demands selection of a level of quality suitable to the needs of the market, the adoption of an appropriate market positioning and the formulation of an operations strategy and process which ensures that there is 'conformance to specification' (Slack, 1991).

Achrol (1991) outlines the value of adhocracies and vertically disaggregated firms in which employees play different roles according to changing needs, the accompanying rotation and variety promoting trust, commitment, and culturalization. In particular, 'marketing coalition' companies are envisaged and defined as:

> Polymorphic organisms (which) adapt to fluctuating coarse-grained environments by developing multiple morphs, each of which is better adapted under a given set of environmental conditions.

Within these coalitions 'staff functions' such as R&D, finance and product assembly are surrounded by marketing which, in turn, liaises with customers through distribution channels, the whole structure promoting transactions with operational units. Classifying marketing coalitions as quasi-organizations, examples provided by Achrol include NASA and modern research universities. He sees these acting as functional alliances, controlled by a 'transorganizational polity' which is based on power sharing through information accessibility. Although Achrol (1991) contends that such organizational evolution may bode a new era for marketing he does draw a note of caution:

> Ultimately, these quasi-corporations will be successful to the extent they realize their fundamental promise – the promise of the purest kind of customer – and market-driven organization yet known.

Implicit in this statement is the fear that such optimal organizational forms, based on the essentially rational objective of maximizing customer satisfaction, will fall foul of well understood and documented management problems. Furthermore, if the superiority of a specific organizational form is so obvious it will be readily copied, thus eroding any advantage which may accrue to it.

The environment–strategy axis

Most definitions of strategy tend to focus on internal dimensions of organizations and draw strong associations between plans and/or patterns of activity. Quinn (1980a), for example, describes strategy as 'the pattern or plan that integrates an organization's major goals, policies, and action sequences into a cohesive whole.' Despite the predominantly internal focus of its definition, strategy is essentially an environmental construct, i.e. it formulates an approach of the organization to those clusters of variables in the external environment upon which it is dependent but over which it has limited or no control. A broader-based definition of strategy is offered by Ansoff (1987), who describes it as a 'system concept which gives coherence and direction to growth of a complex organization.'

Rather than explaining the pros and cons of strategy and strategic planning as a rational approach *per se*, it is perhaps more appropriate to look to the implementation of strategic planning in practice. Quinn (1978) has noted that strategy formulation has been developed by companies as a formal analytical and rational course of action, a process heavily reliant on quantitative data as its key input. This overemphasis on quantitative data is at the expense of what he describes as the 'vital qualitative, organizational, and power-behavioural factors which so often determine strategic success.' Quinn's notion of 'logical incrementalism' is derived from a logic which demands a flexible and to some extent experimental progression from broad concepts to specific commitments. The latter are delayed as long as possible as the best available information is collected to reduce uncertainty. Although the process can be criticized as slow and unwieldy, Quinn claims that the overall aim is to foster a common sense of identity with the company's strategic direction.

This latter point is crucial. The normative approach which character-izes much of the marketing and strategy literature more often than not neglects the behavioural issues and/or organizational constraints on strategy implementation. As Johnson notes (1988b), the core theme underpinning the 'incrementalist' thesis is that current business practice and perceptions of organizational competence are grounded in a politi-cal and historical context.

The incrementalist approach, then, while expedient for conditions of relative environmental stability, is likely to be unacceptable in periods of discontinuous change. The rapid demise of Nixdorf Computer and Wang Computer (*The Economist*, 1991c, 1992e) should have sent strong warning signals to IBM that, in their case, 'more of the same' was wholly inappropriate in the rapidly changing computer industry. In the event, IBM chose to persist with proprietary systems in the mainframe sector (where the trend was towards open systems) and a high price/strong image in the personal computer business where the trend was towards highly rational, well-informed price–performance purchasing.

Mintzberg (1987) has challenged the orthodoxy of strategy as a guide to future behaviour. He has argued that managers, when discussing strategy, tend to describe the consistency of past behaviour in terms of 'a pattern in action over time'. From this perspective, strategies are not an output of a deliberate process; rather, they have emerged over time:

> To manage strategy is to craft thought and action, control and learning, stability and change ... most of the time senior managers should not be formulating strategy at all; they should be getting on with making their organizations as effective as possible in pursuing the strategies they already have.

Furthermore,

> No stability means no strategy (no course to the future, no pattern from the past). Indeed, the very fact of having a strategy, and especially of making it explicit (as the conventional literature implores managers to do), creates resistance to strategic change.

Disagreement emerges, therefore, as to the degree to which strategy should be crafted out of the environment or out of the organization. In a contribution to the debate, Hamel and Prahalad (1989) criticise the strategic fit model (environment–strategy) and promote the alternative approach which centres on the problem of leveraging resources (organ-ization–strategy). From this they offer the following proposition: 'The two are not mutually exclusive, but they represent a significant differ-ence in emphasis – an emphasis that deeply affects how competitive battles get played out over time.'

They argue that the first approach involves a matching process of ambitions to available resources whereas the alternative places empha-sis on levering resources to reach seemingly unattainable goals. This argument reiterates a common theme which recognizes constraints and reduced degrees of freedom when implementing strategic change. The emphasis on organizational constraint is accurately reflected in the authors' further conceptualization of strategy as 'stretch and leverage' (Hamel and Prahalad, 1993). In this theoretical development they discuss the need to deconstruct established managerial frames of reference from a starting point which addresses the core question of 'what is strategy?':

> For a great many managers in large Western companies, the answer centres on three elements: the concept of fit, or the relationship between the company and its competitive environment; the allocation of resources among competing investment opportunities; and a long-term perspective in which 'patient money' figures prominently.

In stating this they argue that managers tend to translate fit into match and, in so doing, are often lulled into a false sense of security. Fit can be defined as 'qualified to be or worthy of being chosen' whereas *match* can be defined as 'one that is equal to another in status, achievement, value meaning or effect'. Fit can therefore been seen as either coping behaviour or opportunistic reaction to an unchangeable reality. A hypothesis can be put forward that the most successful organizations in an era of discontinuity will be those which make the fewest compromises during the development and implementation of strategic change, there being a correlation between degrees of freedom lost and tightness of fit achieved. With this in mind Hamel and Prahalad (1993) contend that the leverage of strategy should embrace five resource deployment processes:

1   *Concentrating resources*   Strategic intent is needed to focus resources and converge thinking on how to achieve the next advantage.
2   *Accumulating resources*   Knowing now to extract knowledge and use the knowledge better than competitors as well as learning to 'borrow' resources is an important aspect of leverage.
3   *Complementing resources*   Blending skills, functions and ingenuity and balancing innovative production and delivery services.
4   *Conserving resources*   Recycling, co-opting and shielding involves optimizing resource strengths as well as maximizing leverage from the weaknesses of competitors.
5   *Recovering resources*   Involves reducing the time between the expenditure of resources and their recovery.

Such initiatives are deemed to have the common goal of creating what Hamel and Prahalad (1993) describe as a designed chasm between ambition and resources. In the context of the above discussion, this could be interpreted as placing strategy in the context of the business environment in terms of the opportunities or ambitions it provides managers and within the organization in terms of the actions taken in the process of accumulation and exploitation of internal resources.

Given the ambiguity of the construct, the difficult question remains as to how the ephemeral nature of strategy can be grasped in more practical terms. Strategy is commonly divided into a process of strategic analysis, strategic choice and strategic implementation (e.g. Johnson and

Scholes, 1993). This approach can be considered to mirror the environment–strategy–organization nexus (strategic analysis representing the 'environment', strategic choice the 'strategy' and strategic implementation the 'organization'). Such division, however, tends to ignore the interrelatedness and interdependence of the three elements by viewing them in a linear and hence sequential fashion.

Conceptually, then, strategy does appear to be the weak link in the environment–strategy–organization nexus. While executives can readily express their perceptions of business environment and organizational issues, the intangibility of strategy is likely to result in varying definitions of the strategy construct and differences in opinion as to the optimal way to proceed in developing a strategic direction. The strong likelihood is that the functional differences in the roles the executives play will drive their definitions. Agreement as to the meaning and worth of strategy in any one organization/industry at any point in time might therefore decrease the risk of losing organizational degrees of freedom in forming strategic options and making effective and manageable choices.

Strategic planning

The preceding discussion highlights the superiority and universality of the dynamic attributes of the environment–strategy–organization nexus when compared with static and/or linear models such as those adopting the strategic analysis, strategic choice and strategic implementation approach. The nexus perspective permits a wider scope when considering the organizational aspects of strategy in its environmental context. In particular, it allows consideration of two behavioural dimensions of strategy, i.e. not only do people *do* strategy – resulting in organizational resistance to strategic change at the implementation stage – but people *formulate* strategy and start with a particular and often collective mind-set.

Without acknowledging this mind-set and analysing it, strategic choice will be constrained by not knowing the degree to which the perceptions of the strategic planners are 'clouded', both in their perceptions of the business environment and the organization's capabilities. In this respect, Mintzberg (1994) comments on the need to differentiate between strategic planning and strategic thinking, the former being analysis, the latter, synthesis. He identifies three key fallacies of strategic planning: (i) its attempt at prediction in the era of discontinuity; (ii) its typical detachment, in practice, from operations; (iii) the general point that formalized approaches are unable to forecast discontinuities. To solve the problem, he advocates the following approach: (a) the use of planning as a process of operationalizing strategy; (b) the recognition of the ability of all employees to promote strategic change; (c) the promotion of planners as catalysts, thus stimulating line managers to question conventional wisdom; (d) the acceptance and exploitation of the differentiation between creative thinkers and analytical planners; (e) a consideration of the behavioural aspects of over-formalizing the strategy

process. This most recent contribution of Mintzberg (1994) is comprehensive in scope, scathing in its critique of strategic planning in practice
but ultimately constructive in its conclusions. A fuller elaboration is
given in Chapter 7.

From the above discussion, it emerges that 'strategy' appears to be a
function of organizational interpretations of the environment and the
role and meaning of the term itself. This behavioural facet of strategy
arguably has two phases, the first surfacing during formulation and the
second during implementation: (i) the managerial perceptions and
attitudes which mould the process of formulating strategy; (ii) the loss
of meaning and communications impetus that occurs as strategic direction is 'downloaded'.

From this, it can be hypothesized that, in an era of discontinuity, the
risk of these behavioural issues negatively affecting performance will
increase as: (i) the scope for interpretation widens, thus increasing the
intra-executive range of perception; (ii) the complexity of the process
increases, thus making intra-organizational cohesion more arduous. To
constrain strategic choice in an era of discontinuity is therefore inevitable
but is also detrimental to organizational prowess.

Strategic intent

In their review of the literature, Johnson and Scholes (1993) found that,
in managing change, the need for clarity of direction and relevance to
the changing environment within strategic choice is essential. They argue
that superior performance rests in management's ability to sense the
critical forces at work around them and in how they manage change by
building a capability for organization-wide learning and adaptation.

An insight into how organizational learning can be encouraged is
provided in the definition of the term provided by Garvin (1993): 'A
learning organization is an organization skilled at creating, acquiring,
and transferring knowledge, and at modifying its behaviour to reflect
new knowledge and insights.'

There appears to be a strong consensus that strategy should be guided
by an open-minded view of the environment and that this should be
achieved by reducing cross-functional barriers to a minimum in order
for change management to be effective. Garvin (1993) argues for a
supportive context with boundaries opened to stimulate idea formulation and an atmosphere that eliminates barriers which impede learning.

Recent debate in organizational theory has focused on learning or
knowledge-based organizations but, despite this, the literature has yet to
offer much practical guidance as to how such knowledge or learning can
be created. That the construct is important is not at issue. As Nonaka
(1991) has argued, 'In an economy where the only certainty is uncertainty, the only one source of competitive advantage is knowledge.'

The concept of the learning organization has had a major influence on
the change management literature, a point we develop when returning
to a more detailed examination of strategic change in Chapter 5. In the

next sections we present a more holistic view of the environment–strategy axis, profiling first the practice of strategic management and then identifying the distinguishing characteristics of the strategic manager.

Strategic management

In practice, it has been argued that strategy has two dimensions (Ansoff, 1987):

- *Portfolio strategy:* the selection of product–market sectors the firm wishes to compete in, i.e. corporate decisions regarding *where* to compete. The most common analytical tools dealing with this question are the various portfolio matrices (e.g. the 'Boston Box', the GE multifactor market attractiveness/competitive position 'screen', Hofer's fifteen-cell product–market evolution framework) and, generically, the 'Ansoff Matrix' of product–market growth vectors.
- *Competitive Strategy:* the nature of competitive advantage exercised at the product–market interface, i.e. business unit decisions regarding *how* to compete. Porter's (1980) generic competitive strategies are the more commonly known approaches to this question although there is a wealth of literature from the marketing and strategy disciplines which provide a range of guidelines for action (e.g. Hooley and Saunders 1993; Brown 1993; Day 1990; McKiernan 1992).

Mintzberg (1988) has criticized the above category dichotomy as false, claiming that portfolio strategies merely deal with extensions of business strategy while the competitive strategy literature focuses almost exclusively on the identification of potential business strategies. He proposes an integrative classification of five generic strategy types:

1. *Locating the core business*   In what position in the value system does the organization wish to be located (e.g. raw materials versus finished goods)?
2. *Distinguishing the core business*   How can the organization distinguish itself from competitors?
3. *Elaborating the core business*   How can the core be developed (new products and/or new markets)?
4. *Extension of the core*   Integration up or down the value system and questions of diversification.
5. *Reconceiving the core*   Decisions regarding the reconfiguration of the core business.

Clearly, then, the concept of strategy and the importance of its relationship with competitive environments and organizational competencies is a complex one. As Ansoff (1987) contends, 'In summary, strategy is an elusive and somewhat abstract concept.'

Many authors have researched the axis between environmental characteristics and strategic choice. Ansoff (1987) draws the link between environmental turbulence and strategic approach, arguing that stable environments facilitate logical incrementalism while a turbulent context demands discontinuous strategic behaviour, what he describes as a change in the company's historical growth vector. Miles and Snow (1978) have also examined the dynamic between a firm's strategy and its 'domain', a combination of environment and life-cycle position. From this they proposed a typology of four strategic styles:

- *Domain defenders*   These companies attempt to achieve stability in response to the demands of the environment.
- *Domain prospectors*   These companies pursue more dynamic strategies, developing new products and seeking new markets in response to the environment.
- *Domain analysers*   These companies consider their environmental problems as a balance between maintenance of a stable product and customer base and the simultaneous identification and exploitation of new market opportunities.
- *Domain reactors*   These companies are purely reactive to the environment and are generally unwilling to take risks and exploit opportunities.

At the end of the day, companies are managed by people and, though the vast majority of the strategy literature tends to ignore this fundamental fact, it is essential to understand the issues at this micro level of analysis to comprehend fully the practice of strategic management.

The strategic manager

The above review concluded that the ephemeral nature of strategy can be made more tangible by interfunctional learning and knowledge creation at every level within the organization, breaking down barriers internally and externally. Ultimately, though, this will require a particular orientation among the people involved in the task of management. At the level of the individual manager, Hinterhuber and Popp (1992) identified the following characteristics possessed by 'strategically inclined' managers: (a) an entrepreneurial vision; (b) a corporate philosophy; (c) an ability to encourage employees to act freely in the interest of the whole company; (d) the drive to build an organization that fits their vision; (e) the confidence to involve line managers in strategic planning; (f) the ability to integrate their strategies with the corporate culture; (g) the inclination to point out directions and take new approaches; (h) luck; (i) the willingness to contribute to society and themselves.

Quoting a military strategist, General Helmut von Moltke, chief of the Prussian and German general staffs from 1858 to 1888, Hinterhuber and Popp (1992) have argued that the most important characteristics of a strategist are twofold: (i) the ability to understand the significance of events without being influenced by current opinion, changing attitudes, or personal prejudices; (ii) the ability to make decisions quickly and to take the indicated action without being deterred by a perceived danger.

Regardless of their distinctive characteristics or personality traits it must be acknowledged that, to be successful, a strategist must have clear goals and that, in business practice, these must embrace the core purpose of strategic management: the creation of customer value (Drucker, 1954).

Creating customer value

Normann and Ramirez (1993) argue that the principal role of strategy is 'the art of creating value'. Strategy, they argue, provides a company with direction and, if that direction is customer oriented, strategy can funnel energy towards creating and delivering value to customers. Their point of departure from traditional studies is the value chain as conceived by Porter (1985). Porter's model was devised to profile the process of adding value to resources in a structured fashion which would enable companies to map, build and sustain competitive advantage. Value chain analysis identifies differences in production costs and the price to be charged to the next customer, thus allowing strategies to be developed which could capture any surplus which is available. A key advantage of the tool is that value chains proposing alternative ways of satisfying the same need can be formulated for comparison. Value chain logic also highlights the potential to redefine the business through substitution of parts of the chain to add value. Finally, it can reveal transaction barriers which, if removed, promote purchase behaviour. By analysing all of the company's activities the value chain also has the potential to provide a holistic view of resource allocation, thus providing an integrated perspective on competitive strategy. Despite its prominence in the literature, the relevance of Porter's value chain concept in the age of discontinuity has been challenged by Normann and Ramirez (1993):

> This understanding of value is as outmoded as the old assembly line that it resembles and so is the view of strategy that goes with it. Global competition, changing markets, and new technologies are opening up qualitatively new ways of creating value. The options available to companies, customers, and suppliers are proliferating in ways Henry Ford never dreamed of.

Normann and Ramirez propose an alternative model, one which is claimed as more appropriate by virtue of its dynamic nature. The justification for a 'new' model is the observation that many companies are no longer confining themselves to adding value: the most successful are re-creating value through recognition of a 'value constellation'. This latter concept derives from the notion that transactional processes have become less sequential, more reciprocal and synchronous as well as more entwined in mobilized informed networks. Examples provided by the authors include Ikea, the Swedish furniture company, and the private network of pharmacies operating in Denmark. The latter transformation resulted in the complete reconfiguration of the operating business system, in the process making the pharmacies much more than just an outlet for drugs. Healthcare cost containment was placing the pharmacies at risk of being nationalized while at the same time patients were becoming more demanding.

The pharmacies built on their core strengths, creating a service which established new relationships based on healthcare information provision. Initiatives included expanding the range of products on offer, upgrading their customer-information services, creating an anti-smoking campaign backed by courses, offering newly developed home health-care services and the development of a database on drug side-effects and interactions. Many traditional members of the healthcare value chain felt that the pharmacists had encroached on their part of the 'production line', but the extraordinary success of the reconfiguration was an illustration of extracting more value from the supply chain.

Does strategic fit provide market-driven value?

The notion of strategic and/or organizational fit suggests a stagnant model which is arguably inappropriate for an era of discontinuity. The latter phenomenon, by definition, describes the constant changes between and within the relationships that form the nexus of environment–strategy–organization. However, uniting continuity and change identifies the core strategic management problem: value must be created without losing degrees of freedom within the triangle, i.e. without distorting its delicate equilibrium. The solution to the problem is less clear-cut than the simpler task of its identification. The key challenge, though, is to prevent loss of degrees of freedom between cross-functional areas in the minds of the strategists, this to be achieved by fostering organizational learning and sagacity rather than constant pursuit of some notion of universal wisdom. Normann and Ramirez (1993) draw together several themes when they explain the need for organizations to 'reposition or reinvent the company's offerings to create a better fit between the company's competencies and the value-creating activities of its customers.'

Wikstrom and Normann (1994) address the concepts of knowledge and value in a model which integrates the concept of value stars, customer orientation and organizational learning to provide an 'active generative knowledge function'. The aim is to improve systemic opportunities for the identification and absorption of external knowledge. This is particularly apposite when coping with discontinuity:

> The accelerating rate of change and the increasing complexity of the corporate environment both call for greater flexibility on the part of the company. Corporate knowledge bearers must learn quickly to create, absorb and apply new knowledge. A fundamental condition for the generation and maintenance of new knowledge is that organizational boundaries become blurred and penetrable.

The authors conclude with a biological analogy in which cross-functional knowledge generation is compared with cross-species pollination, thus bearing new fruit. A better analogy lies within the domain of genetics in which the transfer of DNA produces mistakes known as mutations. These create change which, if beneficial, is likely to pass onto the next generation – the evolutionary gameplan of survival of the fittest. In a management context the analogous loss of fitness is organizational entropy. Theory in social science is based on interpretations of good and bad practice. From their research, Normann and Ramirez (1993) concisely summarize the Darwinian implications of disequilibrium in the environment–strategy–organization nexus: 'In the new logic of value, this dialogue between competencies and customers explains the survival and success of some companies and the decline and failure of others.'

Maintaining dynamic equilibrium in the environment–strategy–organization nexus

It is clear from the preceding discussion that the nexus of environment, strategy and organization is dynamic in nature and that organizational success is a function of managerial ability to maintain equilibrium among the three system components. As the pace of change in the environment quickens so the speed of reconfiguration becomes critical. Johnson (1988a) has demonstrated that, in turbulent environments, companies pursuing an incrementalist approach to strategy will experience strategic drift. In these instances the firm's strategy – and, by inference, its structure – has not kept pace with environmental change. Explaining this phenomenon, Johnson (1988a) argues that the organization is constrained by a cultural paradigm which does not accommodate the admission of threats that might require the paradigm to change. In practice, a flawed perception of reality emerges, key environmental dynamics are filtered out and seen as unimportant, thus suppressing the appropriate strategic response. In a similar vein, Pascale (1990) has explained the failure of Peters and Waterman's (1982) excellent companies as a function of strategic drift, arguing that their strategies did not change as quickly or as much as environmental dynamics demanded.

In proposing the strengths of incrementalism, Quinn (1980a) argued that the organization's paradigm was itself flexible enough to change incrementally, i.e. to update itself in response to environmental change. In practice, however, Johnson (1988b) has demonstrated that such incremental paradigm change simply does not happen. At an even more fundamental level, Mintzberg (1987) has suggested that the very existence of an explicit strategy is likely to create resistance to strategic change, another factor creating the antecedents of strategic drift.

In outlining their 'Quantum Theory of Strategic Change', Miller and Freisen (1984) have argued that many large companies follow their original strategic positioning for very long periods, interrupted by occasional but sudden and substantive strategic reorientation. Research by Greiner (1989) has demonstrated that organizational growth cycles are not smoothed patterns of continuous expansion; rather, they are character-ized by alternating periods of long-term evolutionary (incremental) development and much shorter periods of revolutionary (discontinuous) change. Tushman *et al.* (1986) examined patterns of organizational devel-opment, noting a long process of 'converging change' (incremental system change) with interruptions in the form of 'frame breaking change' (revolutionary system change).

From the preceding discussion it can be seen that a consensus has emerged among researchers that, over time, organizations constantly strive to change both strategy and structure in response to dynamic environmental contexts. They do so with varying degrees of success, constrained to a greater or lesser extent by past experience. The process of adaptation has been characterized by continuity and change, with the latter occurring in contrasting periods of incrementalism and discontinuity. Kanter (1983) has noted that the time periods between discontinuous changes are decreasing, arguing that environmental turbulence is increasingly multidimensional whereas in the past it has principally been a function of one key driver, for example technology. Peters (1987) supports this view, arguing that the interactions between change variables are more important than the individual changes themselves.

The notion of combinations of individual incremental changes driving discontinuous change more generally also has roots within different research disciplines. Within mathematics, for example, catastrophe theory has been developed from the subset of topology, the aim being to explain discontinuous change by the interactions among several continuous changes. A simple 'catastrophe' occurs where only two variables (control factors) change smoothly but yield discontinuous behaviour. Woodcock and Davis (1978) have drawn on catastrophe theory to explain a variety of outcomes from disparate activities, for example crowd behaviour, aggression in dogs and, in an economic context, the relationship between competition and prices. More gener-ally, the profusion of 'chaotic' behaviour has stimulated intense interest among researchers from the 'pure' and 'social' scientists, a common objective being to explain unpredictable behaviour originating from systems whose output would otherwise appear to be entirely predictable (e.g. Peters, 1987; Pascale, 1990; Gleick, 1988; Stewart, 1989).

Pascale (1990) has argued that the establishment of a good fit between strategy, structure and environment does give a sharp focus to an organ-ization. However, it can also threaten it with stagnation. The principal problem is rooted in the organization's historical paradigm and, more specifically, it is an outcome of the pursuit of what he argues is the satis-ficing objective of achieving consensus as a means to reconcile and avoid contention. Eventually this suboptimal strategic management process locks the organization out of the new paradigms which might be essen-tial for its survival. The stagnation effect identified by Pascale is supported by empirical evidence from a number of other researchers (e.g. Peters, 1987; Johnson, 1988a; Hurst *et al.*, 1989) and a good descrip-tion of the process in action is offered by Tushman *et al.* (1986):

For those companies whose strategies fit environmental conditions, convergence brings better and better effectiveness ... Convergent periods are, however, a double edged sword. As organizations grow and become more successful, they develop internal forces for stability. Organizational structures and strategies become so interlinked they only allow compatible changes.

Pascale (1990) proposes the concept of conflict between opposites to enable an organization to cope with a rapidly changing and discontinuous environment: 'This is because each point of view represents a facet of reality, and these realities tend to challenge one another and raise questions.' He develops his approach through analysing the combination of constructs which he describes as 'Fit', 'Split', 'Contend' and 'Transcend':

- *Fit* refers to the consistency and coherence of an organization.
- *Split* relates to a variety of techniques the organization uses to sustain autonomy and diversity. In practice this often means breaking a bigger organization into smaller units, providing a sense of ownership and identity. Such units could be decentralized profit centres, stand-alone subsidiaries, multifunctional task forces or new venture teams.
- *Contend* refers to the acknowledgement of the presence and value of constructive conflict. It argues for 'inescapable' interfunctional conflict to be harnessed rather than suppressed.
- *Transcend* refers to the different mind-set required for successful management of the complexity associated with the orchestration of fit, split and contend. It sees the dynamic synthesis (tension) of contradictory opposites as the engine of self-renewal.

While transcend can be described as the superordinate task, it is contend which allows the managerial approach proposed by Pascale to work in practice. Contend, then, deals with the management of the tension between fit and split: 'Fit contributes to coherence – but too much of it risks over-adaptation. Split helps to instil vitality and focus – but too much of it diffuses energy ... Contention management is essential to orchestrate the tension that arises.'

Building on this proposition Pascale identifies seven domains of contention (modelled on the 7S framework), each of which represents a conflict which requires resolution:

The forces that we have historically regarded as locked in opposition can be viewed (through a different mind-set, or paradigm) as apparent opposites generating inquiry and adaptive responses. This is because each point of view represents a facet of reality, and these realities tend to challenge one another and raise questions.

Dialectic analysis of the type proposed by Pascale has deep roots in social science, with Hegel's thesis/antithesis construct being amongst the most influential. In a managerial context the literature is heavily laden with dialectical phenomena, Peters and Waterman's (1982) 'simultaneous loose–tight properties' being among the most widely disseminated examples.

In a similar vein, Kanter (1989) described the need for a 'post-entrepreneurial' response within companies to enable tightly controlled companies to 'loosen up' and loosely managed companies to 'tighten up' their management approach. The aim is clearly to establish and maintain balance between the loose–tight dialectic proposed by Peters and Waterman as a facilitator of excellence. Despite this, recognition of dialectics will not in itself be adequate to secure organizational survival and success. As Pascale (1990) notes, each of the seven dialectics he has identified must be attacked simultaneously as the organization 'transforms' itself through paradigm change:

> With discontinuous change, leadership leaps into the unknown ... the choices are abstract; their results cannot be predicted ... Transformation is the managerial equivalent of Rubik's cube. If you go left first and right second, you come out in a different place than if you had moved right first and left second.

Concluding remarks

The previous sections have outlined the need for flexibility in organizational response to ensure ongoing success in turbulent environments. This 'survival of the fittest' notion is powerful but does tend towards a reification of organizational form. At the end of the day 'organization' is an abstract concept; an organization is simply a collection of human and capital assets with a rationale. Remove the rationale and the organization will cease to exist. The challenge of organizational change, then, is, as Peter Drucker (1974) has argued, a challenge of management. A variety of contemporary environmental factors have raised the importance of the change dimension as a significant factor impacting upon organizational survival. These, in turn, have led managers to re-evaluate the whole range of business processes and, more specifically, to seek ways of 're-engineering' them. In the next chapter we examine the general failure of this approach as a preface to a more detailed discussion of the strategic priorities and organizational inertias associated with change programmes.

4
Panaceas and pitfalls in the practice of strategic management

Introduction

In their struggle for superiority or survival firms constantly strive to seek better ways of doing business alongside keeping a sharp look-out for lucrative opportunities they can tap into and exploit ahead of rivals. The most exciting (and best selling) books on strategy have tended to focus on this latter element, in many cases drawing on military metaphors to map out the nature of the strategic game. A typical example is James (1985). Seeing business as a sequence of wargames, a battle where 'if you don't fight you can't win', James argues that the role of strategy is to enable the effective conduct of conflict:

> Since both armies and companies are competitive systems trying to secure an advantage over adversaries, they are conflict oriented and strategy is used as the policy tool for planning aggression against opponents.

The suggestion of a zero-sum game here is typical of the genre of 'winner takes all' contributions to the strategy literature and is normally associated with prescriptive solutions for achieving competitive edge. When it encroaches on the field of strategy this is the area where the marketing literature finds its natural home. Unfortunately, the examples given in support of the warfare analogy tend to be one-off and anecdotal, snapshots in time which ignore the background of events and the sustainability of outcomes.

Analysing the practice of strategic management

A classic example of difficulties encountered in interpreting strategic management practice is found in the alternative explanations given of Honda's marketing success with its motorcycles in North America. The Boston Consulting Group (1975) presented this success as a highly typical Japanese approach to market penetration, an aggressive and rationally calculated frontal attack which exploited the company's dominant position and low-cost base in its domestic market. Pascale (1984), meanwhile, has convincingly argued that the whole episode boiled down to luck. In his account, the real spur to sales of Honda's motorcycles came from an entrepreneurial Sears buyer and a University of California undergraduate who coined the phrase, 'You meet the nicest people on a Honda'.

These disparate interpretations of the 'same' series of events should not detract from Honda's undoubted competence and it must be acknowledged that Honda's growth and continued success can hardly be explained away by cumulative chance (Kay, 1993a). As the golfer Arnold Palmer once noted, 'The more I practise, the luckier I get'! The important point raised by the Honda example is that strategy should be seen as a process, an outcome of complex behavioural patterns within companies which closely reflect the political and cultural dimensions of organizational life (Pettigrew, 1977). As we saw in Chapter 2, inherent conflicts and inevitable trade-offs constrain a company's ability to take optimal decisions, satisficing behaviour being the norm.

Regardless of whether or not firms are able to implement rationally developed strategies, they must still strive to maximize the efficiency of their operations. Productivity gains remain the most powerful driver of competitiveness and they underpin the dynamics of economic growth. As we saw in Chapter 1, relative performance in enhancing productivity is a major factor used to explain international competitiveness, a lesson not lost on American industry as it spent the 1980s coming to terms with gains which had been made by its global rivals. Particularly impressive has been the relentless pursuit of productivity advantage among Japanese companies, a competitive edge greatly enhanced by the use of industrial robotics to deliver the manufacturing holy grail of low cost/high variety. Large increases in the capital intensity of production in Japan followed by technology transfer to lower labour cost countries has driven the process of continuous productivity gain, a manufacturing advantage enhanced further by the early adoption of the *kanban* system of JIT production processes and the successful achievement of zero inventories. In the light of these developments the key strategic issue is a sharp focus on corporate capabilities, real or required. As Stalk *et al.* (1992) argue:

> Competition is now a 'war of movement' in which success depends on anticipation of market trends and quick response to changing customer needs. Successful competitors move quickly in and out of products, markets, and sometimes even entire businesses – a process more akin to an interactive video game than to chess. In such an environment, the essence of strategy is *not* the structure of a company's products and markets, but the dynamics of its behaviour.

Once again, we see the notion of organizational competence being advanced to explain competitiveness. A growing awareness of this basic reality has spawned a host of 'business solutions' ranging from simple and small-scale change programmes to agendas aimed at radical restructuring of an organization's entire business systems. The management literature is notoriously prone to fashion and fad, with catch-all panaceas frequently being offered to reinvigorate corporate performance. A contemporary example of an idea which has achieved rapid diffusion within the corporate community is the concept of Business Process Re-engineering (BPR). The basic premise is simple enough: corporate transformation based on 'clean sheet' reinvention of business processes leads to huge productivity gains and enhanced competitive performance (Hammer and Champy, 1993). The key words describing BPR are *fundamental, radical* and *dramatic,* the overall objective being to make quantum leaps in performance (Hammer and Champy, 1993):

> Re-engineering is about beginning again with a clean sheet of paper. It is about rejecting the conventional wisdom and received assumptions of the past. Re-engineering is about inventing new approaches to process structure that bear little or no resemblance to those of previous eras. Fundamentally, re-engineering is about reversing the industrial revolution.

Behind the success stories, however, there are growing question marks regarding the usefulness of the concept. In subsequent sections we examine the claims made by BPR's proponents, profile the 'triggers' which have stimulated its rapid ascendance as a business tool and critically evaluate its claimed role in effective strategic management. Before this, however, it is important to place BPR in its more mundane context. In the next section we examine the antecedents of the BPR phenomenon, focusing in particular on earlier renditions of agendas which had organizational change as their central theme.

Programmed approaches to organizational change

Wilson (1992) describes 'programmed' approaches to organizational change as those which deal with the 'how' of change rather than objectively considering its processes or its outcomes. He identifies four levels of analysis within this change category: (i) programmes aimed at individual organizations (e.g. Total Quality Management); (ii) programmes tailored for individual managers (e.g. management training and development); (iii) macro structural programmes of change (e.g. joint ventures and strategic alliances); (iv) economic programmes for change (e.g. deregulation and privatization). In this book we are concerned with the first three, although we have considered the impact of (iv) on certain sectors in specific countries (e.g. the US airline industry) and in discussing models of competition (see Chapter 1). The following sections deal with (i). The issues associated with management development are discussed in the broader strategic context in the next chapter. The issue of cooperation and collaboration is such a major topic of contemporary management that it forms the substance of a chapter in its own right (Chapter 6).

Examining organizational change programmes

Total Quality Management (TQM) is the most commonly encountered organizational change programme. In many ways it advocates the type of radical organizational transformation now associated with the proponents of BPR, a contention supported by examining a standard definition of the construct (Oakland, 1989):

> Total Quality Management (TQM) is an approach to improving the effectiveness and flexibility of businesses as a whole. It is essentially a way of organizing and involving the whole organization; every department, every activity, every single person at every level. For an organization to be truly effective, each part of it must work properly together, recognizing that every person and every activity affects, and in turn is affected by, others.

Despite its obvious potential and Oakland's demands that TQM become 'a way of life in most organizations', the most striking characteristic of TQM is the virtual certainty that the projects will 'run out of steam' or fail within 18 months to two years of pursuit of the endeavour (Smith *et al.*, 1994). The programmable elements of TQM as a business process reveal its organizational limitations. Reporting longitudinal research among executives from a broad cross-section of industries attending management development programmes, Wilson (1992) profiled the following critique of change programmes directed at TQM principles. The list is ranked according to level of disillusionment with TQM by executives involved in its practice.

1   *The problem of intangible benefits*   TQM creates a tremendous amount of activity but often delivers little which is tangible, standard accreditations aside. Little organizational change occurs from this most frequently employed of change programmes.
2   *TQM creates sectional interests*   This is a particular problem when interest in the process fragments between those who are 'evangelists' and those who are much less enthusiastic.
3   *The customer first/customer as judge syndrome*   While it is accepted that a customer-first focus is laudable, the common situation whereby the customer is sole judge of TQM success can alienate and de-motivate those responsible for initiating the original programme.
4   *The sponge phenomenon*   The scale of TQM programmes expands to the extent that they end up soaking up more problems they were designed for or could be realistically expected to handle. This can generate a self-fulfilling prophecy whereby TQM is 'bad' because it never works, despite the disparity between design and execution.
5   *The problem of re-creating the rigid organization*   TQM programmes which are perceived as successful forestall further essential change, as managers enjoy the comfort of an apparently fruitful status quo.
6   *Blurred boundaries between means and ends*   TQM programmes have a tendency to become an end in themselves rather than a means to systematic organizational change. This is a particular problem for

critical path, sequential-type processes wherein one stage needs fulfilling before further change stages are embarked upon.

7 *TQM programmes make things worse* TQM is not a panacea and, paradoxically, it is likely to be of greater benefit to those companies in a relatively healthy state prior to its inception. It is not an appropriate process for companies facing crises (massive strategic change) and, in fact, could seal the fate of those companies facing absolute decline in economic performance.

8 *Lack of generalizable empirical evidence* There is a paucity of strong support for TQM success, particularly in a European context. Generalizability is a problem, particularly the transferability of TQM principles from the manufacturing sector which, to date, has been the major application source of the concept. Furthermore, the adaptation requirements for disparate international cultures are not well accommodated in traditional TQM manifestos.

The first in the recent flurry of process solutions for organizational change, then, has failed to deliver on its early promise. In the light of such dismal and recent experience one would have expected a reluctance among executives to be overly enthusiastic about a concept which offered a similar panacea and, like its predecessor, wore a three-letter acronym as its distinctive label. Indeed, there is a growing body of evidence that the concept of Business Process Re-engineering (BPR) is viewed with growing scepticism by both practitioner and academics. Despite this, the concept has enjoyed a rapid ascendance as *the* management tool, a phenomenon not witnessed since the swift diffusion of 'excellence' in the early 1980s. With this in mind we examine its foundations and force.

BPR – rationale and role

The strategic management literature has yet to catch up with the BPR phenomenon, publications to date largely emanating from the consultancy organizations which are promoting its use. It is fitting that we review one such tome since it allows us to subject the managerialist perspective of BPR to a more sober academic investigation. We review here one of the more respected books on the topic, that written by Coopers and Lybrand consultant Henry Johansson and his colleagues (Johansson *et al.*, 1993). These authors claim that the pressure for process solutions is driven by four customer-based 'value-metrics' of enhanced quality and/or service and reduced cycle time and cost to the customer. The value-metrics are shown in Figure 4.1.

BPR is aimed at radical rather than continuous improvement and as such is given a strategic role. It is proposed as an umbrella concept which encompasses the core competencies of the organization and employs 'tools' such as JIT and TQM to improve operational effectiveness, secure control of the supply chain and to provide new market opportunities.

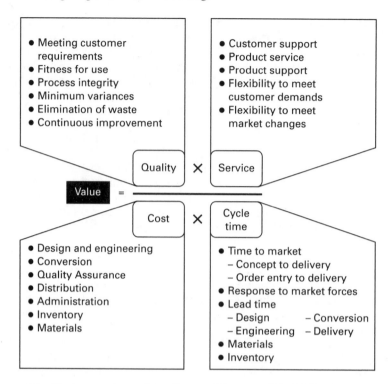

Figure 4.1   *Customer value metrics (Source: Johansson, H.J., McHugh, P., Pendlebury, A.J. and Wheeler III, W.A. (1993),* Business Process Re-engineering: Breakpoint Strategies for Market Dominance, *Chichester: Wiley)*

While the push to BPR is seen as externally driven – customers, competitors, cost, technology shift, shareholders – the greatest challenge to its implementation is identified as organizational. The authors are particularly critical of the suboptimization they see as a distinguishing characteristic of the functional structures found in many Western companies, a weakness upon which the BPR panacea is built:

> This kind of organizational linking needs to be broken apart and rebuilt as a process-oriented business, where everyone understands the ultimate goals, the ways of getting there, and the way in which success will be measured; where everyone regards working in cross-functional teams as the norm; where everyone understands and appreciates the value others add to the organization; and where everyone knows that the key goal is to produce a service or product that the marketplace perceives to be the best.

This ambitious agenda requires a paradigm shift, described by Johansson *et al.* as 'breaking the china' which, in turn, requires that management has a new outlook on the key 'enablers' of BPR within their organization: (i) people ('renaissance' employees); (ii) management and leadership (to deal with the angst of radicalization); (iii) organizational culture (vision, shared values, teamwork, constituency relationships, strategic intent); (iv) functional expertise (cf. bias); (v) technology stockpiling (keeping one-step-ahead); (vi) instantaneous reaction (to exploit strategic windows); (vii) asset management (intangibles and excess capacity); (viii) performance indicators (which must be value-metric-based).

Within this context BPR is proposed as a holistic and radical solution to three key management challenges: (i) cost reduction; (ii) renewed competitiveness (to achieve parity or best practice); (iii) achievement of competitive dominance. Regarding cost reduction, BPR claims greater sophistication than the more traditional route of functional downsizing, since redesigning a process, as a value-added construct, is seen as creating more value for less cost. A powerful argument is advanced which states that the key to success in carrying out BPR is adoption of a rigorous methodology, posited by Johansson *et al.* as a three-phase approach, each of which is now considered in turn.

* *Phase 1: Discover*   Subtitled 'a strategic plan for dominance', the first phase aims to identify the potential for and scope of re-engineering within the organization. A cross-functional multidisciplined team is created and employs techniques such as process mapping, systems analysis and customer satisfaction surveys to identify re-engineering opportunity. In this phase a 'culture audit' is undertaken to identify positive forces for change alongside a recognition of potential cultural obstacles to the re-engineering effort. The key processes to be changed are documented alongside the identification of improvement potential in related and/or supporting processes. Finally, top management commitment to the effort required to implement the long-term re-engineering and to accept the radical changes it will generate has to be reconfirmed.
* *Phase 2: Redesign*   Subtitled 'detailing the re-engineering process', the core process(es) selected for re-engineering are examined in much greater detail, using more sophisticated, activity-based process mapping techniques. The project team will tend to recruit specialist members and the goal will be to generate a conceptual design of the core business process after re-engineering has been undertaken. Analysis of the effect of the change in operational processes alongside an evaluation of the redesign on supplier and customer relations is essential at this stage. The change management issues must be identified, the conceptual design must be engineered in a detailed way and a formal recommitment from top management to the process must be secured.
* *Phase 3: Realize*   Subtitled 'time to implement', the project team in this phase is responsible for a broad range of activities, including the creation of the appropriate organization, introduction of operational targets, setting up of appraisal and reward systems and installation of processes that will facilitate further step-changes in performance improvement. The emphasis at this stage relates to the fact that BPR is a company-wide effort, the objective being to 'create a top-to-bottom transformation of the business's operations'. Effective

communication of 'milestones' is essential, roles and responsibilities of participants must be clearly defined and a feeling of shared ownership of the re-engineered solution should be fostered.

Johansson *et al.* detail the 'special case' of using BPR to 'search for break-points', defined as 'the achievement of excellence in one or more value-metrics where the marketplace clearly recognizes the advantage, and where the ensuing result is a disproportionate and sustained increase in the supplier's market share.'

To summarize this section and to give a feel for the managerialist perspective on the BPR 'phenomenon' the basic principles of the construct as proposed by Johansson *et al.* are quoted here in full:

1   Think of the entire core process, from the time the customer makes a connection with your company through the connections with suppliers and back to the customer.
2   Challenge everything that is done, constantly asking 'why?'. The improvement group members more often than not received the typical answer: 'because that's the way it's always been done.'
3   Process improvement efforts cannot be allowed to push problems upstream on to suppliers: the goal should be creating 'virtuality' in the process by including the supplier and its expertise in an effort to streamline and upgrade the entire process. Relations with suppliers need to be 'win–win'.
4   Take the process improvement to the marketplace; use the business process re-engineering effort to capture and control markets, or to seek out new markets.

Evaluating BPR – breakthrough or bauble?

The power of labels to stick in the managerialist literature is well documented, the catchy phrase being surpassed only by acronyms and alphanumeric mnemonics. The BPR label originated in a short *Harvard Business Review* article whose focus was an attack on the overlaying of IT systems on fundamentally deficient business processes (Hammer, 1990). The principal beneficiary of the concept to date would seem to be the consultancy profession, as a *Management Today* report caustically notes (Oliver, 1993):

> There is a new-look menu over at The Consultant's Café. Good old soupe du TQM and change management pâté are off. Perhaps you would care to try some business process re-engineering (BPR) instead? Corporate diners beware. BPR, that nouvellest of consultant cuisine, bears no resemblance to a standard Saturday night take-away.

The following 'sound bites' from three leading consultants in the field (interviewed in *Management Today*) hint at the shallowness of the construct. Terry Finerty (Arthur Anderson) comments:

The new aspect of BPR is its holistic nature: strategy, process, technology and people are aligned to achieve outstanding results ... we often call it 'bold moves by careful people that deliver lasting results.'

James Kelly (Gemini Consulting) argues:

BPR often involves abandoning traditional hierarchical best practices and replacing them with more lateral, more networked, more self-managed people who can both perform their own functions well but also connect effectively and efficiently with other functions.

Meanwhile, John Houlihan (Booz Allen and Hamilton) notes:

The reason to re-engineer ... is not necessarily to do with how successful you are today, but where you want to be tomorrow.

There is nothing inherently wrong with these statements, but there is certainly nothing new. The methodologies being employed by the consultants interviewed were strikingly similar to each other (and that of the Johansson group) and, in practice, bear a strong resemblance to the traditional managerial approach of systems analysis and operations research (see, for example, Dyson, 1990).

Conceptually, BPR is also difficult to disentangle from traditional value chain analysis and configuration (Porter, 1985) and, indeed, the latter approach is arguably much stronger, particularly on the mapping of external linkages. Although O'Sullivan and Geringer (1993) have proposed the use of value chain analysis as a constituent part of the re-engineering process it can be argued that too much faith is placed on BPR's ability to deliver the cross-functional operationalization essential for enhanced performance. The 'breakthrough' unanimously claimed for BPR as a business concept is its 'quantum-leap' potential (Hammer and Champy, 1993). In support of this claim a good deal of evidence of extraordinary successes achieved by firms adopting BPR principles has emerged. Although largely anecdotal it is worthy of examination since its very existence provides the bedrock of the BPR phenomenon.

BPR's successes

The claims made for BPR certainly seem impressive. Johansson *et al.* (1993) offer the following success stories: in a BPR cost reduction exercise Dun & Bradstreet were able to save $7m annually, achieve staff reductions of more than 200, at a modest one-off cost for new technology; Coca-Cola & Schweppes Beverages Limited achieved 'break points' in supply chain management, capacity utilization, product cost and inventory management; the 'Couplings Company' (like many BPR examples, a pseudonym) reduced lead time from between 28 and 32 weeks to between 10 and 11 weeks, reduced headcount by 29 per cent, achieved an $8m inventory reduction potential, reduced input costs by $530,000 and maintained sales volume in a market which declined by 20 per cent.

The consultants interviewed by *Management Today* each had their success stories to sell. Terry Finerty (Arthur Anderson):

> An example of BPR success is a telecommunications client which reduced its product development cycle from four years to six months, reduced administrative process costs by 50 per cent, increased sales rep productivity by 300–1200 per cent and increased customer satisfaction by 35–95 per cent.

James Kelly (Gemini Consulting):

> As an example of the success which can be achieved, one of our telecommunications clients introduced a '2-3-4 programme', i.e. $200m of cost savings, $300m of revenue enhancement and $400m of capital cost reduction. It is now the most cost effective telephone company in the industry, has the least number of employees per access line, the lowest number of faults per 1000 lines, fewer complaints than its competitors and has successfully expanded its revenue base into new fields.

And, finally, John Houlihan (Booz Allen & Hamilton):

> An example of successful re-engineering is the Kingston Hospital Trust which is embracing the concept of patient focus. The concept of patient focus means that two or three people are trained to have full, continual, total service responsibility for the patient from the beginning to the end without hand-offs. The BPR programme is organizing all aspects of patient care along the lines of patient service as opposed to functional hierarchies. An estimated 55 per cent increase in levels of direct care provided is expected using the BPR approach, without any increase in total personnel-related costs.

In a 'case' study forming a central part of the *Management Today* feature, a profile of Sun Life Assurance Society demonstrated the successful outputs of a three-year BPR project, a 'missionary zeal' led by the company's management director. The company achieved 40–90 per cent improvements in process turnaround times, 10 per cent reduction in the unit costs of key processes and 50–80 per cent improvements in service quality (defined as work performed right first time).

Launching a series of articles on the topic of BPR in the *Financial Times*, Lorenz (1993a) profiled the following success stories: Bell Atlantic reduced connection lead times to long distance carrier services from 2–3 weeks to 3 days, the final target being a few hours; an AT&T subsidiary supplying personal computer manufacturers reduced its design delivery cycle from 53 to 5 days within two years; IBM credit reduced the time taken to approve and issue financing deals from a week to four hours. In a more detailed case analysis, Lorenz (1993b,c) profiled the 'change conundrum' experienced by Rank Xerox, a company which had demonstrated top management commitment to BPR but which had struggled to approach anything like successful implementation. As one senior executive observed, BPR 'hit an invisible wall of all sorts of barriers:

cultural, hierarchical, structural and functional'. Despite the struggle and the loss of senior executives, and in the context of poor financial performance, Xerox raised the ante with a new BPR initiative, this time seeing the redesign of business processes as one element in a four-pronged approach to enhanced performance, the other three elements being adaptation to the group's formal organizational structure, its people and skills and, finally, its informal networks, behaviour and culture. After years of 'flirting' with BPR, then, Rank Xerox intends a more serious approach with the goal of becoming, in the words of its Managing Director, Bernard Fournier, 'the most productive company in our industry in the world ... we need dramatic improvements in performance which will be achieved through re-engineering of our business processes.' In a classic exposition of the BPR concept, seven uniform basic processes are being designed to span functional departments across Europe. These embrace a broad range of core activities, including 'time to market', 'market to collection' (customer order, installation and payment) and the all-important 'service support' (product maintenance). In contrast with the tardiness associated with the company's previous BPR adventure, the organizational hurdles are being tackled head-on. Sponsorship of each business process by a cadre of top management and senior executives is being introduced to ensure the effective design and operation of each new process. Fournier anticipates a struggle in the implementation phase as the 'process owners' encounter the traditional organizational structure, which remains heavily functional. Despite the difficulties, top management is determined to drive through its new approach of overlapping its functional (vertical) structure with its cross-departmental (horizontal) business processes. A policy statement outlining 'The New Company Culture' is guiding a number of behaviour and culture change initiatives, and the philosophy of change is being inculcated through a senior executive leadership programme and work-team workshops. The company has created the role of director of business processes and information management and the incumbent, John Drinkwater, emphasizes the scope of the current BPR initiative: 'Now we're re-engineering not just a few processes, but the whole company.' Among other benefits, the company hopes to achieve reductions in annual overheads of approximately $200m (£130m).

An alternative approach to BPR might be anticipated in a non-manufacturing context. In the *Financial Times* series on the topic, a profile of the financial services group, the National and Provincial Building Society, supports this contention (Michaels, 1993a). N&P began its reorganization with an emphasis on the company's organizational structure and culture, the aim being to foster top management commitment ('process leadership') ahead of making radical changes to its front-line processes. Although little has changed in practice as yet, the company has certainly adopted the BPR lexicon. The board has become the 'direction management team' and business operations have been reorganized into a 'direction management process'. Directors of 'customer engagements' and 'customer requirements' have replaced traditional functional and business directors, the people involved undertaking an extensive review and redesign of core business processes. As part of the culture change programme, fortnightly meetings (termed 'team events') are held to communicate top-level updates to area staff and the high level of involvement encouraged is, according to one young manager, fostering a collective vision and commitment to change: 'Everyone used to be trying to get brownie points for themselves. Now it's very much teamwork. You feel part of something that's going somewhere.' To date, the most tangible outcome of the change process has been the loss of 25 senior managers but a very clear objective has been set, i.e. to reduce eight levels and 20 grades of management to three levels and four grades.

The UK operation of the US insurance company Cigna also recognized the potential resistance to BPR from middle management and, based on the experience of its US internal re-engineering team, installed a culture change programme ahead of its re-engineering initiatives (Michaels, 1993b). The company anticipated and by-passed intransigent middle managers (losing some in the process), involved junior staff in a 'do it, test it, fix it' principle of process design and linked remuneration to team performance. Performance improvements were impressive. Quoting (for group health insurance) was cut from 12 days to 2 and staff are now processing between 75 and 90 claims a day compared with previous figures of between 35 and 40. £1m has been shaved from costs and the operation has moved into profit from a loss-making situation.

Evaluating BPR: an enduring or ephemeral construct?

We can build our critique of BPR at two levels of analysis: (i) from within its own frame of reference; (ii) from the broader context of strategic management, wherein its proponents stake their flag. Considering each in turn, a useful starting point is the summary of the topic by Lorenz (1993d) in the concluding article of the *Financial Times* series on the BPR phenomenon. Pointing to the 'widespread chorus of rude and cynical noises ... bursting forth in the US and Europe about the fashion for re-engineering', Lorenz provides an appropriate balance between empathy for its proponents – and how they have been misunderstood – and acknowledgement of the genuine market-derived challenges which are forcing companies to become more efficient and effective through the adoption of BPR principles. Regarding the former, he cites Champy's complaint that the BPR concept is habitually appropriated and readily bastardized: 'The term re-engineering is misapplied widely – almost to any sort of change programme.' This theme is picked up by McKinsey's Heygate, who lays the blame for the modest achievements of BPR firmly at the door of those entities he feels could benefit most from its adoption:

> What all but a few companies are doing is really just total quality management – fixing certain processes from the bottom up. So it's not surprising that well-publicized gains in individual processes are failing to be translated into dramatic improvements in the performance of the whole organization.

Champy, a co-founder of the re-engineering 'movement', develops this theme of lambasting management, arguing that they are ignorant of the scale of change required in organization structure and managerial behaviour and, more generally, that executives 'do not really have an appetite for discontinuous change'. This problem is compounded, according to Champy, when the organization cannot visualize its future operating model or determine its sustainable source of competitive edge. In the lexicon of BPR, the latter challenge is posited as the creation of a value proposition deriving from an offer which carries the provision of superior customer service, manufacturing efficiency or innovative products and services. According to the BPR evangelists, many firms struggle in BPR because of their more general failure to develop a sharp focus for their efforts – a factor which, argues Boston Consulting Group's David Hall, leads to BPR resource allocation on 'non-critical elements of the business'. Champy also points to management's limited ambitions regarding BPR, a particularly strong critique given BPR's 'quantum leap' aspirations. Summarizing the key problems of the application of the principles of BPR in practice, Hagel (of McKinsey) has identified a number of 'red flags' (a common feature of the project management literature) which give early-warning signals of the impending failure of BPR programmes: (i) inadequate management attention; (ii) inadequate urgency and stamina; (iii) inadequate focus.

Concluding the *Financial Times* series, Lorenz (1993d) takes a sober view of BPR's contribution, particularly the claims it makes regarding major and rapid impact on corporate performance: 'By the standards of conventional "change management" programmes, [the] target of completion within three years looks over-optimistic for anything more than the redesign of a single core process; most companies have found from bitter experience that it takes far longer than that to accomplish successfully a broad programme of radical change.' Commenting on the BPR phenomenon, *The Economist* takes a wry view of its impact: 'Re-engineering is the fad of the hour, as many re-engineered dole claimants know to their cost. But is it doing any good?' They note its 'rampant' adoption in labour and capital intensive industries and its diffusion towards the service sector, particularly insurance and banking. They summarize the general critique of BPR as having a twofold focus. Firstly, there is nothing new about BPR: its core concepts (customer first, teams, empowerment, tearing down divisional walls, performance-related remuneration) merely represent the conventional wisdoms which have permeated throughout organizations during the past two decades. Secondly, and more profoundly, they cite evidence that re-engineering simply doesn't work, with as many as 85 per cent of projects failing to achieve their objectives. As the article concludes, 'companies are putting themselves through an enormous amount of pain for little or no gain.'

The *Economist* feature reports the results of a survey carried out by CSC Index (the consultancy firm which founded the BPR concept) and finds it bizarre that the first major assessment of the BPR phenomenon comes from an organization which has such a vested interest in its sustenance: 'the report is a cunningly constructed document, critical enough of its subject to inspire confidence in its methods, but enthusiastic enough to quell cynics'. The CSC Index survey acknowledged some failure in the practice of BPR and, in its conclusion, identified three essential requirements for successful BPR implementation. Firstly, effective project management coupled with an emphasis on the 'softer' side of BPR (i.e. winning over the workers) is essential since a major obstacle to its implementation is the fear of management and workers and their tendency towards 'turf protection'. Secondly, BPR projects require the unhesitating support of senior management, not least because functional managements (e.g. engineering, design) will fiercely resist the consultant's endeavours. This is particularly the case where installation of IT systems is the prime focus of the re-engineering project. Thirdly, executives must have ambition: 'If re-engineering is worth doing, it is worth doing on a grand scale'. Flirtations with re-engineering will deliver pain, not gain, and a target of massive improvements is more likely to deliver successful outcomes, even if the original objectives are not met. Summarizing the CSC Index report, *The Economist* (1994) draws attention to its limitations, not least its strategic myopia and the overemphasis of BPR on productivity enhancement: 'switching to a new business may be more sensible than simply doing the old one more efficiently. It is clearly time to re-engineer the re-engineers'.

Considered within its own frame of reference, then, BPR appears more bauble than breakthrough. The consultants who are its main proponents universally lambast their clients for their lack of ambition and inability to give their organizational structures and cultures the short, sharp shock necessary for successful implementation of the re-engineered solutions. Cursory investigation of the anecdotal evidence reveals a paucity of support for the notion that re-engineering achieves 'quantum leaps' in performance improvement or that BPR is anything other than reactive tinkering around the fringes of business activity in the grand tradition of Taylorism. Bobbing below the surface of the construct is the suspicion that BPR is a sophisticated packaging solution created by consultants to fill dwindling coffers by exploiting ingenuous executives, a fact hinted at by the managing directors of one of the leading players in the field (Thackray, 1993). Such executives should be on guard, since they are rapidly becoming the targets of the leading BPR guru's next salvo (Champy, 1994):

> I am often asked whether workers will be able to perform in the re-engineered jobs ... The more serious question is whether managers can make the transition. The answer will determine whether it will take five or 50 years to reverse the errors of the industrial revolution.

In the following sections we make a more sober evaluation of the true impact of BPR, taking a perspective which assesses its claims to offer a major *strategic* breakthrough for ailing organizations and which critically evaluates its more outrageous assertions.

BPR: strategic management or muddling through?

Evaluating BPR in a broader strategic management context reveals a fourfold critique: (i) nothing new; (ii) nothing tangible; (iii) nothing strategic; (iv) nothing happens.

Nothing new

A common characteristic of capitalist economies is their cyclical nature. Long periods of growth and well-being tend to be followed by 'recessions', i.e. absolute falls in economic growth. During the 'good times' firms tend to accumulate what economists describe as x-inefficiency, i.e. they develop a gap between the minimum attainable supply cost and the actual cost base they achieve. In the behavioural theory of the firm this supply cost 'gap' is described as organizational slack, i.e. companies carry layers of cost within the firm rather than take the harsh trade-off decisions created by ongoing operations (see Chapter 2). Faced with certain economic 'triggers' (e.g. recession, intensifying competition, technological substitutes) companies must reduce this excessive cost base. A good example of x-inefficiency is the £400m cost reductions Denys Henderson, chairman of ICI, promised shareholders when the company appeared threatened by the Hanson Corporation. Similarly, a strong example of the removal of organizational slack is BT's ability to shed tens of thousands of jobs while actually enhancing its overall levels of customer service. Indeed, one of the principal outcomes of deregulation and/or privatization is the pressures on the industrial sectors concerned to remove organizational slack. The coincidence of the emergence of BPR with prolonged recession in US and European markets suggest that it is essentially a transitory phenomenon. The recovery literature is replete with examples of the 'triggers', both internal and external, which force firms, at any point in time, to reconsider their core activities, both strategic and operational (e.g. McKiernan, 1992; Grinyer and Spender, 1979; Grinyer *et al.*, 1988), and there is a rich literature on the barriers to doing so (e.g. Hambrick and D'Aveni, 1988). In the sense that it is nothing new, then, BPR is a bauble, a packaging solution to the core problems facing the consultancy industry as it struggled to sell its growth packages during the recession of the early 1990s.

Nothing tangible

We can keep this brief. There is *no* robust, generalizable evidence that BPR has made any significant impact on business performance. The evidence given in its support is partial and anecdotal. Where evidence is available it suggests short-term, one-off, incremental type changes, not the 'breakthrough', 'path-breaking', 'quantum-leap' solutions claimed by BPR proponents.

Nothing strategic

The biggest claim for BPR is its 'strategic' orientation. Herein lies its major weakness. Strategies are 'ten-a-penny', readily peddled by management gurus and roving consultants. As Galliers (1995) notes, the altogether trickier task is assessing their appropriateness and feasibility in the context of given organizational constraints:

> While there is much useful advice to be had in terms of identifying strategic opportunities and while the BPR literature has developed from early exhortations simply to 'think discontinuously' – to recognize and break away 'from outmoded rules and fundamental assumptions that underlie [current] operations', there remains the problem of *how* we might go about implementing that change and deciding whether radical change is indeed feasible and appropriate.

Much of the re-engineering literature reviewed above makes the implicit assumption that appending a change programme (more of which later) to the BPR process will achieve the task of implementing the re-engineering project. This conflation of process and implementation is a very common but very flawed feature of the strategic management literature (see Mintzberg, 1994, for a comprehensive critique). Fundamentally, the arbitrary combination of these two disparate constructs is conceptually inept. Describing the nuances of the divide, Wilson (1992) is worth quoting at length:

> To understand the *implementation* of change is to place the management ... of individuals at centre stage. This means implementing preconceived models of change, all with the aim of achieving a particular set of expected, predetermined and desired outcomes. To understand the *process* of change is to examine critically the context, the antecedents and the movement and history of changes, keeping at the same time an analytical eye on the organization theories-in-use which inform such an analysis.

Wilson describes a conceptual impasse between 'contextualists', who aim to characterize and understand the complexity of the process environment, and the 'implementers', who are keen to define roles, competencies, skills and managerial techniques for the successful achievement of stated objectives. The obvious complexity of managing change and the critical challenge of strategy implementation often appear to defy analysis. What is clear, however, is that simple solutions packaged as radical agendas are unlikely to break the mould of organizational inertia. If a strategy cannot be implemented it is not a strategy at all.

Nothing happens

The available evidence on BPR fails to demonstrate any significant and sustainable advantage accruing to the application of its principles. Hammer and Champy (1993), for example, open their discussion with a success story relating to IBM Credit, a subsidiary of a company which has had its overall strategic sloppiness savagely exposed in the early 1990s. As mentioned above, appending a change programme to BPR will not lead to the achievement of radical transformation. Organizations are far more likely to 'muddle through', to adapt incrementally rather than 'reinvent' themselves. Understanding why this is the case and, in particular, comprehending the organizational routines which shape such behaviour must be the starting point of planning strategic change. In the next section we examine insights into why it is that organizations are so prone to inertia. We also draw attention to some fundamental principles which must be addressed if a strategic reorientation via process solutions is to be successfully implemented.

Defensive routines and double loops: unravelling the learning dilemma

Argyris (1985) has drawn attention to a characteristic structural problem which is common to most organizations, a phenomenon he describes as 'defensive routines'. Environmental threats are dealt with by defensive reasoning and what he describes as 'defensive theories in use', thus inhibiting effective response to external stimuli. According to Argyris, defensive routines are the major barriers to organizational learning yet they are rarely acknowledged by top management teams and their advisers. Defensive routines are a crippling source of malaise and, over time, they build an immunity to the many and varied corrective actions which are taken to eliminate them. Thus, many change programmes introduced by consultants will rapidly lose impetus after a brief, top-management-led flurry. Furthermore, attempts to by-pass defensive routines by top management will invariably fail, any short-term successes merely leaving a legacy of 'polluted organizations' for future management teams. Expanding and applying the concept of defensive routines in later work, Argyris (1994) defines the construct as follows:

> [They] consist of all the policies, practices, and actions that prevent human beings from having to experience embarrassment or threat and, at the same time, prevent them from examining the nature and causes of that embarrassment or threat.

Such organizational defensive routines sustain a learning paralysis, a pathological condition compounded by the defensive reasoning of individuals within a cultural universe which is governed by four basic propositions:

> All of us design our behaviour in order to remain in unilateral control, to maximize winning and minimize losing, to suppress negative feelings, and to be as rational as possible, by which we mean laying out clear-cut goals and then evaluating our own behaviour on the basis of whether or not we've achieved them.

Such reasoning is defensive since its purpose is to avoid giving the appearance of vulnerability and incompetence, while simultaneously reducing risk and potential embarrassment. In this sense, according to Argyris, it provides 'a recipe for anti-learning, because it helps us avoid reflecting on the counter-productive consequences of our own behaviour.' The key problem is that defensive reasoning is tacit behaviour and this, in turn, is severely detrimental to organizational learning when routinized within day-to-day management practice. The problem becomes acute in discontinuous environments when once-latent threats are perceived by managers as very real events with potentially damaging consequences. Under these circumstances, the communication patterns and information flows which sustained organizational life in times of stability are inappropriate, since they tend to reinforce single-loop learning, i.e. one-dimensional responses to one-dimensional questions. Put simply, the questions asked of managers and employees are answered (for example, regarding morale, satisfaction, remuneration, etc.) but the assumptions which underpinned the questions are not. This, in turn, leads to a range of predictable pitfalls encountered when trying to establish essential truths about problems which are perceived as threatening or embarrassing. Argyris argues convincingly that, in this context, and facing the challenge of examining the behaviour of subordinates and/or their own behaviour, managers are likely to demonstrate the following behavioural patterns: (i) to reason defensively and to interact with others who are reasoning defensively; (ii) to get superficial, single-loop responses that lead to superficial, single-loop solutions; (iii) to reinforce the organizational defence routines that inhibit access to valid information and genuine learning; (iv) to be unaware of their own defences because they are so skilled and automatic; (v) to be unaware that they are producing any of these consequences, or, if they *are* aware of defensiveness, to see it only in others. Taken together, these pitfalls demonstrate a deep-seated and intangible resistance to change. The challenge, then, is to foster 'double-loop' learning, a process which asks questions regarding the nature of things as they are (single-loop) but also questions the assumptions, rationale and motives underpinning such interpretations of an apparently objective reality.

Drawing on his extensive research and consultancy experience, Argyris argues that internal communications should be more focused on self-awareness and responsibility, requiring employees to scrutinize critically their own roles and responsibilities. They should include a frank appraisal of individuals' own behaviour and motivation and facilitate information sharing and genuine empowerment: 'The problem is not that employees run away from this kind of organizational self-examination. The problem is that no-one asks it of them. Managers seem to attach no importance to employees' feelings, defences, and inner conflicts.'

Concluding remarks

The perceptive observations given by Argyris provide substantive support for our contention that BPR and other partial solutions to organizational survival and success are doomed to failure from the outset. A cruel dilemma confronts organizations which need to change to survive and it is not surprising that the BPR phenomenon has captured the imagination of the management community. But we must acknowledge its limitations and comprehend the enormity of the challenge of organizational change. In the next chapter we present a strategic perspective on the management of change and present a range of insights and agendas for companies to observe when embarking on their search for organizational advantage.

5
A strategic perspective on managing change

Introduction

A striking feature of the business and management literature in recent years has been the pervasiveness of the concept of 'change'. Despite the proliferation of change models its dimensions are essentially twofold: (i) antecedents, i.e. those factors which 'trigger' the need for change; (ii) change as process, i.e. a set of management actions which transform organizations from a given to a desired state over a period of time. We will discuss each in turn, but first a caveat. One of the most respected writers on change management is Kanter, whose early work (1983, 1989) essentially defined the topic or at least brought it to its broader public domain. In a more recent text she draws attention to the shallowness of much of the discussion of change and, in the light of the analysis presented in the previous chapter, she is worth quoting at length here as a preface to the challenges we will encounter in the following sections (Kanter *et al.*, 1992):

> ... the danger lurking in many discussions of organizational change is that the whole thing starts to sound much simpler than it is. Too much credit is given to leaders when things go well, and too much blame when they go poorly. Yet, despite decades of very good advice to organizations about change, we are struck by how many failures there are and how much can go wrong. Even though both the reformers and the revolutionaries are, in their own way, utopians, believing in organizational perfectibility, the sad fact is that, almost universally, organizations change as little as they must, rather than as much as they should.

The dimensions of change are captured on two axes of our adapted nexus model. The change antecedents, the so-called 'triggers' of change, are rooted in the relationship between the organization and its environmental context. The change process, meanwhile, is rooted within the organization–strategy axis and is modelled in the 'dropped' process box shown in Figure 5.1. We consider each in turn in the following sections.

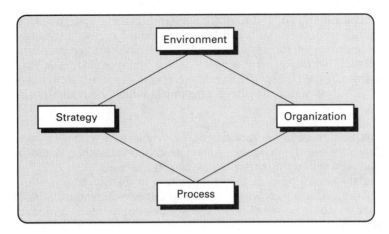

Figure 5.1   *Reshaping fit: the process solution*

Mapping change antecedents: dynamics of the environment–organization axis

The first point to emphasize here is the importance of the phrase 'dynamics' in this section's title. It is intuitively appealing and, to a large extent, empirically proven (see Chapter 2) that stable environments deliver stable organizational form, normally postulated as mechanistic-type structures, while turbulent environments require flexible, or organic, type structures. The key points of debate, however, are how far the *level* of turbulence in the business environment can be objectively measured and to what extent organizations can sensitize themselves for effective monitoring and evaluation of such turbulence. Considering the former, different perceptions of a notionally objective reality could lead to a strategically inappropriate response, in the sense of either strategy–market fit and/or organizational competence. For example, flight from a (perceived) mature domestic market by internationalization is seen as the key growth vector for a company and acquisition is proposed as the most appropriate route to achieve it. In market terms, the resource could have been better allocated on organic development and concentric diversification, thus exploiting strong customer loyalty. In terms of organization, the fact that the company has had no previous experience of large-scale post-acquisition integration and management suggests a weak 'fit' between the 'opportunity' and organizational competence. In this example failure becomes predictable, at least to the outside, impartial observer. At a deeper level of analysis, however, identifying the principal cause of failure is a trickier task: (a) the economic signals emanating from the domestic market (market growth, concentration, size, etc.) could have been misread; (b) the acquiring company certainly lacked acquisition experience; (c) the acquired company possibly had a cadre of influential managers who fiercely resisted the change to be imposed on them; (d) the management information systems of the two companies (for coordination and control) could have been incompatible; (e) the cultures of the organizations could have proven impossible to assimilate. This is a good example – and a real one (Marks & Spencer's acquisition of the US retailer Brooks Brothers) – to illustrate what Kanter *et al.* (1992) describe as three dynamics which activate the change process:

1   The motion of the organization as a whole as it relates to motion in its *environment* – change that is *macro-evolutionary*, historical and typically related to clusters or whole industries.
2   The motion of parts in the organization in relation to one another as the organization grows, ages, and progresses through its *life-cycle* – change that is *micro-evolutionary*, developmental, and typically related to its size or shape, resulting in co-ordination issues.
3   The jockeying for power and struggle for control among individuals and groups with a stake in the organization to make decisions or enjoy benefits as an expression of their own interests – change that focuses on *political dimensions* and involves *revolutionary* issues.

This trichotomy also reinforces the fundamental theme of this book, i.e. that 'strategic management' is essentially an amalgam of industrial economics (strategic imperatives) and organizational behaviour (strategic impediments). This, in turn, suggests an economic determinism, a perspective which lies at the heart of the change debate, i.e. the extent to which a firm shapes, or is shaped by, its environmental context (e.g. Bettis and Donaldson, 1990). In a competitive economic model (e.g. capitalism) the causation is typically the latter route, i.e. environments have primacy and shape strategic choice and organizational form. A key question which then emerges is how far managerial response is a proactive or reactive posture, an issue characterized by Kanter *et al.* (1992) as Looking Backward or Looking Forward: 'Ultimately, despite the limits upon what people can control, it is still up to people to act, and in acting they do more than predict the future, they invent it'. The notion that organizational futures can be created provides the 'strategic' focus of this chapter. In the remaining sections the emphasis will be on the issues associated with *management* of the change process within given organizational contexts.

Managing the change process

To reiterate from Chapter 2, at the macro level organizations strive, with differing levels of success, to create 'fit' with the dynamics of their environmental context. This concept of fit was classified by Miles and Snow (1984) as a fourfold framework:

1   Minimal fit among strategy, structure, and process is essential to all organizations operating in competitive environments. If a misfit occurs for a prolonged period, the result usually is failure.

2   Tight fit, both internally and externally, is associated with excellence. Tight fit is the underlying causal dynamic producing sustained, excellent performance and a strong corporate culture.

3   Early fit, the discovery and articulation of a new pattern of strategy, structure, and process, frequently results in performance records which in sporting circles would merit Hall of Fame status. The invention or early application of a new organization form may provide a more powerful competitive advantage than a market or technological breakthrough.

4   Fragile fit involves vulnerability to both shifting external conditions and to inadvertent internal unravelling. Even Hall of Fame organizations may become victims of deteriorating fit.

These authors are unambiguous in their interpretation of the importance of fit:

> Successful organizations achieve strategic fit with their market environment and support their strategies with appropriately designed structures and management processes. Less successful organizations typically exhibit poor fit externally and/or internally.

Miles and Snow (1984) conclude that achieving minimal fit is essential for survival and that tight fit is associated with corporate excellence. Developing environmental analysis to a sensitivity which allows early fit secures entry to the 'organization Hall of Fame', a sporting metaphor to characterize organizations who develop sustainable competitive advantage through achieving unmatchable organizational break-throughs. Like many contingency theorists, Miles and Snow support the notion of fit without developing a discussion of how it might be achieved or, more specifically, how it can be reconfigured as and when environmental conditions demand. In the next sections the microlevels of analysis required to understand the process of how organizations can effectively reshape fit are outlined.

It was an attempt to rectify fundamental weakness of the change literature which underpinned the previously cited research and publications of Kanter and her Harvard colleagues (Kanter *et al.*, 1992). Consistent with the three dynamics of change discussed above, the Harvard School proposes three *forms* of change and three categories of *role* which are characteristic of the change process. We consider each set of three in the next two sections, drawing on additional literature sources where appropriate.

A typology of change: three forms

The first category of change in the typology is *identity*, defined as substantive changes in the relationship between the organization and its environment. Such change embraces the market (and market segments) the company serves, the company's physical and intangible assets and its relationships with customers, suppliers, investors and governments. In an extreme case the organization 'becomes something entirely different' but, more commonly, this type of change relates to the subtle changes an organization makes to its identity as a function of macro-evolutionary forces, dynamic environments and organizational competencies.

The second category of change in the typology is *coordination*, more often than not relating to micro-evolutionary dynamics as a firm progresses through its life-cycle. In the light of emerging empirical evidence in the change literature this categorization would seem wholly appropriate, particularly with respect to the structural changes involved in the change process. Olsen and Terpstra (1992), for example, have demonstrated that organizations which make *successful* transitions from start-up to growth phases undergo dramatic structural change, including greater complexity, greater formalization and growing decentralization. This, in turn, poses a particular set of challenges for those individuals involved in organizational development, whether they be managers or consultants.

Kanter *et al.* (1992) acknowledge the need for planned intervention for this type of change, arguing that, 'whatever the source of the problem, the need to change the organization's internal configuration, rather than simply to let it evolve, may ultimately result in deliberate *reshaping or revitalizing.*'

The third category of change in the typology relates to changes in *control* and encompasses those responses that impact on the political dimension of organizations. This change category encounters dominant coalition interest sets and deals with the fundamental issue of corporate governance. Such change is often revolutionary in character, carrying the hallmarks of an approach described as 'makeover through takeover'.

An action perspective on change: three roles

The first role category identified by Kanter *et al.* are *change strategists*, those individuals responsible for the organization's general direction as it responds to identified macro-evolutionary forces. This role typically occurs at the outset of a change process and is normally within the domain of the company leadership. Leavey and Wilson (1994) point to the major role of leadership in bringing about strategically significant outcomes and, in longitudinal research, they have identified it as a function of both symbolic and substantive dimensions; in other words, leaders can (and often do) have a major impact on radical strategic change.

Despite this, leaders are increasingly being focused upon as the source of organizational malaise in the more complex and turbulent business environment of the 1990s. Hamel and Prahalad (1994), for example, have launched a scathing attack on the short-termism driving many large organizations, a characteristic that must lie, they argue, in the fact that top management are not fully in control, nor do they have a compelling view of corporate direction: '[leaders] must admit what they know today – the knowledge and experience that justify their position in the corporate pecking order – may be irrelevant or wrong-headed for the future'.

This situation leads, in practice, to an obsession with restructuring and re-engineering *what is* (today's businesses) rather than shaping *what might be* (tomorrow's industries), a focus on core *processes* rather than core *strategies*. In this sense, it is important to recognize that leadership may well be strongly linked to change but that such change is often not strategic in the sense outlined by Kanter *et al*. Indeed, it could well be that a change in leadership is required as an antecedent to strategic change itself. Leavey and Wilson (1994), for example, found that a change in CEO could enhance both the symbolic and substantive impact of leadership on strategic change. The tendency of organizations in severe commercial turmoil to bring in outsiders is supportive of this stance, a contemporary example being IBM's replacement of 'insider' John Akers by 'outsider' Lou Grestener.

The second action role identified by Kanter *et al*. is the one responsible for the microdynamics of change effort development, a task undertaken by *change implementers*. It involves execution of change programmes and project management and is generally carried out at middle management level. While strategists can be implementers, and while this might be desirable, the distinction is generally robust. This contention is supported from evidence in the wider literature. Middle managers in large and complex organizations represent a plurality of coalitions, one or more of which might be dominant at any specific point in time or in response to any particular event. Managing the change process in this context is likely to be more akin to herding cats than systematically implementing new ideas. It is this pluralism which creates incremental rather than radical organizational and/or strategic change. As Quinn (1980b) notes, incremental management processes do not necessarily reflect Machiavellian politicking or incompetent management: 'Instead, they represent an adaptation to the practical psychological and informational problems of getting a constantly changing group of people with diverse talents and interests to move together effectively in a continuously dynamic environment.'

The third action role proposed by Kanter *et al*. arises towards the end of the change sequence and is typically manifested at the lower levels of the organizational hierarchy. The role incumbents are labelled *change recipients* and, paradoxically, it is this role cluster who are most effective but least involved in the change process, i.e. they tend to be passive recipients of change outcomes with little control over what is happening around them. This factor, in turn, accounts for the large amount of anxiety often associated with change programmes, a tension created by the inherently different perspectives of those who initiate and implement change and those who are on the receiving end of the process. This perceived powerlessness often leads to or stirs up collectivism among individuals (e.g. union activity). In extreme cases, such employees might demand control in exchange for their cooperation, particularly where such individuals are well educated and organized. Recent examples of industry restructuring in the American passenger airline industry is a case in point. The joint impact of deregulation and Gulf War-induced recession has created a need for radical cost reductions, a notable feature of these change programmes being the transferring of equity to airline workers to ensure their cooperation and the corporation's future.

The typical *sequence* of change proposed by Kanter *et al.* (1992), i.e. top-down, middle implemented, lower-level affected, has elsewhere been identified as an inhibitor of change. Beer *et al.* (1990), for example, argue that while top managers understand the *necessity* for change they often misunderstand the essential approach to bring it about. Thus, an added complexity of managing the change process relates to the *sequence* of activities which surround it, these twin dimensions of change programmes often being underpinned by two common but flawed assumptions: 'that promulgating company-wide programmes – mission statements, "corporate culture" programmes, training courses, quality circles, and new pay-for-performance systems – will transform organizations, and that employee behaviour is changed by altering a company's formal structure and systems.' This quote leads us to evaluate two principal streams of investigation surrounding the strategic management of change: (i) to evaluate what Beer *et al.* (1990) describe as 'the fallacy' of programmatic change; (ii) to understand the constraining influence of corporate culture on the change process.

The critique of TQM by executives charged with its adoption or exposed to its impact (Wilson, 1992) is testimony to a general problem associated with what Beer *et al.* (1990) describe as 'programmatic change'. Consistent with Wilson's 'evangelical' critique of TQM discussed in the previous chapter, Beer *et al.* (1990) argue that a key weakness of programmed change processes is their fundamental proposition that the starting point of change is the knowledge and attitudes of individuals. The assertion that individual *behaviours* will inevitably change is false, since 'conversion experiences' whereby people 'get religion' is the reverse of observed habits: 'In fact, individual behaviour is powerfully shaped by the organizational roles that people play. The most effective way to change behaviour, therefore, is to put people into a new organizational context, which imposes new roles, responsibilities, and relationships on them.' In the latter case, a situation is created which 'forces' new attitudes and behaviours on people. In the absence of new roles and responsibilities or top-level commitment to a set of assumptions characterized as 'task alignment', change programmes sow the seeds of their own failure. Beer *et al.* (1990) propose three interrelated factors which together constitute the challenge of corporate revitalization. *Coordination* is essential for delivering innovative high quality/low cost products or services, particularly in fostering a sense of teamwork among personnel from marketing, product design and manufacturing departments. Close coordination is also an essential characteristic in the generic relationship between management and labour. To operationalize this, a high level of *commitment* is essential to secure the levels of effort, initiative and co-operation essential for achieving coordinated action. Finally, new *competencies* are essential for team-based problem solving.

These will include a more holistic knowledge of the business, interpersonal skills and a broader base of analytical skills.

The authors state that absence of any of these three elements will negate the change process. With this in mind, they argue that only one or two of these core elements are addressed in typical programmatic change projects, particularly where such programmes are company-wide (a common feature):

> Just because a company issues a philosophy statement about teamwork doesn't mean its employees necessarily know what teams to form or how to function within them to improve coordination. A corporate reorganization may change the boxes on a formal organizational chart but not provide the necessary attitudes and skills to make the new structure work.

The authors are particularly scathing about the support programmes which typically accompany change processes. In particular, they target the fact that many training programmes deal with *competencies* but ignore a company's coordination patterns. In a quote which will engender empathy from executive trainers, Beer *et al.* point to the futility of partial programmes:

> The excitement engendered in a good corporate training programme frequently leads to increased frustration when employees get back on the job only to see their new skills go unused in an organization in which nothing else has changed. People end up seeing training as a waste of time, which undermines whatever commitment to change a programme may have raised in the first place.

Beer *et al.* acknowledge the role of subsidiary activities such as changes in remuneration, organizational structure and corporate philosophy and also the importance of support activities such as training. However:

> The problems come when such programmes are used in isolation as a kind of 'magic bullet' to spread organizational change rapidly through the entire corporation. At their best, change programmes of this sort are irrelevant. At their worst, they actually inhibit change. By promoting scepticism and cynicism, programmatic change can inoculate companies against the real thing.

At this juncture the 'real thing' must be identified, delineated and assessed. In a strategic sense, competitive environments add tremendous complexity to the external and internal work environments of an organization's managers (Hendry and Pettigrew, 1992). As noted earlier in this chapter, the external complexity tends to trigger change processes which, in turn, requires that managers undertake a complex task set they are often unprepared for. In our critique of BPR we noted the virtual absence of focus on the management of people in the change process. Longitudinal research, however, has demonstrated convincingly that a strategic perspective on the human resource function is a distinctive characteristic of organizational survival and structure (Pettigrew and

Whipp, 1993). The 'real thing' of change, then, takes as its starting point the fundamental proposition that organizations are clusters of assets and people, that it is people who manage and undertake business processes and activities and that it is to people whom change programmes should be directed.

In a critique of change programmes which are directed at individual managers, Wilson (1992) notes the lack of advance in management development practices over the last two decades, particularly with respect to doing things differently (as in change programmes) and specifically regarding the dominance of competency training:

> No mention is made of the degree of change, of the different contexts and antecedents which surround the process. Is change viewed as a process at all, or is it a goal or an outcome? When does a manager know how to 'switch on' his or her 'appropriate' competencies?

In the next section we address the important topic of the management of people in the change process. From a systems perspective we can visualize the change process as a chain of events and note, in passing, that any chain is only as strong as its weakest link. It is increasingly acknowledged that the weakest link of the change process is neglect of the human resource and a growing research base is now addressing this basic fact of organizational life.

The human resource challenge of strategic change

In profiling a strategic role for human resource management (HRM) Hendry and Pettigrew (1992) place the challenge at the locus of the relationship between the internal and external work environments of employees, a nexus of coherence and appropriateness: 'that is, whether aspects of the employment system are internally consistent with one another and are aligned with business strategy.' They see HRM as a holistic approach, one which encompasses a sophisticated knowledge of the dynamics of strategic and operational effectiveness while at the same time proactively dealing with a context of continuous change. Regarding the latter, 'This includes the continuing process of adjusting personnel systems to organizational needs, and also the complex processes that integrate strategy–structure–culture change'. Modelling HRM and its linkages between strategy and structure within a framework of context, content and process, Hendry and Pettigrew (1992) capture the complexity of strategic change. The conceptual framework they have developed is shown in Figure 5.2

In a series of case studies of companies undergoing major transformations Hendry and Pettigrew (1992) demonstrated that HRM was closely linked with business performance, was strongly associated with structural change and, significantly, arose out of the process of strategic change. This latter finding, in particular, raises a classic chicken-and-egg paradox: does strategic change lead HRM or does HRM lead strategic

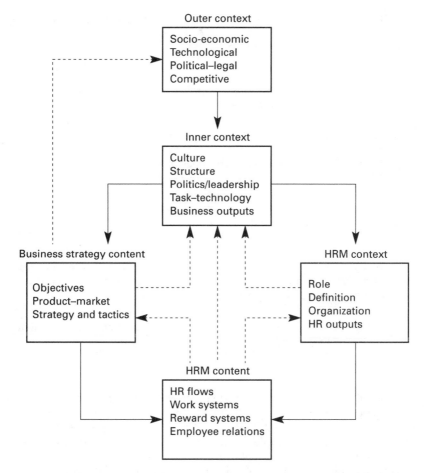

Figure 5.2   *A conceptual model of strategic change and human resource management (Source: Hendry, C. and Pettigrew, A. (1992), 'Patterns of strategic change in the development of human resource management',* British Journal of Management, *3, 3, 137–156)*

change? If the former, will a proactive HRM approach enable more effective implementation of strategic change programmes? The answer seems to be positive, particularly in the context of another chicken-and-egg enigma, the structure versus strategy directional debate. Where structure *must* precede strategy (for example, to remove entrenched power centres) HRM can play a central role in initiating and managing structural and cultural change. The authors propose a process-centred agenda for HRM, arguing strongly for a tight relationship with strategic goals. It is worth quoting in full their series of hypotheses relating to the conditions supporting a HRM philosophy in its fully developed sense:

1 Increasing complexity in the product portfolio, but a complexity matched by coherence, in which increasing variety in product-markets stops short of the unrelated product situation.
2 Increasing complexity in internal organization structures to manage the portfolio situation.
3 The use of decentralization and similar structural devices to devolve responsibility and increase employee involvement.
4 A shift in preoccupations from industrial relations 'fire-fighting' to the development of skills and competencies.
5 The existence or survival of a central personnel function.
6 The role of crisis in focusing the need for new approaches.
7 The importance of top leadership in legitimizing ideas.

The idea that the human resource should form a central plank of strategic change programmes is not new, nor is the notion that organizational structures and people are uncomfortable bedfellows (e.g. Argyris, 1957, 1964). In a memorably titled chapter, 'Man Waiting for Motivation', Peters and Waterman (1982) draw attention to the latent potential of the human resource within organizations alongside offering a critique of traditional approaches to organizational structure:

> The central problem with the rationalist view of organizing people is that people are not very rational. To fit Taylor's old model, or today's organizational charts, man is simply designed wrongly (or, of course, vice versa, according to our argument here).

With this observation in mind, and considering Hendry and Pettigrew's third hypothesis regarding devolved responsibility and employee involvement, we now briefly consider one of the most pervasive themes in the 'management of people' literature, both academic and practitioner: empowerment. Described by Lorenz (1992) as 'Power to the People', empowerment is the process of shifting authority down the organization, 'freeing employees from instructions and controls, and allowing them to take decisions themselves.'

Although empowerment has proved extremely difficult to implement as a corporate philosophy its proponents argue that it is essential for companies to adopt, especially in the context of global competition. Lawler (1992), for example, has described the process of empowerment – or 'high-involvement' – as the ultimate source of competitive advantage for global organizations. His thesis is based on the premise that location, market access, technology procurement and access to capital are no longer sustainable sources of advantage since they are readily available to most global companies. Organizational style and management systems which focus on participative decision-making, teamwork and which foster a sense of collective responsibility are much harder to copy, hence the notion of 'ultimate' advantage. Lawler demonstrates his argument with profiles of global companies such as Hewlett Packard, Digital Equipment, Procter and Gamble and Motorola.

The difficulties faced by British companies in emulating Japanese human resource policies and their chronic inability to build sustainable advantage provides further support for Lawler's arguments. This is true at all organizational levels and there is even evidence that the successful role model of a 'Euro-manager' – if he/she can be identified at all – is more likely to be found in an American or Japanese company rather than a British one (*The Economist*, 1992f)!

It is at the shopfloor level where the greatest efforts have been placed to instil a 'best practice' approach to human resource management, more often than not based on some derivative of Japanese management approaches. Oliver and Wilkinson (1992) have documented the 'Japanization of British Industry' over the past five years and, in a second edition of their book, they identify the lack of progress made by companies over the period. They describe the boasts of British manufacturers who claim Japanization as more often than not being merely corporate 'wish statements'. Rather than being measures of actual progress, they argue, 'there is something of a gap between rhetoric and reality, and there is probably more of the former than the latter.' Despite this pessimism and, for that matter, despite severe recession in the economies of most advanced industrial nations, the nature of work and its inherent attractiveness has emerged as a major theme of contemporary management debate (e.g. Handy, 1994).

Considering the emerging debate within the field of human resource management, then, it is clear that executives of large organizations will face formidable challenges over the coming years. This is particularly the case for companies attempting to globalize their operations. In a review of the key issues Vanderbroeck (1992) has evaluated the actions which global companies must take to address them. Among the priorities he lists are: (i) creating entrepreneurial and relatively small business units to attract graduates and highly motivated employees; (ii) constant training and extensive job rotation to maintain employee flexibility and foster multitask abilities; (iii) recruit and promote more women; (iv) drop parochialism in recruiting policy and employ foreign nationals in their home countries and throughout the organization; (v) avoid 'ageism' – employ older managers and recognize the quality of their experience; (vi) have flexible retirement policies allowing high-quality staff to remain after normal retirement age; (vii) acknowledge that 'de-layered' organizations require an infrastructure of horizontal and diagonal career pathways; (viii) base remuneration packages on skill and contribution, not on hierarchical position, budget size or number of subordinates; (ix) provide a range of service supports for the spouses of expatriate managers, e.g. adult and child education, relocation (or dislocation) allowances and placement service on return from the assignment. This problem is especially acute when both partners are working and difficult choices regarding who should have the 'lead career' have to be made; (x) develop rapid and two-way communications lines.

The issue of quality of working life has become a major concern even throughout the prolonged global recession. Even in Japan, so long derided for having citizens who 'work like ants', there is a growing demand for leisure, particularly, as *The Economist* (1992g) notes, among 'younger managers and shopfloor workers who want to play as well as toil' .

In contrast with previous periods of economic pessimism, quality of life demands from employees are increasing rather than decreasing. Indeed, where firms have offered voluntary redundancy packages there has been a startling response to such offers, not least among skilled employees and middle management. In a special edition of the *International Journal of Quality & Reliability Management* King (1992) has tackled this phenomenon. She argues that the debate should move away from 'availability of work' issues to the more fundamental and long-term questions associated with the quality of working life. She identifies a neglect among companies to inform employees of the impact of strategic decisions on their working lives and she highlights the key role of effective communications to ensure the implementation of strategic direction. The implementation problem and the need for the communications solution becomes particularly acute in periods of radical restructuring, rapid change, adoption of new technology and turbulent economic conditions. Where an organization has regional operations controlled by central headquarters (as is the case for many international organizations) King argues for a 'communications code' which should include the following: (i) a regular dissemination of updated organizational charts and explanations of the role of senior managers; (ii) advance notice of change, the reasons for the change and the benefits associated with it; (iii) the development of procedures to facilitate feedback; (iv) an open recognition of strong regional performance; (v) consultation on operational matters.

A constant theme of King's thesis is that companies (not just employees) will benefit from such communications codes, i.e. that there is a potentially genuine win–win opportunity from shared information. While this is certainly consistent with the themes introduced in this chapter, it only touches the surface of what more innovative companies are developing in their approach to human resource management. Although loaded with ambiguity and misinterpretation, the concept of 'empowerment' is rapidly being adopted by organizations as an approach to managing and implementing radical change programmes. Like many of its change predecessors, however, the biggest challenge for empowerment as a sustainable concept will be its battle with the intangible yet potent force of organizational culture.

Understanding organizational culture

The importance and impact of organizational culture is a pervasive theme of most writings on strategic management. It is a particularly contentious construct in the context of change. As Wilson (1992) notes: 'Not only is the concept of organizational culture multifaceted, it is also not clear precisely how culture and change are related, if at all, and, if so, in which directions.'

The paradox of culture is that it has been shown to resist change, to facilitate change (i.e. it is a static construct) or, alternatively, it has been argued that it is in a constant state of flux. In a paper addressing this conceptual enigma, Meyerson and Martin (1987) propose three paradigms of culture and examine organizational change as a function of changing patterns of behaviour, values and meanings. With this approach, the authors encapsulate some of the core themes emerging from this book, namely: (a) structure is a manifestation of *and* constraint on organizational behaviour; (b) strategy is an outcome and a determinant of interactions and ideas; (c) leadership shapes and is shaped by organizational meaning and values; (d) as a construct, culture is defined by how it is perceived and enacted.

Paradigm 1 in the Meyerson and Martin schema is *integration*. This defines culture as a set of *shared* attributes which identify the organization as being unique. Three central tenets of this approach to understanding culture are consistency (of culture manifestation), consensus (e.g. shared values) and a focus on top management as the creators of the organizational culture. A characteristic of this definition is that culture is persistent, it encourages worker commitment, it enhances organizational effectiveness and it places a high degree of control in the hands of management. A corollary of these factors is that there is an apparently inevitable tendency towards organizational inertia and that within the organization there emerges a strong resistance to change. When change occurs it is revolutionary, characterized by a sequential process of organization-wide collapse and replacement by a new monolithic perspective. The 'excellent companies' of Peters and Waterman (1982) fall broadly within this category, the notion of 'shared values' often being posited as the glue binding the remaining Ss of structure, strategy, style, etc. Noting that the publication of *In Search of Excellence* elevated the role of culture in enhancing organizational performance to new heights, Wilson (1992) also draws attention to the lack of intellectual justification for the basic construct, both theoretically and empirically. Regarding the theoretical problems there are four broad issues regarding the cultural aspects of the excellence construct:

1   It assumes a 'one best way' of organizing.
2   It assumes a simple causal relationship between culture and performance.
3   It is generally dominated by a top-management view of the organization.
4   It lacks a well argued theoretical basis, preferring to borrow selectively from other work.

From an empirical viewpoint, there are also four broad issues undermining the cultural aspects of the excellent construct:

1   The failure of many excellent companies to sustain corporate success.
2   The availability of alternative explanations of success (such as monopoly position in the market).

3   Mostly poor sampling among the studies, so that it is not known how far the organizations are representative.
4   The virtual omission of key business sectors, such as petrochemicals, motor manufacturing, financial services, etc.

In summarizing the 'integrative' culture school, Meyerson and Martin (1987) draw attention to its 'blind spots' and go on to examine culture through 'alternative lenses'. In this vein, paradigm 2 in their classification of the culture literature is termed *differentiation*. Paradigm 2 researchers identify inconsistencies, lack of consensus and non-leader sources of cultural content in a perspective which is characterized by differentiation and diversity. They identify a broader base of constituencies, subunits of groups and individuals based within and outside the organization. Emphasizing a diversity of nested subcultures, this paradigm argues that complex organizations mirror the heterogeneity of broader societal cultures, including occupational, hierarchical, class, racial, ethnic and gender-based associations. Subcultures can be counter-cultural in nature and/or may reflect functional or project affiliations, a problem compounded when subunits within these affiliations fanatically support top management values. Paradigm 2 perspectives on culture have some conceptual links with the integrative paradigm, particularly with respect to the consistency and consensus demonstrated by the subcultures (e.g. workers and managers share similar values within their subcultures). A major point of departure between the two, however, is to be found in their contrasting perspectives on cultural change. The paradigm 2 position represents an open systems perspective – cultural change is closely linked to other sources and types of change and, in general, it is localized and incremental. Triggers of cultural change are seen as diffuse (rather than management-led) and often unintentional. They are typically stimulated by external environmental factors and their impact on organizational function is localized. A corollary of this is that subunits are linked more tightly to their immediate environments but more loosely to each other. Such 'loose coupling' stifles information flows between subunits, encourages localized adaptation and experimentation and accommodates deviance. While loose coupling can dampen the shocks of environmental turbulence it can also inhibit organization-wide change, particularly 'top-down', management-led efforts. Furthermore, the restricted information flows heavily circumscribe organizational learning efforts.

Many prescriptive change programme solutions implicitly or explicitly acknowledge the paradigm 2 perspective on organizational culture. Beer *et al.* (1990), for example, argue that effective corporate transformations start at the periphery, where energy for change is focused on the work itself, 'not on abstractions such as "participation" or "culture".' Traditional change programmes, they argue, focus on attempts at changing the content of individuals' attitudes and ideas and view the desired behavioural changes as a function of this new shaped vision (a paradigm 1 perspective): 'Once people "got religion", changes in their behaviour will surely follow.' In contrast, Beer *et al.* argue that individuals' behaviour is a function of the organizational roles they play (a paradigm 2 perspective): 'The most effective way to change behaviour, therefore, is to put people into a new organizational context, which imposes new roles, responsibilities and relationships on them.' The approach Beer *et al.* champion is described as 'task alignment', an alignment of 'employee roles, responsibilities and relationships to address the organization's most important competitive task'. They acknowledge that task alignment lends itself to small unit operations and identify the key management challenge as promoting task-aligned change across a diversity of such units. In operationalizing a solution they identify a critical path of six overlapping but distinctive steps, a sequential approach which delivers a self-reinforcing cycle of commitment, co-ordination and competence. The process they propose is outlined briefly below:

1   *Mobilize commitment to change through joint diagnosis of business problems*   The use of a 'task force' which represents a cross-section of stakeholders in the organization (e.g. managers, engineers, production workers, union officials) gives a shared diagnosis of the core problem and its potential solutions.

2   *Develop a shared vision of how to organize and manage for competitiveness*   With consensus on problems and solutions a general management-led, task-aligned definition of new roles and responsibilities will coordinate information flows and work across interdependent functions at various levels within the organization.

3   *Foster consensus for the new vision, competence to enact it, and cohesion to move it along*   Strong leadership from the general manager is essential at this stage since commitment to change will always be uneven. After allowing appropriate time for adjustment, individuals who have difficulty working in the new, participatory, organization may have to be redeployed or asked to leave. The issue is obviously very sensitive and management supports (e.g. counselling, internal consultancy) must be made available. In this stage core competencies have to developed, although these are 'forced' to some extent by the participation, collaboration and information-sharing characteristic of the shared goals and accountabilities of the new work teams.

4   *Spread revitalization to all departments without pushing it from the top*   While new insights have been learned from the team-based approach, they cannot be packaged and forced onto other departments. This would be to make the same fundamental error of those pushing programmatic change, i.e. it would short-circuit the change process. As the authors note: 'members of teams cannot be effective unless the department from which they come is organized and managed in a way that supports fully-pledged participants in team decisions.' The departments themselves must be left to recreate their roles and authority in the organization.

5   *Institutionalize revitalization through formal policies, systems and structures*   Until this stage the team structure have been learning the structural and functional interdependencies in an ad hoc manner, a

process essential to ensure cohesion, commitment and, more mundanely but equally important, to identify operational essentials such as information flows. At this stage the knowledge needs to be captured and formalized through appropriate changes in systems and structures.

6   *Monitor and adjust strategies in response to problems in the revitalization process*   The output of the above process is a new asset, 'a learning organization capable of adapting to a changing competitive environment.' The trick now is to sustain its success by continuous monitoring of its behaviour, i.e. learning to learn.

The six-stage approach of Beer *et al.* (1990) has been presented here in a relatively uncritical manner, but it is conceptually more robust than many examples from the prescriptive change management genre. Its provocative title, 'Why change programs don't produce change', is a snipe at leadership-inspired visionary-type programmed transformation attempts. It implicitly acknowledges the limitations suggested by Meyerson and Martin's paradigm 2 perspective on culture, but proposes a solution and methodology for instilling company-wide culture change, the panacea offered by the paradigm 1 perspective. Beer *et al.* (1990) identify a clear role for top management in their orchestration of company-wide transformation. It has three dimensions: (i) create a market for change, setting demanding standards and holding managers accountable to them; (ii) use successfully revitalized units as organizational models for the entire company, facilitated by visits, conferences and educational programmes; (iii) develop career paths that encourage leadership development, since successful corporate transformation is dependent as much on effective change leaders as effective organizational development.

The ideas outlined above do leave some fundamental strategic questions unanswered, for example the appropriateness of a company's product–market portfolio for competitive success. It also leaves some fundamental cultural questions unanswered, for example, the international dimension. Despite this, the proposed solution of task forces and project teams to deal with the plurality of interests identified in the paradigm 2 perspective on culture and culture change is insightful.

Meyerson and Martin's paradigm 3, by their own admission, does not typically feature as a perspective adopted by mainstream researchers on culture. This is not too surprising given the lack of association between culture seen this way and the more tangible representation incorporating structural divisions and the permanent linking roles which are so characteristic of formal organizations. The amorphous nature of culture as seen from the paradigm 3 perspective sees change at the individual level, characterized by adjustments in patterns of attention and interpretation of environmental fluctuations. The paradox of cultural adaptation in this paradigm is that it is both continuous and obscure, a corollary being that cultural change is virtually uncontrollable. In certain settings, though, the autonomy this culture bestows is beneficial where creativity and experimentation are valued, a typical example being research laboratories.

The three-paradigm model proposed by Meyerson and Martin (1987) is extremely useful as a diagnostic framework for both academics and senior executives. In essence, it allows one to see where a culture change proponent 'is coming from', whether this approach is presented in a research paper or a consultant's proposal. The authors are not saying that culture can only exist in one dimension. Far from it – any organization, at any point in time, is likely to demonstrate elements of all three. The key foci of the general critique are cultural analysts and the blinkered outlook brought about by their paradigmatic closure:

> If cultural change is perceived and enacted from only one paradigmatic perspective, then other sources and types of change may not be considered. If researchers and members focus on 'top-down' organizational-level processes, they will miss 'bottom-up' sources of change. If they attend only to locally based changes, they will miss global patterns and masked ambiguities. And, if ambiguities are ignored or hidden, experimentation and 'playfulness' may be inhibited.

In conclusion, Meyerson and Martin (1987) argue that a better understanding of how organizations change will only come about from adopting their multi-paradigmatic view to interpret the complex dynamics of culture alongside an awareness of the myriad of change processes shaping, and being shaped by, such dynamics. Accepting the framework proposed by Meyerson and Martin and drawing on the more practical work of Beer *et al.* (1990) allows us to examine another panacea of the contemporary strategic management literature, the concept of the 'learning organization'.

The learning organization

The emergence of 'new ideas' in management theory is invariably paralleled by conflicting claims for the original structuring of the idea. This is certainly true of 'the learning organization', an idea which has rapidly diffused throughout the academic community and business practitioners. The learning organization is a concept which has rapidly grown in awareness but which still lacks definitional clarity (Jones and Hendry, 1994). One of the most fully developed versions of the concept to date has been articulated by Peter Senge of MIT. In the following sections we adopt his definition and examine his propositions before critically analysing the conceptual and practical limitations of his broader thesis. For Senge (1990), then, learning organizations are:

> organizations where people continually expand their capacity to create the results they truly desire, where new and expansive patterns of thinking are nurtured, where collective aspiration is set free, and where people are continually learning how to learn together.

Senge sees two principal driving forces behind the emergence of learning organizations, one deterministic, the other humanistic. Regarding the deterministic dimension, it is claimed that globalization of the world economy and the increasingly dynamic and complex context of international business demands that the organization and the work processes it encompasses become more 'learningful'. The humanistic perspective emerges from the inherent capabilities of organizations to meet higher order societal needs, as evidenced by the following statement from a corporate president: 'Why can't we do good works at work? Business is the only institution that has a chance, as far as I can see, fundamentally to improve the injustice that exists in the world. But first, we will have to move through the barriers that are keeping us from being truly vision-led and capable of learning.' Senge argues that the conditions for such learning are now in place as the core capabilities such organizations must have are increasingly being understood. The key, though, is mastery of 'the disciplines of the learning organization'.

Commercializing the learning organization

Drawing on a classic engineering metaphor, whereby invention constitutes the *creation* of an idea while innovation describes the *commercialization* of an idea, Senge argues that the notion of organizational learning has only reached the former state. As a way of doing business, however, he claims that organizational learning is ripe for harvesting in its second sense by firms who can harness the following five disciplines to capture sustainable organizational advantage:

1   *Systems thinking*   Senge notes the tendency of managers to focus on individual events – snapshots in time – rather than considering broader-based patterns of change.
2   *Personal mastery*   Characterized as a 'special level of proficiency', personal mastery is posited as the cornerstone of the learning organization, its 'spiritual foundation'. Like Peters and Waterman (1982), Senge notes the 'vast untapped potential' of people: 'Here, I am most interested in the connections between personal learning and organizational learning, in the reciprocal commitments between individual and organization, and in the special spirit of an enterprise made up of learners.'
3   *Mental models*   These are the subconscious assumptions and generalizations which guide managers' interpretations and actions. They are deeply ingrained and frequently prevent companies from seeing, let alone executing, market opportunities. They also provide a major barrier to appropriate changes in outmoded organizational practices. The challenge, then, is to 'unearth' these internal pictures and scrutinize them in a balanced process of inquiry and advocacy.
4   *Building shared views*   The vision should be genuine and encourage people to excel and learn. The discipline of shared vision involves unearthing 'pictures of the future', it requires a detailed set of principles and guiding practices and must foster commitment and enrolment. Attempts at dictating a vision and seeking compliance in the absence of belief will be counterproductive.

5   *Team learning* The discipline of team learning is underpinned by effective dialogue, a process which requires that team members 'suspend assumptions' and identify those patterns of interaction that undermine learning. This discipline is seen as vital since teams are the fundamental learning unit in modern organizations, yet individualism remains pervasive and team members tend to be very defensive. As Senge questions: 'How can a team of committed managers with individual IQs above 120 have a collective IQ of 63?'

Developing his engineering metaphor, Senge equates 'discipline' with technologies, i.e. those components which constitute the entity. In the concept of the learning organization, then, disciplines embrace 'a body of theory and technique that must be studied and mastered to be put into practice.' Disciplines are tangible in the sense that they provide a developmental path for the acquisition of appropriate skills and competencies. The disciplines outlined by Senge depart from the traditional management disciplines of accounting since they embrace additive and collective learning and deal with how individuals think and interact with one another. In this sense, the disciplines of the learning organization are more akin to artistic disciplines than the traditional, science-based disciplines of management. By definition, the process of developing the learning organization is continuous since, as the disciplines converge, they trigger a new wave of experimentation and advancement.

The 'Fifth Discipline' of Senge's title is systems thinking, the integrative agency which underpins the relationship of the disciplines with each other and to the outside world. The systemic perspective empowers managers to believe that they can shape the company's future, but it also challenges them to see how their own actions create the problems they experience, i.e. it forces them to seek explanations, not proffer excuses.

Senge acknowledges that, while the concepts of the learning organization are well grounded, the practice of building learning organizations remains unexplored. Moreover, systems thinking cannot be appended to an organization as a panacea for curing past and current ailments. Putting the principles of the learning organization into practice requires *'metanoia'*, a shift in mind-set that builds on learning as adaptation to embrace learning as generative. Put simply, it enhances the organization's capacity to shape the future. In developing the concept of the learning organization, Senge identifies seven institutional *barriers* to its adoption. He describes these as 'learning disabilities', arguing that they are characteristic of many organizations and that, in large measure, they tend to go undetected. These hurdles to effective adoption of the learning organization concept are outlined briefly below:

1   *'I am my position'* Over time people have a tendency to confuse what they do with who they are. This has two key implications. Firstly, if the nature of work changes, individuals often lack the capacity to change. This is a particular problem, and has been since the onset of the industrial revolution, when new technologies redefine work processes. Secondly, when individuals focus only on

their positional task, for example component assembly, they feel little responsibility for the finished product. If the latter works fine but fails to sell, the component assembler passes blame elsewhere. In many cases positions are institutionalized by unions into 'demarcation' formats, whereby refusal to move beyond the boundaries of positional tasks is legitimized. This was a major problem for many British manufacturers attempting to build in flexibility in work practice in response to the harsher competitive environment of the 1970s.

2   *The enemy is out there*   This disability is a manifestation of the previous one, since the reluctance of individuals or groups to accept responsibility for failure normally means that the blame has to be assigned elsewhere. This could be directed internally so, for example, blame shifts between manufacturing and marketing. Or it could be external, for example 'the unions', 'the management', 'the government', 'the Japanese' or – in the worst case – 'the customers'! This tendency of 'passing the buck' prevents the core problem from being identified and, worse still, restricts exploitation of the organization's potential to master its external environment.

3   *The illusion of taking charge*   Challenging the myth of the proactive manager, Senge argues that proactiveness is more often than not reactive management in disguise. While it might be pre-emptive, it often involves nothing more than taking a more aggressive stance towards the 'enemy out there', the mythical threat introduced above. Conceptually, true proactiveness involves analysis of how managers and organizations contribute to their own problems, i.e. it should be seen as a way of thinking and not, as is so often the case in management practice, an emotional state.

4   *The fixation of events*   This disability is a function of psychological conditioning and fundamentally underpins the short-termism typical of many organizations. Seeing life as a series of events leads managers to seek one obvious cause for each happening. Since the most serious threats to organizations come from slow gradual processes – from combinations of events converging over time – a focus on discrete items inhibits correct diagnosis of core problems. This inability to 'see the wood for the trees' is a major barrier to creativity and prevents generative learning, the fundamental concept of the learning organization thesis.

5   *The parable of the boiled frog*   This story is often told to demonstrate the terminal impact of failing to see the cumulative effects of the gradual processes discussed above. The frog is conditioned by nature to be responsive to sudden environment changes (single events). Place one in a pan of boiling water and its instinct will impel it to clamber out. Place the frog in a pan of water at room temperature, turn up the heat and witness a transformation from contentment to death. The frog becomes impervious to its surroundings and, in particular, the latter's shift from being favourable (warmth) to hostile (intense heat). The parable is used to describe the demise of both companies and industries, an example of the latter being the

inability of the American car industry to perceive the threat of new entrants (the Japanese) or innovative substitutes (smaller cars).

6 *The delusion of learning from experience* Although 'learning by doing' is one of the most powerful developmental tools it requires experience of consequences, not just actions. This is the fundamental premise of 'trial and error' learning techniques, whereby competence is formed through continuous adaptations as a result of cumulative experience. If the consequences of our actions are not readily apparent, or are beyond our 'learning horizon', then the feedback shortage which occurs creates what Senge describes as the core learning dilemma confronting organizations: 'We learn best from experience but we never directly experience the consequences of many of our most important decisions.' This problem is compounded with regard to the most critical decisions, since the impact of these have consequences throughout the organizational system for many years. To cope with systemic complexity organizations create functional hierarchies, a division of labour to facilitate decision making and experiential learning. An unfortunate corollary of this is that functions become fiefdoms, learning is confined and constrained, and an organization's most complex problems – cross-functional in character – are handled badly or simply ignored.

7 *The myth of the management team* A common solution organizations take to the above dilemmas is the creation of 'top teams', a broad cross-section of senior managers who represent different functions and areas of expertise. In practice, however, such teams spend a disproportionate amount of time 'fighting for turf'. While giving an appearance of cohesiveness, the reality is somewhat different. Team members avoid contributions that will put them in a bad light; they avoid public statements of serious reservations; and, when there is disagreement, it is presented in a way which lays blame elsewhere, often polarizing opinion and failing to challenge core assumptions. The series of problems associated with 'top teams' becomes particularly acute when the nature of the tasks is complex, embarrassing or threatening.

Senge's contribution, with its emphasis on a systems perspective, an integrative set of disciplines and recognition of a suite of disabilities preventing its execution, is to date the most cohesive exposition of the learning organization concept. Despite this, Senge's fifth discipline concept suffers the same fate which many sociological, psychological or economic labels encounter when attached to 'organization': it reifies what is at best an abstract concept. The tendency to refer to organizations as 'things', rather than an entity composed of groups and individuals, is a common feature of the management literature (Jones and Hendry, 1994). In the learning organization literature this has been a particular problem, leading to a conceptual and definitional ambiguity which has stifled the practical adoption of what could otherwise be an extremely powerful idea.

Jones and Hendry (1994) have addressed this issue by looking in more depth at the 'learning' dimension of the construct, making a useful distinction between the 'learning organization' and 'organizational learning'. The latter concept, they argue, has a research base dating back to the 1920s and, although the literature has expanded the core principles and broadened the debate to embrace action-learning concepts, organizational culture and strategic change management, its emphasis 'on HRM, training and knowledge and skills acquisition tends to obscure the real issues behind the learning organizations'. In concluding their review of the distinctive characteristics of the learning organization, Jones and Hendry (1994) point to the lack of general awareness regarding how companies could develop strategies for becoming learning organizations and, more pertinently, *when* they should attempt to do so. As mentioned previously, the unclear construction of the learning organization has limited its practical use. Addressing this issue Garvin (1993) chides the proponents of the learning organization concept for failing to provide a framework for action: 'Their focus is high philosophy and grand themes, sweeping metaphors rather than the gritty details of practice.' To operationalize the concept he offers a threefold agenda: (i) meaning; (ii) management; (iii) measurement. In the following sections we examine each of these dimensions in more depth.

The meaning of the learning organization

Reviewing the concept and its history, Garvin finds consensus among researchers that organizational learning is a continuous process of knowledge acquisition and performance improvement but he argues that there are fundamental disagreements on a broad range of conceptual and practical matters. The following quotes are illustrative of the debate (year of publication in brackets; original references can be found in the Garvin article): 'Organizational learning means the process of improving actions through better knowledge and understanding' (1985); 'Organizational learning is a process of detecting and correcting error' (1977); 'Organizations are seen learning by encoding inferences from history into routines that guide behaviour' (1988); 'Organizational learning occurs through shared insights, knowledge and mental models ... [and] builds on past knowledge and experience – that is, on memory' (1989); 'An entity learns if, through its processing of information, the range of its potential behaviours is changed' (1991). Collectively, these citations encompass a range of what is, why things are as they are, what might be and how things might be achieved. They embrace attitudinal and behavioural change (although they differ on causality) and once again draw attention to the scope and ambiguity of the learning organization concept. Garvin (1993) cuts a path through this 'cacophony of voices' and proposes a two-stage definition. Firstly, 'A learning organization is an organization skilled at creating, acquiring, and transferring knowledge, and at modifying its behaviour to reflect new knowledge and insights.' This definition takes as its starting point the 'simple truth' that for learning to take place new ideas are essential. Ideas, though, do not create learning organizations: 'Without accompanying changes in the way that work gets done, only potential for improvement exists.' This 'stringent test' of applicability embraces Peters and Waterman's (1982) discussion of latent human potential ('man waiting for motivation') and Beer *et al.*'s (1990) emphasis on the structure of work processes to enable change ('task alignment'). Garvin argues that successful learning organizations, by his definition, lay down distinctive policies and practices to manage the learning process, i.e. it is instilled by design, not chance. He describes these as 'building blocks', and these constitute the second element of his learning organization agenda: management.

The management of the learning organization

Successful organizations integrate five key activities within 'the fabric of daily operations', supported through the creation of appropriate systems and processes and characterized by a distinctive mind-set, tool kit and patterns of behaviour. The five building blocks are as follows: (a) systematic problem solving, employing the philosophies and methodologies developed by the quality movement, striving for disciplined thinking, challenging received wisdom and fostering a sharp attention to detail; (b) experimentation, using scientific methods to search systematically for and test new knowledge, either as part of ongoing programmes (continuous improvement) or as demonstration projects (holistic, systemwide change). The task of both is to elevate superficial knowledge to a deeper understanding; (c) learning from past performance, a systematic review and objective evaluation of past successes and failures, documented in a way which can be readily communicated to employees; (d) learning from others, looking outside the immediate environment in a structured and systematic discipline of benchmarking best-in-class companies at specific business processes (i.e. not necessarily industry-specific), and holding detailed and ongoing conversations with customers; (e) transferring knowledge, the aim being to disperse locally-based expertise through a variety of techniques, including reports, tours, site visits, personnel rotation programmes, standardization programmes and education and training programmes.

Collectively, the five 'building blocks' defined by Garvin move organizations away from a reliance 'on happenstance and isolated examples' towards a more structured and effective management of the learning process. In a point of departure from most studies of organizational learning, Garvin addresses the important question of *measurement*. He makes the subject much more tangible by accommodating the important managerial task of evaluation.

Measuring the learning organization

In the course of time management theories are judged, among managers at least, by the demonstrable results they deliver. The abstract nature of 'learning' is difficult to capture and, therefore, to measure. Traditional measurement methods have tended to deal with outputs not processes, obscuring causality and thus, paradoxically, learning. Garvin draws attention to traditional measurement solutions but outlines their inherent weaknesses. Measurement constraints such as the learning curve and its industry-wide derivatives, most notably the experience curve, have demonstrated a strong relationship between cumulative output and sharp reductions in costs. In the context of measuring organizational learning, however, such measures are incomplete. The single performance variable employed (cost/price) ignores additional competitive drivers, for example new product developments, logistics and relative quality. Worse still, they describe a relationship but, in a learning organization context, reveal little about the sources of learning or the potential assets which can leverage change.

Garvin profiles an alternative and more flexible measurement tool, the 'half-life' curve. This concept measures internal improvement rates over a much broader range of competitive variables (e.g. defect rates, on-time delivery, time to market) against a time frame (days, months, years) taken to achieve a 50 per cent improvement rate. The value of the half-life curve concept rests in its flexibility, the fact that it is easy to operationalize, that it provides a visible and readily understood measuring stick and that it provides a reliable and highly visible measure for company performance between different business units. Again there is an inherent weakness and its roots are the same. The half-life concept is heavily results-oriented, division-focused and as such tends to foster short-termist and insular behaviour. As Garvin comments, 'Some types of knowledge take years to digest, with few visible changes in performance for long periods. Creating a total quality culture, for instance, or developing new approaches to product development are difficult systemic changes.'

According to Garvin, three complementary and overlapping stages characterize organizational learning, each of which can be monitored and measured to assess progress. The first is cognitive, since organizational members, through exposure to new ideas, broaden their knowledge base and think differently. For this stage the measurement is of attitudes and depth of understanding. The second stage is behavioural, where employees, through internalization of the new insights they are exposed to, begin to change their behaviour. In this stage measurement must include direct observation of employees, typical techniques including 'mystery customers' and the use of independent consultants. The third stage is performance improvement, for example improved logistics, higher market share, higher quality, superior service and so on. Typically, cognitive and behavioural changes precede performance improvements. A complete learning audit, combining surveys, questionnaires, interviews and direct observation, must be undertaken to ensure that the learning process is working and, more pointedly, that it is achieving the company's objectives.

Noting, in conclusion, that building a learning organization is a long-term exercise, Garvin nevertheless identifies immediate steps companies can take to accelerate the process. These include a few essentials, such as cultivating an environment conducive to learning, thus creating space for reflection and analysis. Additionally, artificial functional and divisional boundaries which inhibit information flows must be removed, typical solutions being conferences, meetings, task forces and project teams. Finally, learning forums, designed to tackle specific strategic and operational problems, should be organized. The combined output of the approach proposed by Garvin is a higher order category of continuous improvement, 'a solid foundation for building learning organizations.'

Garvin's contribution is significant, particularly in terms of clarity of definition and attention to a more holistic approach to measurement. Despite this, fundamental questions of structure and culture, while alluded to, are not addressed directly. In the final sections of this chapter, we focus on these core issues, in the process drawing together the threads of discussion to provide an integrative perspective on the strategic management of change.

Culture and structure: alignment and agendas

In large measure, the study of organizational structure and culture has taken different paths. Perspectives on culture were addressed earlier in this chapter, but there was little mention in that discussion of organization structure. Likewise, scholars of organizational design do not tend to have culture among their primary variables. In a similar vein, executives responsible for structural changes such as downsizing, delayering, flattening, merging, acquiring, integrating, and collaborating take decisions which have a tremendous impact on culture, yet this is rarely at the forefront of their minds when they initiate and/or undertake the process. Consultants advising on re-engineering or organizational design pay lip service to the behavioural dimensions of organizations in the full knowledge that they do not have to deal with the cultural flotsam they leave in their wake. An integration of structure and culture, then, is long overdue, particularly in the context of strategic change. Handy (1993), more than most, has addressed this issue. His structural approach to organizational analysis, with its focus on division of labour, the structure of roles within the organization's design and the existence of social networks, allows him to make specific links between structure, culture and change: 'many of the ills of organizations stem from imposing an inappropriate structure on a particular culture, or from expecting a particular culture to thrive in an inappropriate climate.'

Handy profiles four different types of culture and their structural contexts. His analysis is not prescriptive in the sense of proposing one best culture. Rather, it takes an institutionalist perspective where appropriateness of fit is the distinguishing factor, i.e. there is an effective match of people, systems, task and environment and suitable linkages between these four components.

The first of Handy's typology is the power culture. The dominant force is a central power source and the structural dimension is modelled as a spider's web, with rings of power and influence radiating away from the centre. Decision making is politically oriented, the success of the organization being largely a function of the quality of people at the centre. There is little bureaucracy and there are few procedural norms. The culture is strong since like-minded people will thrive in this environment while people who do not 'buy-in' to it will leave or be ejected. The organization is flexible and fleet of foot in response to environmental opportunities and threats, although the direction taken will be more autocratic than consensual. Power cultures are typical of smaller, entrepreneurial companies, an obvious limiting factor to their existence being the size and complexity of the organization. Change management will be difficult and succession is a major problem.

The second culture identified by Handy is the role culture. The dominant force is functional specialism and the structural dimension is modelled as a Greek temple, with tall and strong pillars representing functions (e.g. marketing, production, purchasing, finance), the pediment representing the senior executives who play a coordinating role. Decision making is structured and rational, the quality of decisions being a function of an appropriate allocation of resource and an effective division of labour. Bureaucracy is the norm, rules and procedures being the guiding principles. Roles are defined so that the position within the organization is of more importance than the individual who occupies it. Within these positions lie the principal sources of power within the organization. The role culture and bureaucratic structure work well in conditions of largeness. They are also typically found in situations where organizations can exert influence over their environment, for example in monopolistic and oligopolistic market structures or in public sector institutions such as the civil service.

In turbulent times, however, role cultures, like Greek temples, are inherently unstable. Since visions of the future are so locked into interpretations of the immediate and distant past, directional change of an appropriate nature is difficult to conceptualize, let alone implement. Change management will be difficult since control is so vertical and coordination limited to so few. The problem is compounded when the organization replicates its form in a multi-divisional diversified structure.

The third culture identified by Handy is the task culture. The dominant force is expertise and the structural dimension is modelled as a net, with strong strands representing specialisms for the task at hand, knots representing the source of power and influence. Decision making is team-based, effectiveness being a function of appropriate selection of team members. The task culture is malleable, reflecting the particular job and group member mix. It is responsive and flexible and therefore ideally suited to turbulent business environments and/or in situations where the organization has little control over its external environment. Not all organizations suit a task culture and, in general, they are difficult to control, particularly once projects are up and running. The construct is inherently unstable and there is a tendency for a slow infusion of rules and procedures and, ultimately, a regression towards a role culture, particularly if the organization as a whole is underperforming and/or resources are scarce.

Handy's fourth culture is the person culture. The dominant force is the individual and the structural dimension is modelled as a cluster, 'a galaxy of individual stars'. This culture is rare and can be conceived of as a battle of the individual versus the organization. It is typically a short-term phenomenon since the organization invariably wins through in establishing its own identity. Control and hierarchy are absent and few organizations exist with this culture type. Not surprisingly, people within other organizational cultures aspire to the empowerment the person culture offers, but with rare exceptions they would not survive. A particular expertise (e.g. IT specialists in commercial organizations) or tenure (e.g. professors in universities) might harbour elements of person culture within more traditional culture/structure formats but, even here, pressures would mount for integration.

The strong linkages claimed by Handy between structure and culture provide powerful insights for organizational analysts and those interested in the burgeoning topic of organizational design (OD). For the former, the identification of culture at any point in time and (geographical) space will require a rigorous situational analysis of the following factors (Handy, 1993): (a) history and ownership; (b) organizational size; (c) the nature and intensity of technology; (d) goals and objectives; (e) the environment; (f) the people. Each dimension will suggest its own imperatives, a complexity compounded when the interrelatedness between the variables is taken into account. So, for example, a fast-growing entrepreneurial company dominated by a power culture grows to a level of scale and complexity which requires the standardization, formalization and decentralization dimensions characteristic of a role culture. The transition will be turbulent, since the technologies and people which sat comfortably in the formative years are not necessarily readily transferable.

Regarding organizational design, Handy notes the tendency of contemporary management thinkers to push for the task-based culture/structure, since this is the most appropriate organizational form to deliver the autonomy and empowerment so desirable to individuals while, at the same time, it supposedly facilitates organizational learning and knowledge transfer. In practice, however, 80 per cent of an organization's personnel – including sales, production and the firm's general management infrastructure – are involved in 'steady-state', routinized, programmable activities which lend themselves to a role structure/culture.

Integrating these contradictions and conflicts inherent in organizational analysis and organization design, Handy chastises management theorists and writers for their blinkered adherence to a particular cultural recipe. His four-fold critique resonates with some of the core themes of this book and as such they are cited in full below:

1 Classical management theory was talking about role cultures – the management of the steady state.
2 Modern management thinkers concentrate on the task culture and have found their favourite organizations among the project-based

companies in the US aerospace industries and the innovative ends of more traditional organizations.

3   Journalists, historians and biographers have found the power cultures, centred around a key figure or figures, easier to focus on, more tempting to describe.

4   Sociologists, religious and youth leaders, have been concerned with the clash between the organization and the individual with a 'person' orientation.

The management task, then, is to align appropriate structures and systems with the four cultures to manage successfully four different activity sets, the latter being described as steady state, innovation, crisis, policy creation. This can be effectively handled by careful management of the divergent forces of 'differentiation' and 'integration'. Differentiation is the principle that the cultures and structures of organizations should be aligned closely to the dominant kind of activity being undertaken by the division, department, function etc. So, for example, R&D should have the characteristics of the task culture/structure while continuous process flow manufacturing should have a prevailing role culture/structure. The dilemma of differentiation is fragmentation, i.e. the physical, psychic and political distances which emanate from formal separation of departments and cultures. The challenge here is to design and operationalize integrative devices to limit the harsher realities of fragmentation.

In practice, an appropriate balance of differentiation and integration is rarely achieved, particularly in discontinuous business environments. One culture will typically dominate and this will tend to be the role culture. The power culture is too dependent for its stability on structured information flows and the patronage of the centre, both of which are threatened by growing scale and succession problems. The task culture, with its inherent control problems, also tends towards the role culture over time. From a change perspective, the task forces and project teams which underpin the task culture are often inappropriately constructed and inadequately trained. In practice, firms aiming to inculcate a task- or team-based culture do so through a structural form known as a 'matrix organization'. The inherent weaknesses of such structures and their supportive systems have long been known.

Profiling the matrix structure

Davis and Lawrence (1977) examined the conditions under which the matrix was the preferred structural choice and examined these with reference to matrix structures, systems and organizational behaviour. Three conditions were proposed: (i) *outside pressure for dual focus*, a recognition that organizations are spatially bounded and constrained by competence, i.e. they cannot be everywhere at once or be all things to all people; (ii) *pressures for high information-processing capacity*, a recognition that communications channels become overloaded in the hierarchical pyramids of conventional organizations. The problem is acute when discontinuous environments raise uncertainty, when organizational diversification increases complexity and, finally, when effective response raises interdependence between organizational members from different functions and divisions; (iii) *pressures for shared resources*, a recognition that organizations, when under environmental pressure, need to utilize fully and achieve economies of scale from their 'expensive and highly specialized talents', i.e. their human resource. People should be a shared asset, available to work on more than one task at a time or for redeployment to enable flexible response to changing environments.

For Davis and Lawrence these are the 'necessary and sufficient' conditions for adoption of a matrix structure, and each must be present simultaneously. The benefits of the matrix are clear. Structure is flexible rather than having the stolid and static characteristics of traditional organizations. Since environments constantly evolve, the latter structures, which change infrequently, occasionally have to make discrete quantum leaps to remain viable, in the process severely disrupting established and entrenched behaviour patterns, only to find that the environment has changed yet again. A matrix, however, creates a work environment where the structure is in a state of constant change, thus reducing the severe dislocations and eruptions experienced in contexts of radical change.

Despite these obvious benefits the matrix is not the holy grail which delivers the flexible organization, particularly in the way it tends to be adopted in practice. Three complex behaviour patterns are essential if the three necessary and sufficient conditions outlined by Davis and Lawrence are to be met simultaneously within a matrix structure: (i) focusing human effort on a number of critical organizational tasks simultaneously; (ii) human handling of complex information flows and a 'general management' (balanced response) approach to all business problems; (iii) flexible and rapid employment and redeployment of human resource to a variety of projects. The authors argue that effective and full implementation of the matrix structure is a process which extends over 2–3 years and is not a simple matter of formal design. Rather, it is the result of a complex equation: Matrix Organization = Matrix Structure + Matrix Systems + Matrix Culture + Matrix Behaviour.

The long-term perspective and complex management tasks involved in transforming traditional organizations to matrix structures is clearly a major constraint on their adoption, particularly given the inherent short-termism of commercial organizations. Compounding the problem is the finding that adopting matrix structures actually increases managerial overhead, particularly in the initial stages, at a time when most organizations are desperately trying to reduce fixed administration costs.

Shaping the future

From the preceding discussion it is clear that in the context of change a premium is placed on organizational learning (Vicere, 1991) and, in a more proactive sense, we can argue that the importance of managerial actions comes to the fore. By this we refer to the fact that companies are not merely passive receivers of and reactors to environmental stimuli. They can shape their own future to the extent that their managers can intervene in and successfully interrupt an otherwise 'normal' progression of events.

Taking as his starting point a review of contemporary organization thinking, Dichter (1991) profiled 'the organization of the '90s' and demonstrated the powerful impact of a new set of organizational principles on corporate performance. Dichter's article contributes to a pattern of literature which increasingly proposes organizational advantage as the most sustainable form of competitive edge, particularly where markets are mature and/or deregulated and where technology transfer is complete. In Dichter's view, then, 'the new model' has the following characteristics: (a) customer (versus supervisor) focus; (b) continuous performance improvement (versus meeting periodically defined objectives); (c) teams (versus hierarchical) relationships; (d) flat, flexible (versus vertical, static) structures; (e) empowerment (versus compliance); (f) vision- and value-driven (versus control-oriented) leadership.

Prosperous companies demonstrate some or all of these characteristics and can be differentiated from their less successful counterparts. On the downside, there are far more of the latter as organizations demonstrate their well-known tendency towards inertia. The twin tasks for senior executives are to challenge misconceptions among managers and to foster a working environment which facilitates rather than constrains change. This is particularly true where firms have internationalized and, in the process, face a new competitive challenge from both global and indigenous rivals. In their influential book *Managing Across Borders*, Bartlett and Ghoshal (1989) addressed these issues and warned companies of the dangers of 'administrative heritage' whereby the 'heavy weight of past choices' constrains the appropriate decisions for contemporary and emerging competitive conditions. This becomes all the more apparent when dealing with the 'softer' realities of organizational advantage. Jones (1992) has drawn attention to the rush by Western companies to identify and initiate Japanese product and process innovations (e.g. flexible manufacturing systems and kanban inventory management techniques). In doing so, he argues, they ignore organizational capability, in this sense described as 'the deeper foundation of competence and context'. In the process of globalization companies tend to move beyond the boundaries of their existing knowledge base, from the context of relative certainty to a milieu characterized by ambiguity and – in many cases – distrust. For many companies the task is not merely to learn – more often than not the immediate mission is 'learning to learn'. A requirement for such knowledge transfer applies to both externalities and internal organizational issues, particularly for multinational, multidivisional companies.

Concluding remarks

Changes in strategic direction and its counterpart, organizational restructuring, are not new phenomena, particularly in recessionary periods. The key difference between the current phase of organizational change and those of the past is the greater intensity of competition and the progressive trend towards deregulation and liberalization of markets. As Heygate (1992) notes, 'when competitive pressure reduces the time available for redesigning processes and building skills to a maximum of only two or three years, [the] challenge becomes far more difficult still.'

In addressing this challenge many firms have had the limits of their capabilities exposed. In the next chapter we examine why this is the case. We profile the growth options available to companies and present a critical evaluation of the rise of joint ventures and strategic alliances as apparent solutions to a fundamental paradox of international business: the desire to serve many markets is matched only by an inability to cope with the complexity of the task.

6

The role of alliances and networks in strategic management

Introduction

Firms face a tremendous range of pressures to grow: shareholders seek capital gain, managers pursue ever-increasing spans of control while employees aspire to the security and job potential offered by scale. Economics plays a role too, as we shall see. The desire for growth captures the essence of the capitalist dynamic but also exposes the limitations of the firm. Constrained by its capabilities, the individual company has a limited option set. In most texts on corporate strategy and strategic management this range is modelled on the concept of growth vectors first proposed by Ansoff (1965) in his seminal text on the subject. The Ansoff growth matrix is shown in Figure 6.1.

A factor rarely considered in textbook renditions of Ansoff's matrix is a detailed discussion of the scope of meaning within the 'product' and 'market' categories which constitute the dimensions of the matrix. Regarding the former, product should be taken to include the technologies and processes which supply the product to market and not just, as is often the case, the tangible item or service delivered. Viewed in this

	Present products	New products
Present markets	Market penetration	Product development
New markets	Market development	Diversification

Figure 6.1 *Product–market growth opportunities matrix (Source: Ansoff, I. (1987), Corporate Strategy, Harmondsworth: Penguin)*

way, the sharp constraints on an organization's ability to deliver genuinely new products to their core markets is readily apparent. As mentioned in Chapter 1, a stronger likelihood is that new entrants and/or technological substitutes delivered by entrepreneurial, innovative companies will take market share from incumbent rivals. Much of business process re-engineering activity and its counterpart, time-based competition, is a demonstration of this fundamental fact.

In a similar vein, the 'market' axis of the Ansoff box is regularly treated in a simplistic fashion, more often than not taken to equate to some aggregate of consumers. Stranger still, 'market development' is often taken to include geographic expansion, a bizarre assertion given the fragmented and heterogeneous nature of market structures and consumer needs in most industrial economies (Egan and McKiernan, 1994). A fuller definition of 'market' is essential, not least for the reason that a new market for company A's product is highly likely to be the 'bread and butter' domain of company B. In addition to embracing customer segments and competitors, 'market' should also encompass distribution channels – arguably the greatest structural impediment to market access – and communications channels.

The Ansoff matrix is often used to offer prescriptions for firms seeking synergistic exploitation of their asset base, particularly with regard to the diversification cell. In practice $2 + 2 = 3$ is the more common equation, suggesting a potentially excessive cost of *phantom* synergies. As Day (1990) notes:

> So many diversification efforts fall short of their inflated expectations that the whole notion of synergy as multiplicative combinations of businesses is called into question. In theory, any activity a business excels at can be exported to a new arena. In practice these prospective synergies are often illusions.

Despite the obvious difficulties and appalling failure rates, the diversification cell remains attractive for many companies, often for behavioural more than economic reasons. Placing diversification in a broader context of strategic choice, Kastens (1973) is scathing of its strategic intent: 'The primary principle that must be grasped is that diversification is fundamentally a negative strategy. Diversifiers are always running away from something.' Even Ansoff (1987), the archdeacon of rationality, has proposed the 'grass looks greener in the neighbour's yard syndrome' as a major reason why firms diversify.

The pros and cons of diversification and other growth vectors are not our main interest here. Of far greater concern is the *methods* which firms typically take when striving for growth and the organizational challenges each approach creates. There are essentially three approaches firms take when expanding their operations: (i) organic (internal) development; (ii) acquisitions; (iii) networks. The latter provides the focus of this chapter since the network solution has rapidly emerged as a means of keeping the environment–strategy–organization nexus in equilibrium. This is demonstrated in Figure 6.2 which adapts the core model introduced in Chapter 2.

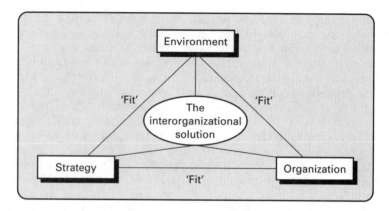

Figure 6.2 *Nexus revisited: the interorganizational solution*

As we will see in the following sections, networks have come to play a major role in the conduct of international business. Many definitional problems are associated with the term networks but, in their broadest sense, they describe *inter-* rather than *intra*-organizational solutions to coping with the dynamics and complexity of the business environment. In Chapter 3 we introduced the work of Williamson (1975, 1985) and, in particular, focused on his propositions regarding the alternative trans-action mechanisms of markets versus hierarchies. Networks provide an intermediate solution. They can offset the uncertainties associated with market-based transactions and they avoid the complexities of integra-tion. They are not without their problems and there are strong criticisms of their existence. A neo-classical critique, for example, would argue that collaboration rather than competition will stifle innovation and allow companies to become inefficient, the customer being the ultimate victim of cartel-like business practices. Organizational theorists will point to the difficult task of managing *within* organizations, let alone *between* them. Despite this, there is growing evidence that network solutions provide extraordinary competitive advantages, whether this be through the giant Japanese *kieretsu* networks or among the exporting networks of Scandinavian producers. In the following sections we explore the network phenomenon, charting its incidence and evaluating its impact on strategic management theory and practice.

Collaboration for competitive edge

For a broad range of reasons many firms are seeking 'strategic partners' to cope with the risks and uncertainties of the contemporary business environment. The number of such alliances has escalated dramatically in recent years and in many cases old rivals are now beginning to collab-orate. A stark example is the formation of a partnership between IBM and Apple to cope with the power and influence exerted by Microsoft and Intel, the latter companies being relative newcomers to the computer business. The trend towards alliances has been particularly apparent within Europe as firms jockey for position in the single market and where a broad restructuring of many industrial sectors is being undertaken.

Doz (1992) has used the European business environment to examine the role of partnerships and alliances in the broader context of strategic management. He identifies three steps which are characteristic of how firms manage the process of growth while coping with the substantive discontinuities they encounter: (i) decentralization, strategic business unit formation, portfolio analysis and planning and a general assessment of the competitive position of each set of business activities; (ii) consolidation of fragmented industrial sectors within countries, often influenced and facilitated by governments, to create so-called 'national champions'; (iii) transnational mergers and acquisitions.

Doz collectively categorizes these strategic moves as 'hard restructuring' and outlines the particular problems firms experience when undertaking them. Since organic growth is too slow in stable environments and too difficult in discontinuous ones the principal route to growth and restructure taken by European companies has been via acquisitions. Despite this, the acquisition route has had a very chequered history, the vast majority not meeting managers' expectations of them. Furthermore, many 'sensible' mergers have not taken place. Regarding the latter point, Doz identifies five obstacles which go some way towards explaining 'missed' acquisition opportunities: (i) public policy restrictions, including the protection of politically sensitive sectors, the protection and promotion of 'national champions' and state ownership of enterprises in sectors otherwise ripe for consolidation; (ii) anti-monopoly concerns which disallow proposed mergers or which discourage companies from pursuing acquisition or merger candidates for fear of becoming embroiled in long and drawn-out public debates; (iii) the size and ownership structure of companies so that, for example, the absolute scale and complexity of the Siemens operation would be impossible to absorb, while companies such as Nestlé and Philips have (or have had) equity voting patterns which virtually preclude their acquisition. This was highlighted in Nestlé's case when the company was in the process of acquiring the British company Rowntree and the whole issue of reciprocity emerged, i.e. a concern that while Nestlé could easily acquire Rowntree, it was virtually impossible for any company to gain a controlling position in Nestlé; (iv) it is difficult to assign a value to an acquisition target and, even where this is possible, there is no guarantee of buyer–seller agreement. The proposed BA/KLM merger ultimately floundered on this issue, BA arguing that the price demanded by KLM (government owned) would have eroded their own shareholder value. This general problem is compounded by the dynamics of the acquisition decision-making process itself; (v) as companies refocus, attractive acquisition targets are few and far between and the risk of paying too much increases accordingly.

As mentioned above, when acquisitions do take place the research evidence suggests that the post-acquisition integration process often fails. Doz argues that three competencies are essential for successful integration and management of the merged companies: (i) bidirectionality, i.e. the willingness of both parties to share competencies, avoiding the imposition of a 'one-best-way' approach by the acquiring firm; (ii) maintaining balance between learning and efficiency, i.e. exploiting potential synergies but giving the acquired company the autonomy and scope to deal with its own business environment; (iii) fostering a sense of mutual interest and flexibility: 'To create the most value, both the acquired and the acquiring companies must usually learn to work together, i.e. both must adapt.'

In practice such lofty ideals are rarely met. Firms pursuing acquisition policies tend to adopt one method of integration, regardless of the specific objectives relating to the particular acquisition. For example, acquisitions are often managed as 'absorptions' – full rationalization – when a partnership approach to the creation of value from combined assets would be more appropriate. Such problems become acute when large firms acquire the skills and knowledge of small entrepreneurial companies and subsume them within the more stifling bureaucratic role culture of the larger organization, in the process destroying the innovativeness they have acquired.

In conclusion, Doz argues that the typical 'hard' approaches to restructuring – organic and acquisition – are inappropriate for the radical restructuring which is essential within the essentially fragmented European industrial base. Organic growth is either too slow or beyond the capability of most organizations. Acquisitions give the impression of a quick-fix solution but are fraught with problems. According to Doz, then, the hierarchical solution in the Williamson sense is problematic. There is, however, an alternative approach:

> In many cases in which mergers and acquisitions may not take place or may fail, partnerships, joint ventures and alliances represent a 'softer' approach more likely to bring the same rationalization and restructuration benefits as mergers are expected to provide.

While there are some clear successes of growth by acquisition (e.g. Tube Investments, Reed Elsevier) many mergers and acquisitions have failed to provide the *'ex post'* gains promised in the *'ex ante'* propaganda. Hence, it could be that, in a strategic sense, 'hard' restructuring through mergers and acquisitions is just too difficult for many firms, a particular problem emanating from the complexities of integrating diverse cultural groupings. 'Strategic' alliances, then, can help to overcome many of the problems that tend to undermine successful outcomes from mergers and acquisitions.

While alliances of some sort emerge as an obvious solution to what appears to be an otherwise intractable problem it is still extremely difficult to evaluate their effectiveness as an approach to strategic management. As with many management issues the immediate problem is definitional. Faulkner (1992), for example, has claimed that the prolific academic writing on alliances in recent years has suffered from the wide variety of terms employed to describe similar or even identical forms of business practice. In a similar vein, Daniel (1991) has argued that although the term strategic alliance is new the strategy of partnership it represents is not: 'Strategic alliances (although not called by that name at the time) were highly topical in the late 1960s and the early 1970s, became less popular and then re-emerged in popularity by the late 1980s.'

In reality there are a variety of interorganizational forms including international coalitions (Porter and Fuller, 1986), strategic networks (Jarillo, 1988), hybrid organizational arrangements (Borys and Jemison, 1989) and industrial systems constellations (Perlmutter and Heenan, 1986). According to Johanson and Mattsson (1988) strategic alliances are a particular mode of interorganizational relationship in which the partners make substantial investments in developing common operations in a long-term collaborative effort. Strategic alliances, then, are not temporary or short-term phenomena. Rather, they involve substantial commitment of resources, mutually acceptable objectives and a sharing of risk from environmental pressures (Root, 1987).

In the debate on definitions Lorange and Roos (1992) place strategic alliances on a continuum which measures the degree of vertical integration on a scale running from 'free markets' to 'internalized hierarchy', a framework we demonstrate in Figure 6.3.

The left-hand side of the continuum represents a situation characterized by complete integration of activities within the organization. Moving towards the right-hand side suggests ever lower degrees of vertical integration to an extreme where all transactions are taking place in an open market context. In addition to the degree of vertical integration it is also useful to define alliances by the degree of mutual interdependence which exists between the organizations in the relationship. In the scale shown in Figure 6.3 the informal cooperative venture would be characterized by low interdependence, the degree of interdependence increasing in line with the degree of integration.

Contractor and Lorange (1988) argue that it makes strategic sense to choose an alliance which is based on compatibility and that a key

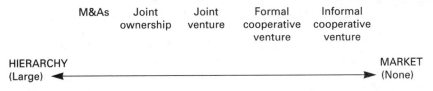

Figure 6.3 *Strategic alliances and degrees of vertical integration (Source: Lorange, P. and Roos, J. (1992),* Strategic Alliances: Formulation, Implementation and Evolution, *Oxford: Blackwell)*

operational imperative is to recognize the need to develop mutual trust and confidence between the parties involved. Given this, they argue that appropriate definitions of alliances should be firmly based on the degrees of vertical integration and mutual interdependence involved. Despite this apparently obvious logic there remains the problem of contrasting perceptions of the true nature of the relationship since each partner can view the alliance from a different perspective and frequently does so. This is why strategic alliances are extremely difficult for academics or business managers to define with any precision: gaining a common viewpoint on the degree of integration and dependence is very difficult to achieve in practice.

Mapping alliance activity

Strategic alliances occur in many different industries and between firms of different sizes. They have numerous purposes and may involve both vertical and horizontal links between firms. In a study of 839 agreements Hergert and Morris (1988) found that most alliances occur in high-tech industries: automobiles (24 per cent), aerospace (19 per cent), telecommunications (17 per cent), computers (14 per cent), and other electrical industries (13 per cent). The largest share of agreements were in joint product development (38 per cent) and the vast majority (71 per cent) were formed between rivals.

There are a number of general drivers in the international economy that encourage firms to cooperate rather than follow Porter's 'compete at all cost' philosophy. These include: (a) increased competitive pressure in the globalization process and the strategic need to gain scale and scope economies; (b) the need to preserve strength in national markets while adapting to the local needs and demands of international markets; (c) technology and knowledge transfer flows at ever-increasing rates, in the process shortening product life-cycles and forcing the need to share R&D activities between companies; (d) sophisticated consumers are demanding more and more specialized packages, thus creating a supply-side need to combine the best technology with the best marketing; (e) overcapacity in traditional industries has led to many businesses repositioning in new markets and seeking partners to aid the transition; (f) many groups have become over-diversified, thus forcing a need to restructure, for example AEG (Germany), Empain Schneider (France); (g) threats of takeover or successfully completed takeovers have forced restructuring, for example Societé Générale de Belgique, Montedison, Plessey.

Lorange and Roos (1992) have proposed a framework which integrates the motivations of individual parties to a relationship and generates a profile of four generic strategic alliance approaches. The first stage of their model is shown in Figure 6.4. The two dimensions of the matrix reflect two key questions. Firstly, is the proposed alliance part of the core activities of the business or is it seen as peripheral? Secondly, what is the firm's relative position in the market that it is in. Is it a leader – larger market share, leading technology or superior quality? If the answer is

Business market position

	Leader	Follower
Core	DEFEND	CATCH-UP
Peripheral	REMAIN	RESTRUCTURE

Strategic importance in portfolio

Figure 6.4 *Generic motives for strategic alliances (Source: Lorange, P. and Roos, J. (1992),* Strategic Alliances: Formulation, Implementation and Evolution, *Oxford: Blackwell)*

yes then the firm would approach a strategic alliance differently than if it only enjoyed a marginal position and was attempting to catch up. In the following, each cell of the matrix presented in Figure 6.4 is profiled. In each case the strategic position is considered alongside the key organizational motive for embarking on the alliance:

1 *Defend – core/leader position*   The typical motive here is defensive, the objective being to give wider access to markets and/or technologies and to secure greater access to key resources (e.g. IBM with specialist software developers). Big players may have strategic alliances with smaller dynamic ones to: (a) keep abreast of technology and other developments (e.g. the alliance between the Swedish company SKF (global market leader in roll bearings) and the French firm SDM to develop electromagnetic bearings); (b) secure sourcing of raw materials and/or inexpensive products; (c) to break into new or emerging megamarkets (e.g. China, India and Japan between 1945 and 1972).

2 *Catch-up – core/follower position*   Companies may have fallen behind in their core businesses and perceive that the quickest way to catch up is through alliances (e.g. SAAB and General Motors).

3 *Remain – peripheral/leader position*   Companies may wish to form strategic alliances to get the maximum efficiency from the business (e.g. Ericsson with GE in cellular radio in 1989 – a business peripheral to both but an alliance which gained Ericsson a significant presence in the large US market).

4 *Restructure – peripheral/follower position*   The main motive here is to restructure the business, perhaps with an eye on creating strength to eventually divest it.

Giving this outline of generic motives allows a classification of strategic alliances into a four-fold typology which we examine in the following sections.

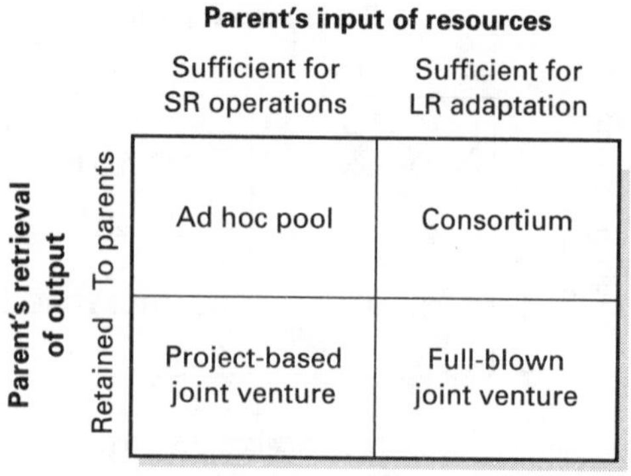

Parent's input of resources

	Sufficient for SR operations	Sufficient for LR adaptation
To parents	Ad hoc pool	Consortium
Retained	Project-based joint venture	Full-blown joint venture

(left axis label: Parent's retrieval of output)

Figure 6.5 *Generic strategic alliance types (Source: Lorange, P. and Roos, J. (1992), Strategic Alliances: Formulation, Implementation and Evolution, Oxford: Blackwell)*

Generic strategic alliance types

Despite the motive, it is important for parent companies to decide how much input of either organizational resource (people, funds, technology) or strategic resource to put into the alliance. Similarly, a decision has to be made on the retrieval of output from the strategic alliance (e.g. to take all the output of the alliance or to leave it within the venture to grow), Figure 6.5 highlights the options, each of which is discussed in turn.

1 *Ad hoc pool*   If parents put in just enough resources to complement each other and these are then ploughed back in their entirety to parents, an ad hoc type of strategic alliance makes sense. An example is an agreement between shipowners to trade ships in a common pattern for a certain time charter arrangement.
2 *Consortium*   Here, parents put in a lot more than in the ad hoc pool, but take it all out again. For example, in an R&D consortium each partner puts in its best technologies, scientists and so on but all the benefits go back to parent companies after any discoveries have been made.
3 *Project-based joint venture*   Minimum strategic resources are committed but the arrangement hinges around creating a common organization. Resources generated do not get distributed to parties except as financial results (dividends, royalties etc.). For example, the creation of such an alliance could facilitate rapid entry into foreign markets.
4 *Full-blown joint venture*   An abundance of resources are donated by each partner and the venture is allowed to retain outputs (except dividends). An example would be a long-term joint venture to develop an entirely new business where the entity would have full strategic autonomy.

Lorange and Roos (1992) stress that it is the parents' perspective regarding strategic positioning as well as the input/output of resources that dictates the form of the strategic alliance. This emphasizes the fundamental fact that strategic alliances are a means to an end, not the end in itself. Considering this latter point, Bleeke and Ernst (1993) see the emergence of alliances as a direct result of companies avoiding the Darwinian game:

> In businesses as diverse as pharmaceuticals, jet engines, banking, and computers, managers have learned that fighting long, head-to-head battles leaves their companies financially exhausted, intellectually depleted, and vulnerable to the next wave of competition and innovation.

For these authors, then, the current turbulent business environments have led to 'the death of the predator', with large multinational corporations delivering better value to their stakeholders, including shareholders, employees and customers, by selective sharing and/or exchanging control, costs, market access, knowledge and technology rather than 'competing blindly'. Indeed, they argue that the strongest predictor of a company's success at internationalization is its willingness and ability to collaborate.

Ohmae (1989) sees a similar global logic behind the growing incidence of strategic alliances:

> Globalization mandates alliances, makes them absolutely essential to strategy. Uncomfortable, perhaps – but that's the way it is. Like it or not, the simultaneous developments that go under the name of globalization make alliances – entente – necessary.

Building on his 'Triad Power' thesis, Ohmae sees three key drivers within the globalization process (i.e. the internationalization of markets, industries and firms) which are making alliances a prerequisite for corporate survival. Firstly, 'the Californiazation of need', the phenomenon which sees a converging of customer needs and preferences, particularly with regard to consumers purchasing the best products available at the lowest possible price. This trend is facilitated by the proliferation of communication channels and the knowledgeable consumer. As we mentioned in Chapter 1, faced with choice, customers exercise it. Furthermore, raise customer satisfaction and you raise their expectations too, in the process forcing an endless pursuit of innovation in the supply base. Secondly, technology has spread rapidly, dispersing so widely that few companies can single-handedly maintain a leading-edge sophistication, nor can any one organization be a master in all the technologies which make up today's complex products. In this sense, globalization marks the death of the fully integrated company, technological pressures forcing ever-increasing levels of 'outsourcing'. As Ohmae notes, 'Nothing stays proprietary for long. And no one player can master everything. Thus, operating globally means operating with partners – and that in turn means a further spread of technology.'

In this context an intriguing example of a network solution to a quite unique market challenge is the case of General Magic, a Silicon Valley start-up company created to exploit the potential of the converging computer and consumer electronics industries. The company is unique in its creation of a network of partnerships, a complex structure which its vice-president of marketing describes as 'a web of relationships in which companies cooperate and compete at the same time' (Kehoe, 1993). The company's founding 'partners' include Apple Computer, AT&T, Motorola, Sony, Matsushita and Philips, each of which has licensed General Magic's technology for use in their emerging communications products and services. The basic premise is that traditional technological rivalries should be transcended, spreading the risk of new industry development and forcing the innovation challenge directly into the realm of marketing.

The third factor Ohmae identified relates to the fixed cost implications of the previous two issues. Ohmae argues that it is no longer possible for individual companies to build multiple entry barriers around a variety of competencies. The capital intensity of production which is a distinguishing characteristic of global industries has eroded the variable-cost solution to international business, forcing companies to maximize marginal contribution to a high base of fixed costs. This, in turn, requires ever-growing sales from a broader base of markets.

Taken together, then, these key drivers are creating a new competitive dynamic which is forcing firms to think and behave differently. Ohmae does not ignore the traditional options of organic development or acquisition but he does question their appropriateness as strategic options in the current climate: 'Experience shows ... that you should look hard – and early – at forging alliances. In a world of imperfect options, they are often the fastest and most profitable way to go global.'

It should be noted that Ohmae here refers to alliances, in the process eschewing equity-based joint ventures as relationships riddled with the 'poisonous desire' and 'imperialistic instinct' of the parent companies to gain control. For Ohmae, the only objective for an alliance should be to maximize contribution to fixed costs, a goal achieved by joint exploitation of assets which bring the venture closer to meeting customer needs. While he acknowledges that some joint ventures do succeed he sees within them an inherent instability. Firstly, the contracts which underpin joint ventures are typically created for a particular set of market conditions. When these inevitably change, and the joint venture performance suffers, the original contract then becomes a club to bludgeon and blame. Secondly, parent companies tend to stifle the aspirations of their joint venture child, particularly with regard to its growth ambitions and especially if these aspirations encroach on their own product/market territory.

In the absence of the control offered by equity-based contracts, Ohmae promotes the logic of entente, the nurturing of a friendly agreement based on an understanding of mutual benefit. He acknowledges the operational difficulties, most notably the fact that most executives equate management with total control and, since alliances mean ceding control, 'management' and 'alliance' are mutually exclusive. This, notes Ohmae, misses a fundamental fact of capitalist life, particularly in turbulent business environments: '... few businesses succeed because of control. Most make it because of motivation, entrepreneurship, customer relationships, creativity, persistence, and attention to the "softer" aspects of organization, such as values and skills.'

Ohmae presents a powerful thesis. It is grounded in the well-established context of the internationalization of the world economy and directly addresses the potentials and pitfalls loitering in and around the global ambitions of large multinational companies. He is suitably critical of the short-termism which is characteristic of many equity-based ventures and he appropriately lambasts the obsession with ROI measurement criteria on the grounds that it demotivates alliance managers and ignores valuable but hidden contributions to fixed costs. Like his McKinsey colleagues (Bleeke and Ernst, 1993) he sees alliance formation and exploitation as a fast and flexible response to a turbulent international business environment.

Despite this, the logic he so eloquently explains leaves serious questions unanswered. Firstly, Ohmae is myopic in the extreme by focusing exclusively on the triad markets, thus ignoring the vast potential markets of the less developed world, a feature of his globalization thesis which has drawn heavy criticism (see, for example, Kotler, 1991). Secondly, he fails to explain adequately why so many of the alliances created in the spirit of entente collapse for the sake of self-interest, the latter motivation being a key aspect of game theory eloquently elaborated by Kay (1993a). Ohmae is too dismissive of equity-based ventures and too supportive of entente-based strategic alliances; in both cases he is devoid of substantive empirical evidence. Finally, he pays lip service to, but largely ignores, the operational detail associated with the ongoing management of strategic alliances. Despite our critique of Ohmae and our general scepticism regarding the sustainability of alliances, it is clear that, in the medium term, they will remain a key feature of organizational life and a hopeful source of organizational advantage. With this in mind, in the following sections we address the key management issues associated with the successful operation of strategic alliances.

What makes strategic alliances successful?

A number of features of success have been established by academics observing alliances and monitoring outcomes (e.g. Doz, 1988; Hamel *et al.*, 1989). We summarize these under six broad headings, a schema which owes much to the integrative work of Doz (1992):

1 *Strategic issues* The strategic interest of each partner toward the alliance, the continued complementarity of their contributions and the ongoing compatibility of their objectives and success criteria are important variables for ensuring success. Alliance stability appears to arise where there is open access to each partner's skills and there

are only limited perceptions of encroachment risk; it is enhanced where there is a strong dependence on the partnership output for independent operations of the alliance members. Strategic compatibility comes about through carefully delineating the boundaries and scope of the partnership. JVC and Thomson, for example, found enough joint value creation to assemble VCRs together and to 'localize' their European manufacturing base, but not to develop them. JVC, the technology leader, would not share its product development know-how but preferred to use it as a source of bargaining power in the alliance.

2   *Learning and convergence*   Mutual trust and knowledge must be the perennial focus of the partners and this can only occur through a process of continuous interaction. This usually requires a distinction between the negotiating and operating teams in order to avoid having what Doz (1992) describes as 'concerns, fears and stereotypes' triggered by an often adversarial negotiation process transferred into the post-alliance collaboration. This convergence process is enhanced by an early start at understanding each other's culture and organizational language which, in turn, enhances the ability to communicate and helps avoid ambiguities. Special, cross-disciplinary task forces, offsite workshops and joint projects can foster the two-way communications process essential for success.

In addition, each partner must understand the speed and delivery of each other's culture. Companies with short-term capital repayment strategies will be inappropriate partners for an alliance which has longer term market-share building objectives. Similarly, the speed with which each partner identifies, communicates and solves problems is critical to avoid alliance failure.

3   *Expectation adjustment process*   Managerial expectations can quickly collapse if negotiations contain over-escalated projections. The reality is frequently different from the image portrayed, creating the familiar problem of dissonance. Furthermore, additional and often unforeseen resources are frequently required before payoffs from the alliance can be gained. A pressure for quick success has to be avoided, especially if the strategic alliance begins from a precarious strategic position (e.g. restructuring or crisis).

An ability to re-evaluate and reassess the relationship frequently and without trauma is one great facilitator of success, but only where openness and frankness provide the foundations of effective communications. Unfortunately, many operating managers conversant with the opportunities and problems of the strategic alliance are also likely to have a stake in its success. This may lead them to deny crises and cover up problems, stressing the positives and suffering from 'role-constrained' learning with all its negative consequences (Levitt and March, 1988). A final success factor in this category relates to situations where the strategic alliance has been managed as an evolutionary relationship which is receptive to adjustment and revision.

4   *Governance process*   Success is a function of the match between the characterization of operations and the way they are governed. If

the task of the strategic alliance is predictable, if it does not involve too much interdependence and if it does not require task-autonomous decisions a contracted arrangement is sufficient. Unpredictability and interdependence, however, probably require some equity arrangement in a joint venture to ensure stability in the relationship.

5   *Capability transfer process*   It is important that sufficient skills are transferred to support the task of the strategic alliance. Despite this, it is essential to maintain an 'exclusivity' clause around each partner's key skills to prevent erosion of the complementary and unique skills which each party brings to the arrangement. The solution must be organizational as well as analytical. The latter can be achieved by clarity of scope and intent and carefully articulated valuation criteria and management structures. The former must be done through people at the operating level. Such boundaries are often built in more subtle ways (e.g. indoctrination). In hi-tech alliances, for example, it is absolutely essential that R&D specialists know the boundaries of knowledge that they must preserve.

6   *Top management monitoring*   Strategic alliances are not a cost-free alternative to organic development or acquisitions. They incur a different mix of costs, benefits and risks that have inherently different trade-offs. They may decrease the risk of being wrong (for example, regarding an acquisition decision) but only at great managerial cost. Alliances require constant managerial attention and persistent efforts to construct genuine value. Short-run risks are likely to be lower, but it must be acknowledged that the risks tend to increase in the long run as a consequence of a higher probability of strategic divergence.

A crude but concise summary for strategic alliance success is contained in the 6Cs: *Clarity* of purpose, processes and roles; *Commitment* of managerial effort and resources; *Collaboration* on vision, objectives and goods; *Culture* in understanding rationalities, styles and intellects; *Control* of direction versus autonomy; *Contingency* of actions, adaptations and exits.

The evidence on strategic alliance success remains patchy but it is a widely held view that many do in fact end up in failure. A summary list of reasons for this failure explains why alliances are certainly not an easy strategic option: (a) failure by either partner to give up autonomy; (b) failure by alliance partners and their management teams to maintain the initial energy put into the start-up negotiations when the more mundane operations phase is enacted; (c) a tendency to focus too much internally on making the alliance work at the expense of monitoring the external environment and the original alliance purpose; (d) too much petty politics; (e) failure to develop the critical 'willingness to learn' from partners; (f) too much dependence on a few individuals; (g) failure to maintain a strong 'black box' of crucial strengths away from partners.

Carl de Benedetti, the CEO of Olivetti, said of strategic alliances in 1990:

If you do not have a reference structure for a network organization, it is difficult to make strategic alliances work. We have to overcome the logic of the octopus and reach the logic of the network. The 'network organization' requires a different organizational structure, and more important, different management processes.

De Benedetti's reference to networks alludes to an agenda for management actions which depart radically from conventional wisdom. Theory must also progress if it is to capture the realities of management practice and offer insights into a broader range of business solutions. In the next sections we examine network theory, an eclectic perspective which draws on evidence from international marketing endeavours and looks particularly at the internationalization process. A major part of its novelty relates not so much to the quality of its ideas and agendas but more to the context from which it has emerged.

Network theory

Theories explaining the internationalization process may have to move into a new, and perhaps 'post-modernist' era to explain the prevailing empirical evidence. A useful starting point could be the Swedish research undertaken by Forsgren (1989) whose insights we are indebted to in the following sections. In his examination of the recent internationalization patterns of Swedish companies the evidence he found rejects the traditional 'stages' approach which suggests that companies become involved in Foreign Direct Investment (FDI) by way of exports, licensing, setting up of foreign sales and marketing branches and eventually the opening of a wholly owned subsidiary. This successive-stage strategy reflected the conventional mode of internationalization for many organizations, particularly in the 1960s and 1970s as many previous empirical studies of the Uppsala School in Sweden bear out (Johansen and Wiedersheim-Paul, 1975; Forsgren and Johansen, 1975; Johansen and Vahlne, 1977). Moreover, the successive-stages model supports a centre–periphery perspective of organizational structure. This view sees the parent company based in its domestic homeland deciding upon and implementing its international expansion decisions and identifies strategic decision making as essentially hierarchical. However, the recent growth in acquisitions, coupled with the long experience of internationalization by many organizations, means that the majority of their assets may not be on domestic shores. This development leads logically to a centre–centre perspective of the organization, i.e. one where decisions to internationalize no longer come from the centre but emanate from well established and experienced foreign subsidiaries.

To understand strategic decisions in the 'centre–centre' structure perspectives must shift from the rational, hierarchical norm to the conceptualization of the organization as a coalition of interests along the lines proposed by Cyert and March (1963) and Pfeffer (1978). An experienced, widely spread, international organization is an interdependent

International firm as:

	Hierarchy	Coalition of interests
Rational planning	Conventional theories of FDI	Political power of subsidiaries
Pattern of activities	Sequential stage process of internationalization	Political view of complex organizations in internationalization, e.g. networks

Strategic behaviour as:

Figure 6.6 *A classification of approaches to international business (Source: Forsgren, M. (1989),* Managing the Internationalisation Process: a Swedish Case, *London: Routledge)*

system embracing both competing and dependent interests. In this model strategic decision making and international expansion affects the whole corporate network and is not just a headquarters/foreign-subsidiary issue.

As we have seen in previous chapters there are two competing perspectives relating to strategy formation: it is either rationally formed and intended or it emerges from within the organization (Mintzberg, 1988). The rational perspective is at the heart of most explanations of the internationalization process but, as Forsgren (1989) argues, 'Foreign investment behaviour should perhaps be described instead as a pattern in a stream of activities which becomes apparent after a while and which is then described by top management as corporate strategy.'

This relatively new perspective has enabled Forsgren to classify a range of approaches to international business which we present in Figure 6.6.

It is within the 'politically' oriented literature that the better interpretations of contemporary empirical evidence relating to internationalization may be found. As Figure 6.6 demonstrates, one key explanation lies in network theory, the fundamental premises of which are as follows:

1   Organizations are related to a network of other organizations and to understand individual organizational behaviour it is necessary to understand these relationships.

2   Organizations are dependent on other organizations for resources and this ties them together in a relationship which is based upon their reciprocal transactions.

3   Resources controlled by individual organizations are not directly comparable. Because of this investments are made in the relationships between organizations which create value in their dependent linkages. Productive and marketing capacities of organizations are adjusted to match those of others in the network by an investment in physical and human assets which reinforces the bonding of the industrial network.

4   The network is in constant flux as suppliers, buyers and customers may enter and exit over time and, more specifically, as their respective objectives change.

5   The strength of the individual organization depends not on company-specific advantages – as suggested by market-imperfection theories of competition – but on links with customers, suppliers, distributors, competitors and so on.

6   Research evidence (Hallen *et al.*, 1987) has shown that information exchange and adaptation processes are key attributes of interorganizational networks.

7   The character of the products of exchange influences the extent of the bonding in the network so that, for example, hi-tech products require much closer liaison between organizations (for example Silicon Glen in Scotland, Silicon Valley in California).

Picking up on the latter point, many writers have argued that the network form is especially pertinent to markets characterized by sophisticated and rapidly changing technology exposed to the continuous shift in international trade and competition (e.g. Miles and Snow, 1986). In this context traditional organizational structures have failed to cope and the network has emerged as a superior form of organizational design. From a more descriptive perspective the network concept has been used as an 'analytical convenience' for understanding industrial systems (Cunningham and Culligan, 1991). This approach allows the application of network concepts such as power, dependency, trust, exchange, money, information and utilities (that flow along the links in the network) to the analysis of corporate behaviour (Thorelli, 1986).

Entire networks are founded as information utilities (e.g. airlines, travel agents and captive computer reservations systems). The market for on-line information services (OIS) is one example of these competence-enhancing relationships. The four basic competencies necessary for the provision of OIS – database supply, data processing, software supply and telecommunications – are illustrated in Figure 6.7. The different players have different roles relating to their areas of competence but, as a whole, they link up in a network of value-added to offer an OIS to the market.

Typical strategic issues resolved in a networking context include: (a) corporate positioning; (b) product positioning; (c) market channels and franchising; (d) turnkey contracts and systems selling; (e) barter and

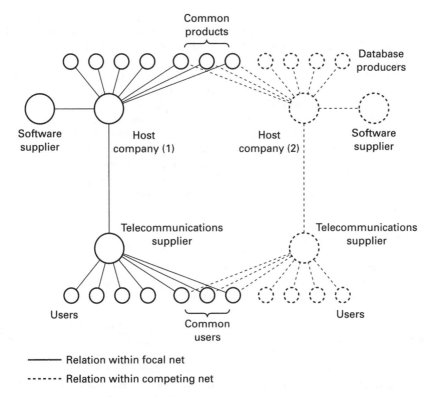

Figure 6.7   *Networks in online information services (Source: Cunningham, N. T. and Culligan, K. (1991), 'Competitiveness through networks of relationships in information technology product markets', in Paliwoda, S.J. (ed.),* New Perspectives on International Marketing, *London: Routledge)*

reciprocal trading; (f) split versus unified sourcing; (g) cartels; (h) interlocking directorates; (i) diversification and vertical integration; (j) joint ventures, mergers and acquisitions; (k) internationalization. As can be seen, the network idea is particularly applicable in international business and industrial and international marketing and this certainly explains why much of the empirical research has come from marketeers working on customer–supplier relationships in an international context (Hakansson, 1982; Mattsson, 1986; Cunningham and Culligan, 1991; Forstrom, 1991; Easton and Lundgren, 1991). While at first sight the emphasis may be seen to be on cooperation the underlying motivation remains the means to the end of gaining a competitive advantage.

From a network standpoint, the traditional view of the internationalization process begins to change. Any strategic investment is meant to obtain, defend or develop a position in the network. In network theory, organizations do not necessarily invest solely to build upon a specific advantage as argued in the traditional models of internationalization.

For experienced organizations, the investments are to strengthen, manage and monitor their positions in already existing international networks. Because the organization is part of a network the importance of any company-specific advantage is much reduced. An organization's strength does not solely depend on a specific advantage but more upon its network linkages so that any asset-specific advantage is constrained by the network in which the organization operates.

Once again we encounter the notion that organizational advantage is a superior and more sustainable source of competitive edge than techno-logical- or product-based competencies. In the situations we have covered in this chapter it can be readily seen that firms are increasingly seeking to keep up with or stay ahead of productivity gains made by rivals in the rapidly internationalizing global economy.

Concluding remarks

A recurrent theme of this chapter has been a demonstration of the impor-tance of interorganizational solutions in allowing companies to cope with the added complexity of the international business arena. Focusing specifically on cross-border alliances, McKinsey consultants Bleeke and Ernst (1991) examined 49 strategic alliances from a cross-section – size, location, industry, structure – of 150 Japanese, American and European companies and sought to identify 'hard' data on alliance performance in comparison to alternative routes such as acquisition. To address the measurement problem the authors defined success according to whether or not ingoing strategic objectives had been achieved by both partners and whether or not both had recovered the financial costs of the capital injected into the project. The results were mixed, with only 51 per cent of alliances being successful for both partners (although only a third ended in failure for both). The study compared alliance performance with the achievement of similar objectives via acquisition, a key finding being that the two approaches have similar success rates (50 per cent) but for different objectives. While acquisition seemed appropriate for developing core businesses in existing geographic areas, alliances were more effective for geographical expansion and related diversifications. Successful alliances shared the following common characteristics: (a) the partnership was undertaken between two strong companies who brought complementary skills and capabilities to the partnership; (b) the alliance was granted autonomy and was given a strong board with the authority to take operational decisions and allowed the flexibility to evolve beyond the original objectives and intentions and so tap into new product–market opportunities; (c) there was a separation of financial ownership from management control, with 50–50 ownership splits to prevent one partner from dominating decision making and to ensure that each alliance member cared about the other's success.

The evidence Bleeke and Ernst offer is partial and offers little insight into the operational aspects of managing alliances. Nevertheless, the 'hard' data they provide, including the fact that most alliances terminate, draws attention to the ephemeral character of the interorganizational solution to business environment dynamics.

In the next and final chapter we address the issues associated with the management of alliances in more depth. This analysis is presented alongside a review of literature which offers insights into effective strategic management practice, the collective theme being the creation of 'balanced solutions' to complex organizational problems.

7

Seeking organizational advantage: balanced solutions

Introduction

Organizational life is such a pervasive feature of modern society that it has attracted scholars from a wildly disparate range of academic disciplines. From the Marxist scholar seeking explanations of appropriation to the industrial geographer advising retail companies on optimal location decisions, the study of organizations and how they are managed is enjoying exponential growth. In developing its focus this book has targeted a fundamental concern, that of organizational survival. Organizations are not living entities but they do die. Within this paradox lies an abundant cavern of imperfect knowledge for researchers and charlatans to scavenge and plunder. Herein lies the rub. What possible sense can be made of such senseless material? How many exceptions to the rule must we have before the rule itself is redundant? How can we predict and plan and make and manage when uncertainty defines our context?

Before offering solutions we must acknowledge the limitations represented by such rhetorical questions. But we should also be aware that within paradox lies discovery and that discovery, in turn, requires an openness of mind. In a vigorous defence of the application of scientific inquiry to the subject of management, Kay (1993b) highlights the myopic character of many of the discipline's critics and draws on a powerful precedent to make his point: 'The Inquisitors who visited Galileo refused to look through his telescope since what he claimed to see could not be there.'

The simplest observation we have made throughout the pages of this book is that organizations, in their struggle for survival, demonstrate a range of coping behaviours. It is our contention that, if we understand the context of this struggle, we can go some way toward suggesting more appropriate behaviour, both in a generic sense and for quite specific environments. Organizations are not passive receivers of Darwinian natural selection since, to a large extent, they can craft their genetic code and genetically engineer their future.

The context we have identified in this struggle for survival is the internationalization of the world economy, the ascendancy of capitalism and the discipline of the market. The label we attach to capture the dynamic nature of this context is discontinuity. This seems appropriate if we consider the milieu of contemporary business in the broad historical sweep of two centuries of industrialization, a period covering the rise and fall of colonization, two world wars, the great Communist experiment and countless skirmishes in pursuit of social, political and/or economic hegemony.

Unlike Fukuyama (1992), the intention is not to peddle an 'End of History' thesis and no determinism is intended for the context we define. Rather, we specify a hiatus, a transitional stage in the tradition of the Hegelian dialectic of thesis/antithesis, a phase which, if understood, can be managed. A working theme for the book has been 'Capitalism – and how to survive it' and it is within the limitations suggested by that phrase which the following prescriptions are made. But the message is clear. Strategy is real, it does matter and it can be managed. Even Mintzberg, the *enfant terrible* of management research, 'the scourge of strategic orthodoxy' (Clutterbuck and Crainer, 1990), has conceded the possibilities of a formalized approach to strategy and it is to him who we now turn for our first insights towards 'balanced solutions'.

A future for strategic planning

Mintzberg (1994) has offered a broad-based critique of strategy and strategic planning, targeting what he describes as its three fundamental fallacies: (i) predetermination; (ii) detachment; (iii) formalization. Within these strategic pitfalls, however, lie solutions and a future for strategy. Regarding the predetermination fallacy, Mintzberg attacks the claims made for forecasting – particularly in environments characterized by discontinuity – since most predictive models rely heavily on extrapolation of recent history:

> There is an interesting irony in the ability of forecasting to extrapolate known trends as opposed to predicting new discontinuities, because the very condition that the planning literature has made so much fuss about – turbulence in the environment – is the one characterized by such discontinuities, and therefore the very one that planning can do least about.

A key problem relating to this irony is that, in practice, strategy and strategic planning deliberately imposes stability on an organization's behaviour so that, when the environment does change, a company is unlikely to have an appropriate 'strategy on demand' to exploit or cope with the discontinuity: 'serious change in strategy generally means a shift in gestalt – the conception of a new worldview, generally based on a permanent change in conditions, or at least the perception of such a change.'

Regarding the detachment fallacy (the separation of strategic management from operations management), Mintzberg attacks the artificiality of separating thinking and doing, particularly with respect to detachment in practice. This practice, he argues, tends to isolate strategic thinkers and charge them with the task of developing the broad overview: 'Effective strategists are not people who abstract themselves from the daily detail but quite the opposite: they are the ones who *immerse* themselves in it, while being able to abstract the *strategic messages* from it.' Thus, the common detachment metaphor – the ability to see the wood from the trees – is flawed since the best opportunities and most serious threats are probably lying under the leaves. A principal problem of detachment is the extensive reliance on 'hard' data, a quantification process which has been facilitated (and therefore increasingly adopted) by developments in information technology. Such hard data is riddled with biases and inaccuracies, it is rarely timely and is often unreliable. The garbage-in-garbage-out (GIGO) syndrome hints at the problems for strategy making, a problem compounded by the physical separation of strategy planners and strategy implementers, the latter continuing to rely heavily on 'soft' information, particularly oral forms of communication.

Regarding the fallacy of formalization, the core critique is based on the complete lack of empirical support that it exists in any form other than name: '... we have no evidence that any of the strategic planning systems – no matter how elaborate, or how famous – succeeded in capturing (let alone improving on) the messy informal processes by which strategies really do get developed'. Mintzberg levels his critique of formalization at its attempts to decompose strategy making into a series of discrete, specified steps in a Tayloresque reductionist pattern. He argues strongly that strategy creation cannot be programmed in a similar fashion to the work process of shovelling coal, claiming that the problem with Taylorism is that it explicitly precludes discretion and deliberately inhibits creativity. As he notes, with a hint of sarcasm, 'Strategic planning set out to do the same thing (its claims notwithstanding), and when it succeeded, the results were devastating.' For Mintzberg, then, strategy formation requires creativity and synthesis which, in turn, needs informed actors empowered to exercise discretion.

Mintzberg's critique of strategic orthodoxy is scathing, particularly with regard to what can be characterized as its 'scientific' bias and claims. The fallacies outlined above relate to a particular dimension of the strategy process – strategic planning – but in developing their detail he paints a broad picture of organizational incompetence. In this sense Mintzberg is too inward-looking and too insular, his focus on planning precluding any structured discussion of the discontinuity he alludes to but fails to delineate. His balance of effort is heavily loaded towards evaluating why organizations *cannot* do strategy at the expense of an examination of why they *must*. Despite this, his critique of normative structured, rational–analytical (planning) techniques is consistent with the theme of this book, i.e. that strategic management is more art than science. In exposing the planning school's grand fallacy – that strategic planning equates with strategy formation – Mintzberg is able to be both radically critical and prescriptively constructive:

Analyses may precede and support synthesis, by defining the parts that can be combined into wholes. Analysis may follow and elaborate synthesis, by decomposing and formalizing its consequences. But analysis cannot substitute for synthesis. No amount of elaboration will ever enable formal procedures to forecast discontinuities, to inform managers who are detached from their operations, to create novel strategies.

Mintzberg subsequently argues that the strategy-making process should be devolved to business-unit managers, although he remains insistent that it can never be carried out as a formalized process. He claims to have identified the comparative advantages of planners and managers, the former having the time and inclination to analyse but little power to act, while the latter shun analysis, preferring instead to act but not reflect. Keeping planners and managers apart consequently separates analysis from intuition and, since each of these management competencies carries its own possibilities and limitations, a solution to the planning dilemma is readily apparent:

In terms of the grand fallacy, analysis may not be synthesis, and so planning may not be strategy formation, but effective strategy formation, especially in large organizations, does depend importantly on analysis, both as an input to the process and as a means of dealing with its outputs. Soft data may be indispensable, but hard data can hardly be ignored.

Mintzberg consequently postulates and profiles roles for (i) planning, (ii) plans and (iii) planners. We consider each role set in turn.

The planning challenge

Arguing that planning cannot generate strategies Mintzberg sees a more constructive role for the process when it is conceptualized as strategic programming, defined as the translation of previously generated and intended strategies into realized ones. Strategic programming is outlined as a process of three steps: (i) *codification of the strategy*, i.e. its clarification and expression in a way that makes it formally operational. A principal concern is how the codified strategy is articulated, with particular attention to the nuance, subtlety and qualification of the strategy being essential to maintain the richness of the strategic intent; (ii) *elaboration of the strategy*, i.e. its decomposition into substrategies, ad hoc programmes and specific action plans. The substrategies can be at the corporate, business unit or functional levels and these, like the programmes and plans which support them, can be scheduled or prepared on a contingency basis; (iii) *conversion of the strategy*, i.e. a determination of the consequences of strategic change on routine organizational operations such as budgets and performance controls. Mintzberg avoids proclaiming strategic programming as a 'one best way' of doing strategy, arguing instead that it is appropriate within clusters of 'necessary' and 'facilitating' conditions. The two necessary conditions are environmental stability and an organization which has an elaborated structure, simple systems and tightly coupled operations. The four facilitating conditions are large size, high capital intensity, industry maturity and external control (e.g. a parent company controlling a subsidiary). Clearly, then, Mintzberg proposes strategic programming for a specific environmental context and with reference to a particular organization form. He limits its suitability further by arguing that strategic learning must have been completed and that appropriate patterns of strategic thinking should have developed in a homogeneous fashion. Taken together these conditions and circumstances categorize the process as contingent: 'Strategic programming makes sense when viable strategies are available, in other words, when the world is expected to hold still or change predictably while intended strategies unfold, so that formulation can logically precede implementation.'

Plans in practice

A role for plans is twofold: (i) to communicate; (ii) to control. Considering communication, plans provide the media through which strategic intent is channelled alongside a portrayal of the roles which individual organizational members will play in achieving it. Plans also convey strategic aims and rationale to an external constituency (e.g. investors, suppliers, governments) to garner their support and commitment to the ideals therein. Considering the control dimension, plans are devices which specify behaviour, monitor adherence and evaluate variance. Plans function internally to monitor whether or not the intended strategy was realized and to establish whether or not the realized strategy (intentional or emergent) was successful. Plans are also used by organizations to exert control over their external environment, including markets, competitors, suppliers, governments, and customers: 'Much planning, in other words, exists for purposes of enactment: to impose strategies on the environment.'

The planner's task

Planners are given a threefold role: (i) as strategy finders; (ii) as analysts; (iii) as catalysts. As *strategy finders* the onus is on planners to hunt down strategies – deliberate and emergent – which are lurking in unexplored organizational domains (fledgling strategies) or are readily identifiable as patterns of action (realized strategies). This role requires a creative and judgemental orientation and is interpretative in nature. Inputs to the programming and control process are ad hoc although comparing 'uncovered' realized strategies with intended strategies requires a more comprehensive and systematic approach. The latter, of course, is an orientation which matches the comparative advantage of traditional planners. Despite this, the danger of 'analysis paralysis' lurks within this role, requiring that planners undertaking the task have intuitive skills to complement their analytical strengths.

As *analysts*, the role of planners anticipates ad hoc contributions to the strategy-making process in the form of analyses of specific issues. In the creative phase of strategy formation, planners as analysts have two potential undertakings. Firstly, they draw attention to issues which managers may have missed, for example market segment dynamics and their implications. Secondly, they can offer models which represent alternative insights into important issues, in the process challenging established and firmly rooted mind-sets. Mintzberg distinguishes three types of strategic analysis. First is external analysis, where the insightful planner can observe, monitor and interpret patterns of events in the organization's environment (e.g. competitor actions) and thus profile strategic opportunities and threats. Second is organizational studies, where internal analysis is undertaken to reveal and evaluate patterns of behaviour and competencies within the organization, whether these are established, emerging or can potentially evoke new 'mental models' among decision makers. Third is the scrutinization of strategies, an ad hoc process of investigating and evaluating strategies in parallel with strategy making. The challenge is to compare and contrast alternatives via an iterative test of the viability of possible strategies everywhere within the organization.

As *catalysts*, the role of planners involves creating a propensity to plan, i.e. to instil among managers a desire to envisage the future in a creative way. The catalyst role focuses on the process of the planner's output inasmuch as it emerges 'when strategic programming shifts from the planner doing it to helping line managers getting it done.' Within the catalyst role Mintzberg sees a place for formalization although he qualifies his enthusiasm by regarding it as a double-edged sword, noting in particular its potential drift from help to hindrance. On the positive side, he argues that formalization has a multifaceted role to play:

> Formalization can pertain to time, to location, to participation, to agenda, and to information, as well as, but with only the greatest of care, to process itself. It can help to focus attention, stimulate debate, keep track of issues, promote interaction and facilitate consensus.

On the downside, as formalization increases, viable support can degenerate into 'the abyss' of intrusive control. The challenge is to avoid arbitrary formalization and to embrace the combined strengths of the 'right-handed' (analytical) and 'left-handed' (intuitive) thinkers in the planning function. Concluding his review of strategic planning and noting its foundations within several decades of research and experience, Mintzberg forcefully draws attention to its theoretical and practical limitations but signposts a future for strategic programming:

> We have ... learned what planning is and can do, and perhaps of greater use, what planners can do beyond planning. We have also learned about our need to solidify our descriptive understanding of complex phenomena – and to face up to our ignorance of them – before we leap into prescription. Only when we recognize our fantasies can we begin to appreciate the wonders of reality.

In the next section we describe one such study of reality and evaluate its cautious prescriptions. While Mintzberg has drawn our attention to the possibilities of thinking and acting strategically he leaves many strategic management processes cocooned within the black box he puts at the centre of his thesis. In contrast, longitudinal cross-sectional research undertaken by Pettigrew and Whipp (1993) has given deep insights into the *strategic process* itself and has drawn empirical links between effective strategic management and competitive success. In the following sections we profile this contribution and consider its implications for the creation of organizational advantage.

Strategic management and competitive success

From a broad examination of competition in automobile manufacture, book publishing, merchant banking and life assurance, Pettigrew and Whipp (1993) drew the following key conclusions:

1   There is an observable difference in the way the higher performing firms manage change from their lesser performing counterparts.
2   A pattern emerges, across the four sectors, from the actions taken by the higher performing organizations.

The patterns explaining higher performance were modelled as five inter-related factors, each of which had distinctive primary conditioning features and a set of secondary actions and mechanisms. The model is shown in Figure 7.1

In the preceding chapters of this book many aspects of Pettigrew and Whipp's framework have been examined in some depth. We review them briefly here as a preface to a more detailed discussion of *coherence*, a key contribution of the Pettigrew and Whipp model to the understanding of strategic change processes.

Pettigrew and Whipp argue that the competitive process and strategy creation emerge from the way that a firm interprets its business environment. Assessment of this environment's complexity and the determination of appropriate responses to the continuity and change dynamics it generates requires that the firm sustains itself as an open learning system, acquiring, interpreting and processing information at all organizational levels and across all functions. This intangible but essential capability for creative environmental assessment contributes a key organizational strength, an asset which demands that leaders facilitate a continuous process of learning and action.

With respect to leading change, the principal conclusions that Pettigrew and Whipp drew were that there are no universal rules and that effective leadership is acutely sensitive to context. They are sharply critical of the 'leader as hero' school of thought, arguing strongly that effective change is a function of actions by people at all levels within the business and that this, in turn, is facilitated by sustained leadership over time. While 'leadership' obviously exists, 'leading change' is chosen to describe the complex and interrelated sets of problems which require resolution at any point in time. The challenge of leadership, then, is not

Environmental assessment

Primary conditioning features

1 Availability of key people
2 Internal character of organization
3 Environmental pressures and associated dramas
4 Environmental assessment as a multifunction activity

Secondary mechanisms

5 Role of planning, marketing networks with main stakeholders
6 Construction of purposive networks with main stakeholders
7 Use of specialist task-forces

Leading change

1 Building a receptive context for change; legitimation
2 Creating capability for change
3 Constructing the context and direction of the change
4 Operationalizing the change agenda
5 Creating the critical mass for change within senior management
6 Communicating need for change and detailed requirements of the change agenda
7 Achieving and reinforcing success
8 Balance continuity and change
9 Sustaining coherence

Linking strategic and operational change

1 Justifying the need for change
2 Building capacity for appropriate action
3 Supplying necessary visions, values and business direction
4 Breaking emergent strategy into actionable pieces
5 Appointment of change managers, relevant structures and exacting targets
6 Rethinking communications
7 Using the reward system
8 Setting up local negotiation climate for context
9 Modifying original visions in light of local context
10 Monitoring and adjustment

Human resources as assets and liabilities

1 Raising HRM consciousness
2 Use of highly situational additive features to create positive force for HRM change
3 Demonstrating the need for business and people change
4 Ad hoc, cumulative, supportive activities at various levels
5 Linking HRM action to business need with HRM as a means not an end
6 Mobilizing external influences
7 Devolution to line
8 Construction of HRM actions and institutions which reinforce one another

Coherence

1 Consistency
2 Consonance
3 Advantage
4 Feasibility
5 Leadership
6 Senior management team integrity
7 Uniting intent and implementation
8 Developing apposite knowledge bases
9 Interorganizational coherence
10 Managing a series of interrelated changes over time

Figure 7.1 *A model of strategic change and competitive success (Source: Pettigrew, A. and Whipp, R. (1993), Managing Change for Competitive Success, Oxford: Blackwell)*

to take premature bold actions but, rather, to create an appropriate context for leading change. Three primary conditioning features are essential for this to occur:

1   The building of a climate within the firm which will be receptive to change, which involves justifying why the change should take place.
2   Similarly, there is little point attempting change without first building the capability to mount that change.
3   Equally, establishing a change agenda which not only sets the directions of the business but also establishes the necessary visions and values is by no means simple. It is a process in itself which may take a series of attempts before completion.

These three necessary conditions for leading change resonate strongly with the challenges of managing strategic change which were presented in Chapter 5 and they reinforce the substance of our critique of 'scientific' process engineering in Chapter 4. The challenge is raised to a higher level when considering the role of leadership as a strong influence in linking strategic and operational change, the third of Pettigrew and Whipp's five central change factors.

The debate surrounding the issue of whether or not strategy is planned or emergent has provided a strong undercurrent to the core themes of this book. By examining the process of linking strategic and operational change Pettigrew and Whipp capture both the intentional and emergent characteristics of strategy by observing how intentions are implemented and transformed over time:

> Indeed, the additive effect of otherwise separate decisions and acts of implementation may be so powerful that they overwhelm the original intentions and even help create an entirely new context for future strategic decision making. Strategies so often therefore are the post hoc labelling of such series of 'successful' operational acts.

Effective management of strategic and operational change requires the creation of an appropriate context, development of a capability for action and the elaboration of an appropriate vision and associate set of values to countenance the chosen strategic intent. This, in turn, requires exacting target-setting, effective communication mechanisms, implanting of change managers throughout the organization, refashioned reward systems and an acute sense of potential political problems. At this point the importance of effective management of the human resource becomes readily apparent.

Pettigrew and Whipp's fourth central change factor concerns the recognition of human resources as assets and liabilities. They compare their own observations of the strategic importance of effective human resource management (HRM) with the paucity of established literature linking this aspect of organizational life with competitive performance. They are also highly critical of the general assumption that HRM is a 'given' and that its positive contributions tend to be taken for granted.

They argue strongly that an HRM philosophy cannot be constructed overnight, the successful practitioners of such an approach having experienced successive development episodes in a long-term learning process. For Pettigrew and Whipp, then, 'Human Resource Management relates to the total set of knowledge, skills and attitudes that firms need in order to compete. It involves concern for and action in the management of people, including selection, training and development, employee relations and compensation.' The binding mechanism embracing these aspects is an HRM philosophy with this, in turn, being created by a general consciousness of its benefits with regard to the business needs of the firm. In a change context knowledge and learning become paramount, the ability to shed anachronistic attitudes and behaviour faster than rivals being seen as 'one of the cardinal determinants of competitive strength in the 1990s.'

The fifth central change factor identified by Pettigrew and Whipp – coherence – depends upon and to some extent integrates the previous four. The identification and articulation of this variable marks a significant contribution of the research to the strategic change literature and plugs some of the conceptual gaps we have identified throughout the chapters of this book. As such, we examine the construct in more depth in the following section.

Continuity, change and coherence

Pettigrew and Whipp identify the problem of coherence as the most common and most elusive concern for those individuals charged with the task of managing change within organizations. Defined as 'the ability to hold the organization together while simultaneously reshaping it', coherence captures the challenge of seeing competition and strategic change as a composite process:

> In our view, the problem of developing a wholeness or consistency in managing strategic change and competition has to embrace both thought and action, intra- and interfirm relations. Such coherence is not easily acquired nor is it a steady-state which is simply maintained. Attaining coherence places a heavy emphasis on the ability to solve the analytical, educational and political problems posed within the process of managing strategic change and competition.

In outlining the concept of coherence Pettigrew and Whipp take as their starting point a critique of the suggestion of constancy and rigidity associated with the notion of 'fit', arguing that it tends to lock together an organization and its strategic direction 'in some timeless fashion'. In contrast, the challenge for organizations is to maintain strategic thinking while reshaping and adjusting to accommodate new and emergent strategies which develop over time. Coherence, then, is critical to a firm's strategic management and competitive performance in three key senses: (i) in the strategic position adopted by the firm; (ii) in the internal and

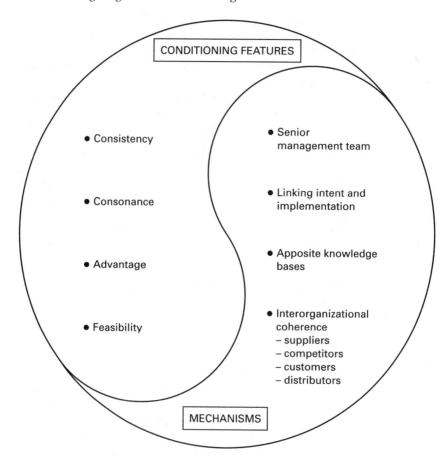

Figure 7.2   *A model of coherence in strategic change management (Source: Pettigrew, A. and Whipp, R. (1993),* Managing Change for Competitive Success, *Oxford: Blackwell)*

external relations of the firm; (iii) in the way that the integrity of (i) and (ii) are developed over time. Taken together, these elements create the competitive bases of the firm and, in defining its strategic orientation, ensure that there are few impediments to implementation of strategic choices.

As with the other four change components in Pettigrew and Whipp's model, coherence has a set of conditioning features and supportive secondary mechanisms. The twin dimensions of coherence are shown in Figure 7.2.

The authors note the simplicity of the four conditioning factors when viewed in isolation but point to their potency when their joint effect is considered. *Consistency* demands that there are no inherent contradictions or conflicting goals within the given strategy. *Consonance* demands that the chosen strategy should be a tangible and genuinely adaptive response to its environment. *Advantage* demands that the strategy should have some clear and sustainable competitive edge. *Feasibility* demands that the chosen strategy does not extend beyond the capabilities of the company to implement it, i.e. it must not create unsolvable problems.

The secondary mechanisms supporting the coherence dimension demonstrate the integrative nature of the Pettigrew and Whipp model and embrace both internal and external dimensions of the nature of competitive performance. Strong leadership and refinement of the senior management team is essential for sustaining coherence, as is the effective linking of strategic intent and strategy implementation. Coherence should also be founded on a strong and appropriate knowledge base and must be extended to embrace interorganizational linkages.

Taking coherence as their integrative theme, Pettigrew and Whipp bestow an appropriate level of complexity on strategic management:

> Achieving coherence in managing change requires the resolution of a whole series of conundrums. Creating a collective capacity to assess a firm's environment, lead change, link strategic and operational change and manage human resources throws up a host of dualities and dilemmas. These have to be resolved while change takes place.

A key output of the Pettigrew and Whipp study is the practical insights it gives to those charged with the responsibilities for recognizing the need for change and managing the change process itself. Given our desire for cautious prescription in this chapter the key findings of the research are discussed here. Four principal observations are made by Pettigrew and Whipp and each is now discussed in turn.

Firstly, the competitive strength of the companies they investigated was demonstrably affected by every one of the five central factors which constitute the model. Firms who have a reliance on a single advantage leave themselves open to attack via imitation and/or aggression on their weak flanks and are certainly no match for companies who enjoy the 'composite capacity' represented by the five-factor model.

The second practical insight is a word of caution relating to managerial expectations. The complexity of competition and strategic change as processes is noted, as is the futility of attempts to implant the five factors in one go. The initial challenge for managers is to recognize the need to conceive problems in the distinctive way suggested by Pettigrew and Whipp before shaping the firm-specific capacity to manage change with reference to its own particular environmental context.

The third level of advice concerns the ability to recognize and develop the intangible assets which underpin the ability to manage change and competition. A key task for managers is to build flexibility and learning into its knowledge base of skills, structures and values and to address the following question: 'Is the organization capable of mounting the creative destruction necessary to break down outmoded attitudes and practices, while at the same time building up new, more appropriate competencies?'

The fourth group of practical insights deal with the central nature of 'energy' within the five-factor model of the change process and three managerial actions are proposed which can assist its flow. The first is the energy created by constructive conflict. This can derive from bringing an outsider into the organization or it can emanate from established managers who are prepared to challenge company orthodoxies and exploit deviant behaviour. The second point deals with the observable reality that sustaining energy flows throughout the change process is an acutely difficult task. A key reason for this is the over-reliance on a single source of leadership, a solution proposed by Pettigrew and Whipp being to create a cadre of change leaders at different organizational levels who should seek to uncover information which confronts established assumptions. This, in turn, will require modified HRM policies and a new approach to performance review and remuneration to reflect the changed responsibilities and to ensure recruitment of appropriate internal personnel to the role. The third point deals with the challenge of avoiding regression in the change process. Pettigrew and Whipp suggest fostering a perception of change as a continuous process rather than as episodes of events and point to the constructive role of communicating 'islands of progress' to show what can in fact be achieved.

The comprehensiveness of the Pettigrew and Whipp model is its greatest strength. It is grounded in a strong research base and has been constructed on a platform of in-depth longitudinal study. When combined with the conceptual insights from Mintzberg's long study we have a view of strategy as a management process which requires a delicacy of touch and a good deal of creative flair. The emphasis on balance between external awareness and internal responsiveness and the recognition of broad clusters of interest and expertise in and around organizations is a pervasive theme of contemporary marketing and strategic management literature (Doyle, 1992; Kaplan and Norton, 1993). Strategy emerges as more art than science but there is a strong feeling that organizations can do much more than just muddle through.

As we saw in the previous chapter, on occasions firms seek a broader range of solutions than the intraorganizational ones addressed by Mintzberg (1994) and Pettigrew and Whipp (1993). In the following sections we return to interorganizational solutions and, in particular, examine research evidence which suggests an approach for their successful management.

Making networks work: the art of alliances

A recurrent theme of this book has been how the behavioural *practice* of management will always tend to undermine attempts to classify business processes scientifically. The artistry alluded to in this section title (borrowed from Kanter, 1994) suggests that this is certainly the case where the management of interorganizational relationships are concerned. The panaceas and pitfalls of network solutions were discussed fully in Chapter 6 and their pervasiveness in contemporary strategic management practice, particularly in the context of globalization, was noted. Despite their ubiquity, there is a paucity of reliable data relating to the number or value of alliances, not least because governments of the major industrialized countries, otherwise such rigorous collectors of industry statistics, largely ignore them. As Emmot (1993) notes, 'All that is clear is that it is a hot topic: books and articles on the subject pour out of business schools and consultancies, and alliances pop up anecdotally where they were not found before.'

Given the deficient and anecdotal nature of the available evidence it is difficult to identify genuine examples of best practice. There is little cross-sectional or generalizable testimony to guide companies in their pursuit and management of network solutions. Fortunately, however, academic researchers are catching up with the practice of network management. Kanter (1994) and her research team interviewed more than 500 people within 37 companies and their strategic partners. The respondents were all involved in the management of the relationship between the organizations they represented and the research spanned a range of alliance types; it was undertaken in eleven countries, it involved large and small firms and covered firms in the manufacturing and service sectors.

Emanating from the research were three fundamental characteristics of successful business alliances: (i) they must yield benefits for the partners, but they are more than just the deal since they are living systems that evolve progressively in their possibilities. Beyond the immediate reasons companies have for entering into a relationship, the connection offers the parties an option on the future, opening new doors and unforeseen opportunities; (ii) alliances that both partners ultimately deem successful involve *collaboration* (creating new value together) rather then mere *exchange* (getting something back for what you put in). Partners value the skills each brings to the alliance; (iii) alliances cannot be 'controlled' by formal systems but require a dense web of interpersonal connections and internal infrastructures that enhance learning.

Kanter urges companies to strive to achieve 'collaborative advantage', a key corporate asset essential to have in the context of the globalization of the world economy. In common with many previous writers on the topic, she uses the marriage metaphor to profile the pattern of circumstances and events which evolve over the life-cycle of an alliance. The first stage is selection and courtship, wherein companies meet, are attracted to each other and determine their compatibility. Selection is crucial to longevity and success and can be enhanced by reference to three key criteria: (i) *Self-analysis*, understanding industry dynamics and undertaking a rigorous and objective evaluation of the company's current and potential competitive position prior to seeking an alliance; (ii) *Chemistry*, the fostering of rapport between key executives of the partners to demonstrate commitment and to secure a pool of goodwill should operational tensions develop; (iii) *Compatibility*, a test of affinity and context, ranging from historical, philosophical and strategic foundations to core values, principles and ambitions for the future.

The second phase of the alliance life-cycle of successful partnerships is 'getting engaged', the institutionalization and public announcement of the venture. It has two key stages: (i) *Meeting the family*, i.e. broadening the base of involvement to include management and employees of the prospective partners and to secure commitment from external stakeholder groups such as investors, bankers and governments; (ii) *The vows*, a formalization of the alliance, typically involving professional input from third-party advisors but still requiring the leader's vision, dedication and personal involvement. This second phase is obviously a critical element on the path to alliance formation, the most successful partnerships demonstrating a threefold commonality. Firstly, a preliminary, small-scale focused joint activity involving real work should be set up, since 'the longer a courtship drags on without consummation, the more likely conditions, or minds, or both, can change and jeopardize it.' Secondly, the relationship should be strengthened and underpinned by 'side bets', exchanges of personal and/or equity swaps to demonstrate levels of commitment and inextricably link the fates of the partners. Thirdly, there should be a clear demonstration of independence in the partners' pre-alliance businesses, so sending signals of continuity to suppliers, customers and shareholders.

The third phase of the alliance life-cycle of successful partnerships is 'Setting up house-keeping', a progression from the romanticism of courtship to the harsher operational realities of living together. In this phase there are three broad stages typically encountered: (i) *problems of broader involvement*, the potential for greater resistance to change as the alliance gathers momentum and grows apart from its initiator's inspirational vision; (ii) a *discovery of difference*, the emergence of management, operational, cultural and systems differences once the venture is under way; (iii) *respect versus resentment*, a critical juncture where trust is established and people 'buy-in' to the process or, alternatively, where stereotyping, culture clashes or perceptions of inequality trigger a vicious cycle of mistrust and poor performance.

The danger throughout the three phases of the alliance life-cycle is that formalization and institutionalization of the venture erode the vision and strategic objectives which initiated it. This is a problem compounded by inexperience and a failure to anticipate fully the coordination and communication requirements for effective ongoing operation of the venture. Concluding her research observations, Kanter argues that the alliance route requires that companies learn to collaborate *actively*, building multiple and multilevel ties and developing structure, skills and processes to bridge organizational and interpersonal differences. The most productive relationships encountered by Kanter achieved five levels of integration: (i) *strategic integration*, involving ongoing involvement of senior executives in discussions regarding the alliance itself alongside general sharing of information regarding the strategic direction of the partner companies. Where possible, individual parties should broadly aim to evolve in complementary directions; (ii) *tactical integration*, the planning of specific activities and projects by middle managers and/or professionals and the identification of organizational and systems development to facilitate coordination and knowledge transfer; (iii) *operational integration*, ensuring that those involved in the day-to-day management of the alliance can achieve their tasks and that they are assured of timely and sufficient access to information and resources; (iv) *interpersonal integration*, establishing deeper and broader networks of bonds, strengthening relationships so that conflicts are spotted and resolved before they escalate and ensuring that current and future surplus value is maximized. As Kanter notes, 'Broad synergies born on paper do not develop in practice until many people in both organizations know one another personally and become willing to make the effort to exchange technology, refer clients, or participate on joint teams'; (v) *cultural integration*, fostering a sense of cross-cultural awareness and building communication skills between partner members which allow them to become both teachers and learners: 'When managers accept technology and learning roles, they demonstrate interest and respect, which helps build the goodwill that's so useful in smoothing over cultural and organizational differences.'

The obvious conclusion to draw from the essential nature of these integrative dimensions is that parties to an alliance will have to allow unprecedented levels of openness and intervention in their own businesses. As Kanter notes, this involves the 'risk of change', and it must be addressed. Relationship managers must be empowered to shape their own procedures and policies and free to take venture-specific decisions. Furthermore, since a principal benefit of alliances is the learning opportunities they offer, it is essential that companies develop an infrastructure for learning; more specifically, they should remove internal barriers to communication and ensure that effective cross-functional systems are in place.

Seeking balanced solutions

Integrating the themes of this chapter suggests an agenda we describe as 'balanced solutions', the combination of creative articulation of the strategic management process and effective employment of networks. Figure 7.3 presents the final revision of our nexus model.

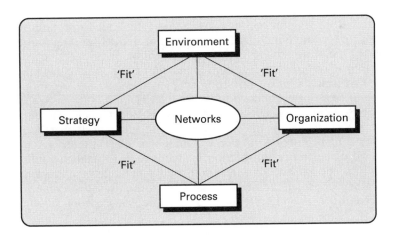

Figure 7.3 *Balanced solutions: markets, hierarchies and networks*

The concept of balanced solutions fundamentally addresses the challenge of securing equilibrium in the environment–strategy–organization nexus. It describes what appears to be happening in strategic management and, given the caveats mentioned above, is prescriptive in nature. We have not shied away from saying what firms *should* do to survive in competitive and discontinuous environments; rather, we have drawn attention to the organizational limitations and inertias which prevent them seeking, let alone attaining, optimal solutions. Our final comments relate to this latter point. There is a growing awareness that if a strategy cannot be marketed internally it will have little chance in the marketplace. The concept of 'internal marketing' has emerged to address this issue and, in the final section, we briefly evaluate its potential as an aid to securing organizational advantage.

Internal marketing

In understanding the factors driving the provision of superior customer satisfaction many insights can be drawn from the services management literature, among the most important being the notion of internal marketing (e.g. Berry, 1981; George, 1984, 1986, 1990; George and Gronroos, 1989; Gronroos, 1981a, 1981b). The concept is operationalized as an approach to business which, as George (1990) notes, 'focuses on achieving effective internal exchanges between the organization and its employee groups as a prerequisite for successful exchanges with external markets.'

A pilot study on internal marketing carried out by Collins and Payne (1991) suggests that formal internal marketing rarely exists. Some of their findings include: (a) internal marketing is generally not a discrete activity – it is implicit in quality initiatives, customer service programmes and broader business strategies; (b) where it exists, internal marketing comprises formal structured activities accompanied by a range of less formal ad hoc initiatives; (c) communication is critical to internal marketing success; (d) internal marketing performs a critical role in competitive differentiation; (e) internal marketing performs an important role in reducing interfunctional conflict; (f) internal marketing is evolutionary, involving the slow erosion of interfunctional barriers.

Internal marketing underpins shared values, a 'soft' concept which permeates much writing on strategic management and organizational behaviour. An important role of internal marketing is to ensure that all employees, but especially those who have regular contact with customers, believe in the company's products and that they are motivated to promote a favourable image of the company. Achieving this level of customer satisfaction, in turn, requires considerable effort and it must be led and underpinned by top management commitment. In this sense, effective internal marketing requires the creation of a 'service culture' throughout the organization. As Gronroos (1990) notes:

> the task of developing and maintaining a service culture and of internal marketing offers an important interface between marketing and organiza-

tional behaviour. Hence, they also offer an arena where marketing practitioners and academics on the one hand, and personnel and human resources development people and academics from the field of organizational behaviour on the other hand, are challenged to work together.

Here Gronroos is underlining the importance of cross-functional integration in the traditional marketing philosophy sense of 'everybody does marketing'. A growing body of evidence is demonstrating that such an approach is among the most effective and sustainable sources of competitive advantage (e.g. Pascale, 1990; Porter, 1990). A recurrent theme of this book has been that the lofty ideal of 'customer first' often breaks down on the failure of organizations to reconfigure their processes to achieve this apparently simple goal. Despite this, many companies are genuinely striving to seek organizational advantage based on a sharper market focus (Slywotzky and Shapiro, 1993). Our final critique is levelled at academics and consultants who have missed this latter point.

Concluding remarks

The previous quote from Gronroos was obviously directed at the commercial organization. But she is also drawing attention to the need for researchers to leave their disciplinary functional silos and engage in collaborative work. Most business schools are structured into departments which closely mirror the functional structures of traditional organizations. Academics and managers must realize that, in discontinuity, sustainable competitive advantage arises in organizational advantage and that this, in turn, requires challenging orthodox thinking on strategic management, particularly its pseudo-scientific claims. As the sociologist Antony Giddens (1977) has argued, 'daunting though the intellectual and practical problems facing us in the late twentieth century may be, it is surely indisputable that they are above all organizational and institutional in character.'

That change is with us, and is discontinuous, and is rapid, is beyond doubt (Drucker, 1969; Ansoff and McDonnell, 1990; Kanter, 1991; Crozier, 1991). Perhaps academic researchers – like Darwin before them – should leave their conceptual baggage behind and return to the field to observe this extraordinary turbulence. Strategic management practice is in the ascendancy; it cannot afford to be weighed down by theoretical constraint or consultants' baubles.

References

Achrol, R. S. (1991), 'Evolution of the marketing organization: new forms for turbulent environments', *Journal of Marketing*, October, 55, 4, 77–93

Anderson, P. F. (1982), 'Marketing, strategic planning and the theory of the firm', *Journal of Marketing*, Spring, 15–26

Andrews, K. R. (1991), 'The concept of corporate strategy', in Mintzberg, H. and Quinn, J. B. (eds), *The Strategy Process: Concepts, Contexts, Cases*, Englewood Cliffs, NJ: Prentice Hall

Ansoff, H. I. (1965), *Corporate Strategy*, Harmondsworth: Penguin

Ansoff, H. I. (1979), *Strategic Management*, London: Macmillan

Ansoff, H. I. (1987), *Corporate Strategy* (2nd Edition), Harmondsworth: Penguin

Ansoff, H. I. and McDonnell, E. (1990), *Implanting Strategic Management* (2nd Edition), Englewood Cliffs, NJ: Prentice Hall

Argyris, C. (1957), *Personality and Organisation*, New York: Harper and Bros

Argyris, C. (1964), *Integrating the Individual and the Organisation*, New York: Wiley

Argyris, C. (1985), *Strategy, Change and Defensive Routines*, London: Pitman

Argyris, C. (1994), 'Good communication that blocks learning', *Harvard Business Review*, July–August, 77–85

Aspinwall, L. (1967), 'The characteristics of goods and parallel systems theories', in Mallen, B. E. (ed.), *The Marketing Channel: A Conceptual Viewpoint*, London: John Wiley

Bartlett, C. A. and Ghoshal, S. (1989), *Managing Across Borders*, Boston, MA: Harvard Business School Press

Beer, M., Eisenhart, R. A. and Spector, B. (1990), 'Why change programs don't produce change', *Harvard Business Review*, November–December, 68, 6, 158–166

Berle, A. A. and Means, G. C. (1967), *The Modern Corporation and Private Property* (originally published in 1932), New York: Harvest

Berry, L. L. (1981), 'The employee as consumer', *Journal of Retail Banking*, March, 33–40

Bettis, R. A. and Donaldson, L. (1990), 'Market discipline and the discipline of the market', *Academy of Management Review*, 15, 3, 367–368

Bhasin, A. and Stern, L. W. (1982), 'Vertical integration: considerations of efficiency, risk and strategy', in Harvey, M. G. and Lusch, R. F. (eds), *Marketing Channels: Domestic and International Perspectives*, Norman Okla: University of Oklahoma Printing Services

Bleeke, J. and Ernst, D. (1991), 'The way to win in cross-border alliances', *Harvard Business Review*, November–December, 127–135

Bleeke, J. and Ernst, D. (1993), 'The death of the predator', in Bleeke, J. and Ernst, D. (eds), *Collaborating to Compete: Using Strategic Alliances and Acquisitions in the Global Market Place*, New York: Wiley

Borys, B. and Jemison, D. B. (1989), 'Hybrid arrangements as strategic alliances: theoretical issues in organisational combinations', *Academy of Management Review*, 14, 234–249

Boston Consulting Group (1975), *Strategy Alternatives for the British Motorcycle Industry*, London: HMSO

Britton, S. (1990), 'Conditions of Progress', *Financial Times*, March 23

Brown, R. (1993), *Market Focus: Achieving and Sustaining Marketing Effectiveness*, Oxford: Butterworth-Heinemann

Burns, T. and Stalker, G. M. (1961), *The Management of Innovation*, London: Tavistock

Buzzell, R. D. (1983), 'Is vertical integration profitable?', *Harvard Business Review*, 61, January–February, 92–102

Cammish, R. and Keough, M. (1991), 'A strategic role for purchasing', *The McKinsey Quarterly*, 3, 22–39

Carlzon, J. (1987), *Moments of Truth*, New York: Ballinger Press

Champy, J. (1994), 'Time to re-engineer the manager', *Financial Times*, 14 January

Chandler, A. E., Jr, (1962), *Strategy and Structure: Chapters in the History of the American Industrial Enterprise*, Cambridge, Mass: MIT Press

Christopher, M. (1992), *Logistics and Supply Chain Management: Strategies for Reducing Costs and Improving Services*, London: Pitman.

Clarke, C. J. (1987), 'Acquisitions – techniques for measuring strategic fit', *Long Range Planning*, 20, 3, 12–18

Clarke, C. J. and Gall, F. (1987), 'Planned divestment – a five-step approach', *Long Range Planning*, 20, 1, 17–24

Clutterbuck, D. and Crainer, S. (1990), *Makers of Management: Men and Women Who Changed the Business World*, London: Guild Publishing

Collins, B. and Payne, A. (1991), 'Internal marketing: a perspective for HRM', *European Management Journal*, 9, 3, 261–271

Contractor, F. and Lorange, P. (eds), (1988), *Cooperative Strategies in International Business*, Lexington, MA: Lexington Books

Coyne, J. and Wright, M. (1985), 'An introduction to divestment: the conceptual issues', in Coyne, J. and Wright, M. (eds), *Divestment and Strategic Change*, London: Philip Allen

Crook, C. (ed.), (1991), 'Survey of the IMF and the World Bank', *The Economist*, 12 October

Crozier, M. (1991), 'The boundaries of business: the changing organisation, *Harvard Business Review*, July–August, 138–140

Cunningham, N. T. and Culligan K. (1991), 'Competitiveness through networks of relationships in information technology product markets', in Paliwoda, S. J. (ed.), *New Perspectives on International Marketing*, London: Routledge

Cyert, R. M. and March, J. G. (1963), *A Behavioural Theory of the Firm*, Englewood Cliffs, NJ: Prentice Hall

Daniel, J. D. (1991), 'Relevance in international business research: a need for more linkages', *Journal of International Business*, 2nd Quarter

Davis, S. M. and Lawrence, P. R. (1977), *Matrix*, Reading, MA: Addison-Wesley

Day, G. (1990), *Market Driven Strategy: Processes for Creating Value*, New York: The Free Press

Dichter, S. F. (1991), 'The organisation of the '90s', *The McKinsey Quarterly*, 1, 145–155

Doyle, P. (1992), 'What are the excellent companies?', *Journal of Marketing Management*, 8, 2, 101–116

Doyle, P. (1993), *Marketing Management and Strategy*, London: Prentice-Hall

Doz, Y. (1988), 'Value creation through technology collaboration', *Aussenwirtschaft*, 43, 175–90

Doz, Y. (1992), 'The role of partnerships and alliances in the European industrial restructuring', in Cool, K., Neven, D. J. and Walter, I. (eds), *European Industrial Restructuring in the 1990s*, London: Macmillan

Drucker, P. (1954), *The Practice of Management*, New York: Harper & Row

Drucker, P. (1969), *The Age of Discontinuity*, London: Harper & Row

Drucker, P. (1974), *Management: Tasks, Responsibilities, Practices*, London: Heinemann Professional Publishing

Dyson, R. (1990), *Strategic Planning: Models and Analytical Techniques*, Chichester: Wiley

Egan, C. and Guilding, C. (1994), 'The dimensions of brand performance: challenges for marketing management and managerial accountancy', *Journal of Marketing Management*, 10, 449–472

Egan, C. and McKiernan, P. (1994), *Inside Fortress Europe: Strategies for the Single Market*, Wokingham: Addison-Wesley

Emmot, B. (1993), 'Holding hands – enemies, friends: who can tell the difference?', *The Economist*, March 27

Faulkner, D. (1992), 'The Rover–Honda alliance – case and instructor's note', in Johnson, G. and Scholes, K., *Corporate Strategy*, Hemel Hempstead: Prentice-Hall

Forsgren, M. (1989), *Managing the Internationalisation Process: a Swedish Case*, London: Routledge

Forsgren, M. and Johanson, J. (1975), *International foretagsekonomi*, Stockholm: Norstedts

Forstrom, B. (1991), 'Competitive distribution networks: the Finnish magazine industry in the UK', in Paliwoda, S. J. (ed.), *Perspectives on International Marketing*, London: Routledge

Fukuyama, F. (1992), *The End of History and the Last Man*, London: Hamish Hamilton

Galbraith, J. K. (1967), 'The concept of countervailing power', in Mallen, B. E. (ed.), *The Marketing Channel: A Conceptual Viewpoint*, New York: Wiley

Galbraith, J. K. (1994), *The World Economy Between the Wars*, London: Sinclair Stevenson

Galliers, R. D. (1995), 'The place of information technology and radical/incremental organizational change in business process redesign', in Grover, V. and Kettinger, W.J. (eds), *Business Process Re-engineering: A Managerial Perspective*, London: Idea Publishing

Garvin, D. (1993), 'Building a learning organization', *Harvard Business Review*, July–August, 78–91

George, W. R. (1984), 'Internal marketing for retailers: the junior executive employee' in 'Developments in marketing science', *Academy of Marketing Science*, VII, 322–325

George, W. R. (1986), 'Internal communications programs as a mechanism for doing internal marketing', in Venkatesan, M. (ed.), *Creativity in Services Marketing*, Chicago: American Marketing Association

George, W. R. (1990), 'Internal marketing and organisational behaviour: a partnership in developing customer-conscious employees at every level', *Journal of Business Research*, 20, 63–70

George, W. R. and Gronroos, C. (1989), 'Developing customer-conscious employees at every level – internal marketing', in Congram, C. A. and Friedman, M. L., (eds), *Handbook of Services Marketing*, New York: AMACOM

Giddens, A. (1977), *Social Theory and Modern Sociology*, Cambridge: Polity Press

Giddens, A. (1984), *The Constitution of Society*, Cambridge: Polity Press

Gleick, J. (1988), *Chaos: Making a New Science*, London: Cardinal McDonald & Co

Greiner, L. E. (1989), 'Evolution and revolution as organisations grow', in Asch, D. and Bowman, C. (eds), *Readings in Strategic Management*, London: Macmillan

Grinyer, P. H., Mayes, D. and McKiernan, P. (1988), *Sharpbenders: The Secrets of Unleashing Corporate Potential*, Oxford: Blackwell

Grinyer, P. H. and Spender, J.-C. (1979), 'Recipes, crises and adaptation in mature business', *International Studies of Management and Organization*, IX, 3, 113–133

Gronroos, C. (1981a), 'Internal marketing – an integral part of marketing theory', in Donelly, J. M. and George, W. R., *Marketing of Services*, Chicago: American Marketing Association

Gronroos, C. (1981b), 'Internal marketing – theory and practice', in Bloch, T. M. (ed.), *Services Marketing in a Changing Environment*, Chicago: American Marketing Association

Gronroos, C. (1990), 'Relationship approach to marketing in service contexts: the marketing and organisational interface', *Journal of Business Research*, 20, 3–11

Hakansson, H. (1982), *International Marketing and Purchasing of Industrial Goods: an Interaction Approach*, London: Wiley

Hallen, L., Johanson, J. and Seyed Mohammed, N. (1987), 'Relationship strength and stability in international and domestic industrial marketing', *Industrial Marketing and Purchasing*, 2, 3, 22–37

Hambrick, D. C. and D'Aveni, R. A. (1988), 'Large corporate failures as downward spirals', *Administrative Science Quarterly*, 33, March, 1–23

Hamel, G., Doz, Y. and Prahalad, C. K. (1989), 'Collaborate with your competitors – and win', *Harvard Business Review*, January–February

Hamel, G. and Prahalad, C. K. (1989), 'Strategic intent', *Harvard Business Review*, May–June, 63–76

Hamel, G. and Prahalad, C. K. (1993), 'Strategy as stretch and leverage', *Harvard Business Review*, March–April, 75–84

Hamel, G. and Prahalad, C. K. (1994), *Competing for the Future*, Boston, MA: Harvard Business School Press

Hammer, M. (1990), 'Re-engineering work: don't automate, obliterate', *Harvard Business Review*, July–August, 104–113

Hammer, M. and Champy, J. (1993), *Re-engineering the Corporation: A Manifesto for Business Revolution*, London: Nicholas Brealey Publishing

Handy, C. (1989), *The Age of Unreason*, London: Business Books Limited

Handy, C. (1993), *Understanding Organisations* (4th Edition), Harmondsworth: Penguin

Handy, C. (1994), *The Empty Raincoat: Making Sense of the Future*, London: Hutchinson

Harrigan, K. R. and Porter, M. E. (1983), 'End-game strategies for declining industries', *Harvard Business Review*, July–August, 111–120

Harris, T. G. (1993), 'The post-capitalist executive: an interview with Peter F. Drucker', *Harvard Business Review*, May–June, 114–122

Haskel, J. and Kay, J. (1990), quoted in Britton, S. 'Conditions of progress', *Financial Times*, March 23

Hendry, C. and Pettigrew, A. (1992), 'Patterns of strategic change in the development of human resource management', *British Journal of Management*, 3, 3, 137–156

Hergert, M. and Morris, D. (1988), 'Trends in international collaborative agreements', in Contractor, F. and Lorange, P. (eds), *Cooperative Strategies in International Business*, Lexington, MA: Lexington Books

Heygate, R., (1992), 'Accelerating front-line change', *The McKinsey Quarterly*, 1, 134–147

Hill, T. (1985), *Manufacturing Strategy: The Strategic Management of the Manufacturing Function*, London: Macmillan

Hinterhuber, H. H. and Popp, W. (1992), 'Are you a strategist or just a manager', *Harvard Business Review*, January–February, 105–113

Hooley, G. and Saunders, J. (1993), *Competitive Positioning: The Key to Market Strategy*, Hemel Hempstead: Prentice-Hall

Hurst, D. K., Rush, J. C. and White, R. E. (1989), 'Top Management Teams and Organisational Renewal' in Henry, J. (ed.), (1991), *Creative Management*, London: Sage

Hutt, M. D. and Speh, T. W. (1988), *Business Marketing Management: A Strategic View of Industrial and Organisational Markets*, New York: The Dryden Press

James, B. G. (1985), *Business Wargames*, Harmondsworth: Penguin

Jarillo, J. C. (1988), 'On strategic networks', *Strategic Management Journal*, No 19

Johansson, H. J., McHugh, P., Pendlebury, A. J. and Wheeler III, W.A. (1993), *Business Process Re-engineering: Breakpoint Strategies for Market Dominance*, Chichester: Wiley

Johanson, J. and Mattsson, L. G. (1987), 'Interorganisational relations in industrial systems: a network approach compared with the transaction cost approach', *International Studies of Management and Organisation*, 17, 185–195

Johanson, J. and Vahlne, J. (1977), 'The internationalisation process of the firm: a model of knowledge development on increasing foreign commitments', *Journal of International Business Studies*, Spring–Summer, 23–32

Johanson, J. and Wiedersheim-Paul, F. (1975), 'The internationalisation of the firm: four Swedish case studies', *Journal of Management Studies*, October, 305–322

Johnson, G. (1988a), 'Processes of managing strategic change', in Mabey, C. and Mayon-White (eds) (1993), *Managing Change* (2nd Edition), London: Paul Chapman Publishing/Open University

Johnson, G. (1988b), 'Rethinking incrementalism', *Strategic Management Journal*, 9, 73–91

Johnson, G. and Scholes, K. (1993), *Exploring Corporate Strategy*, London: Prentice-Hall

Jones, A. M. and Hendry, C. (1994), 'The learning organisation: adult learning and organisational transformation', *British Journal of Management*, 5, 153–162

Jones, D. (ed.), (1993), *The Lean Enterprise Benchmarking Project*, London: Anderson Consulting

Jones, K. J. (1992), 'Competing to learn in Japan', *The McKinsey Quarterly*, 1, 45–57

Kanter, R. M. (1983), *The Changemasters: Corporate Entrepreneurs at Work*, London: Unwin

Kanter, R. M. (1989), *When Giants Learn to Dance: Mastering the Challenges of Strategy, Management and Careers in the 1990s*, London: Unwin

Kanter, R. M. (1991), 'Transcending business boundaries: 1200 managers view world change', *Harvard Business Review*, May–June, 151–164

Kanter, R. M. (1994), 'Collaborative advantage: the art of alliances', *Harvard Business Review*, July–August, 96–108

Kanter, R. M., Stein, B. A. and Jick, T. D. (1992), *The Challenge of Organisational Change: How Companies Experience it and Leaders Guide it*, New York: Free Press

Kaplan, R. S. and Norton, D. P. (1993), 'Putting the balanced scorecard to work', *Harvard Business Review*, September–October, 134–147

Kastens (1973), 'Diversification strategies', *Long Range Planning*, 6, 3 June, 34–47

Kay, J. (1993a), *Foundations of Corporate Success: How Business Strategies Add Value*, Oxford: Oxford University Press

Kay, J. (1993b), 'Art or science? – can the study of management be "scientific"?', *The Economist*, April 24

Kehoe, L (1993), 'Rebels turned diplomats', *Financial Times*, 8 February

Keith, R. J. (1960), 'The marketing revolution', *Journal of Marketing*, January, 35–38

King, N. (1992), 'Improving the quality of working life through communications', *International Journal of Quality and Reliability Management*, 9, 5, 51–58

Kotler, P. (1991), *Marketing Management: Analysis, Planning, Implementation and Control*, Englewood Cliffs, NJ: Prentice-Hall

Lambert, E. W. Jr, (1966), 'Financial considerations in choosing a marketing channel', *MSU Business Topics*, Winter, 17–26

Lawler, E. E. (1992), *The Ultimate Advantage: Creating the High Involvement Organisation*, New York: Maxwell Macmillan

Lawrence, P. R. and Lorsch, J. W. (1967), *Organisation and Environment: Managing Differentiation and Integration*, Homewood, Ill: Irwin

Leavey, B. and Wilson, D. (1994), *Strategy and Leadership*, London: Routledge

Levitt, B. and March, J. G. (1988), 'Organisational learning', *Annual Review of Sociology*, 14, 319–340

Levitt, T. (1960), 'Marketing myopia', *Harvard Business Review*, July–August, 45–56

Lilien, G.L. (1979), 'ADVISOR2: Modelling the marketing mix decision for industrial products', *Management Science*, 25, February, 79–98

Lorange, P. and Roos, J. (1992), *Strategic Alliances: Formulation, Implementation and Evolution*, Oxford: Blackwell

Lorenz, C. (1990), 'The trouble with the "networked" company', *Financial Times*, 22 May

Lorenz, C. (1992), 'Changing corporate cultures: power to the people', *Financial Times*, 30 March

Lorenz, C. (1993a), 'Stepping out in a new direction', *Financial Times*, 24 May

Lorenz, C. (1993b), 'The uphill battle against change', *Financial Times*, 18 June

Lorenz, C. (1993c), 'Time to get serious', *Financial Times*, 25 June

Lorenz, C (1993d), 'Sculptors in jelly', *Financial Times*, 28 July

Mallen, B. E. (1973), 'Functional spin-off: a key to anticipating change in distribution structure', *Journal of Marketing*, 37, July, 18–25

March, J. G. and Simon, H. A. (1958), *Organizations*, New York: Wiley

March, J. G. and Simon, H. A. (1992), *Organizations* (2nd Edition), Cambridge, MA: Blackwell Business

Mattsson, L. G. (1986), 'Indirect relations in industrial networks: a conceptual analysis of their strategic significance', cited in Cunningham, N. T. and Culligan, K. (1991), 'Competitiveness through networks of relationships in information technology product markets', in Paliwoda, S. J. (ed.), *New Perspectives on International Marketing*, London: Routledge

McKenna, R. (1991), 'Marketing is everything', *Harvard Business Review*, January–February, 65–79

McKiernan, P. (1992), *Strategies of Growth: Maturity, Recovery and Internationalisation*, London: Routledge

Meyerson, D. and Martin, J. (1987), 'Cultural change: an integration of three different views', *Journal of Management Studies*, 24, 623–647

Michaels, A. (1993a), 'Taking it from the top', *Financial Times*, 5 July

Michaels, A. (1993b), 'Culture vultures', *Financial Times*, 23 July

Miles, R. E. and Snow, C. L. (1978), *Organisational Strategy, Structure and Process*, New York: McGraw-Hill

Miles, R. E. and Snow, C. C. (1984), 'Organisational fit', *California Management Review*, 26, 3, 10–28

Miles, R. E. and Snow, C. C. (1986), 'Organisations: new concepts for new forms', *California Management Review*, 28, 62–73

Miller, D. (1989), 'Configuration of strategy and structure: towards a synthesis', in Asch, D. and Bowman, C. (eds), *Readings in Strategic Management*, London: Macmillan

Miller, D. C. and Freisen, P. H. (1984), *Organisations: A Quantum View*, Englewood Cliffs, NJ: Prentice-Hall

Mintzberg, H. (1979), *The Structuring of Organisations*, Englewood Cliffs, NJ: Prentice-Hall

Mintzberg, H. (1987), 'Crafting strategy', *Harvard Business Review*, July–August, 66–75

Mintzberg, H. (1988), 'Generic strategies, toward a comprehensive framework', *Advances in Strategic Management*, 5, 1–67, Greenwich, CT: JAI Press

Mintzberg, H. (1991), 'Beyond configuration: forces and forms in effective organisations', in Mintzberg, H. and Quinn, J. B. (eds), *The Strategy Process: Concepts, Contexts, Cases*, Englewood Cliffs, NJ: Prentice-Hall

Mintzberg, H. (1994), *The Rise and Fall of Strategic Planning*, Hemel Hempstead: Prentice-Hall

Mintzberg, H. and Quinn, J. B. (eds) (1991), *The Strategy Process: Concepts, Contexts, Cases*, Englewood Cliffs, NJ: Prentice-Hall

Mitchell Waldrop, M. (1992), *Complexity: The Emerging Science at the Edge of Order and Chaos*, Harmondsworth: Penguin

Morgan, G. (1986), *Images of Organisation*, California: Sage

Morgan, G. (1990). *Organizations in Society*, London: Macmillan

Narver, J. C. and Slater, S. F. (1990), 'The effect of a market orientation on business profitability', *Journal of Marketing*, 54, October, 20–35

Nonaka, I. (1991), 'The knowledge creating company', *Harvard Business Review*, November–December, 96–104

Normann, R. and Ramirez, R. (1993), 'From value chain to value constellation: designing interactive strategy', *Harvard Business Review*, July–August, 65–77

O'Neal, C. R. (1987), 'The buyer–seller linkage in a Just-In-Time environment', *Journal of Purchasing and Materials Management*, 23, Spring, 7–13

O'Neal, C. R. (1989), 'JIT procurement and relationship marketing', *Industrial Marketing Management*, 18, 1, 55–64

O'Sullivan, L. and Geringer, J.M. (1993), 'Harnessing the power of your valve chain', *Long Range Planning*, 26, 2, 59–69

Oakland, J. S. (1989), *Total Quality Management*, Oxford: Butterworth-Heinemann

Ohmae, K. (1982), *The Mind of the Strategist*, Harmondsworth: Penguin

Ohmae, K. (1989), 'The global logic of strategic alliances', *Harvard Business Review*, March–April

Oliver, J. (1993), 'Shocking to the core', *Management Today*, August, 18–22

Oliver, N. and Wilkinson, B. (1992), *The Japanization of British Industry: New Developments in the 1990s*, Oxford: Blackwell

Olson, P. D. and Terpstra, D. E. (1992), 'Organisational structural changes: life-cycle stage influences and managers' and interventionists' challenges', *Journal of Organisational Change Management*, 5, 4, 27–40

Pascale, R. T. (1984), 'Perspectives on strategy: the real story behind Honda's success', *California Management Review*, 26, 3, 47–72

Pascale, R. T. (1990), *Managing on the Edge: How Successful Companies Use Conflict to Stay Ahead*, London: Viking

Perlmutter, H. V. and Heenan, D. A. (1986), 'Cooperate to compete globally', *Harvard Business Review*, March–April

Perrow, C. (1967), *Organisational Analysis: A Sociological View*, London: Tavistock

Peters, T. J. (1984), 'Strategy follows structure: developing distinctive skills', *California Management Review*, Spring

Peters, T. J. (1987), *Thriving on Chaos: Handbook for Management Revolution*, London: Pan Books

Peters, T. J. and Waterman, R. H. (1982), *In Search of Excellence*, New York: Harper and Row

Pettigrew, A. M. (1977), 'Strategy formulation as a political process', *International Studies of Management and Organization*, 7, 2, 78–87

Pettigrew, A. (1985), *The Awakening Giant: Continuity and Change in ICI*, Oxford: Blackwell

Pettigrew, A. (1990), 'Longitudinal field research on change: theory and practice', *Organisation Science*, 1, 3, 267–92

Pettigrew, A. and Whipp, R. (1993), *Managing Change for Competitive Success*, Oxford: Blackwell

Pfeffer, J. (1976), 'Beyond management and the worker: the institutional function of management', *Academy of Management Review*, April, 79–98

Pfeffer, J. (1978), *Organisational Design*, Arlington Heights, Ill: AHM

Pine II, B.J., Victor, B. and Boynton, A.C. (1993), 'Making mass customization work', *Harvard Business Review*, September–October, 108–119

Pondy, L. R. (1967), 'Organisational conflict: concepts and models', *Administrative Science Quarterly*, 12, 2, 296–320

Porter, M. E. (1980), *Competitive Strategy: Techniques for Analyzing Industries and Competitors*, New York: The Free Press

Porter, M. E. (1985), *Competitive Advantage: Creating and Sustaining Superior Performance*, New York: The Free Press

Porter, M. E. (1987), 'From competitive advantage to corporate strategy', *Harvard Business Review*, May–June, 3, 43–59

Porter, M. E. (1990), *The Competitive Advantage of Nations*, London: Macmillan

Porter, M. E. and Fuller, S. (1986), *Conditions and Global Strategy*, in Porter, M.E. (ed.), *Competition in Global Industries*, Boston, MA: Harvard Business School Press

Powers, T. L. (1989), 'Industrial distribution options: trade-offs to consider', *Industrial Marketing Management*, 18, 3, 155–162

Prahalad, C. K. and Hamel, G. (1990), 'The core competencies of the corporation', *Harvard Business Review*, May–June, 79–91

Preston, J. (1993), *International Business: Text and Cases*, London: Pitman

Quinn, J. B. (1978), 'Strategic change: logical incrementalism', *Sloan Management Review*, 20, Fall, 7–21

Quinn, J. B. (1980a), *Strategies for Change: Logical Incrementalism*, Homewood, Ill: Richard D. Irwin

Quinn, J. B. (1980b), 'Managing strategic change', *Sloan Management Review*, 21, 4, 3–20

Reed, M. (1985), *Redirections in Organisational Analysis*, London: Tavistock

Roll, E. (1992), *A History of Economic Thought* (5th Edition), London: Faber and Faber

Root, F. R. (1987), *Entry Strategies for International Markets*, Lexington, MA: Lexington Books

Rosenbloom, R. (1987), *Marketing Channels: A Management View*, Hinsdale Il: The Dryden Press

Rumelt, R. (1991), 'The evaluation of business strategy', in Mintzberg, H. and Quinn, J. B. (eds), *The Strategy Process: Concepts, Contexts, Cases*, Englewood Cliffs, NJ: Prentice-Hall

Schnitzer, M. C. (1994), *Competitive Economic Systems* (6th Edition), Cincinatti, Ohio: South-Western Publishing Co

Senge, P. M. (1990), *The Fifth Discipline: The Art and Practice of the Learning Organisation*, New York: Doubleday

Shipley, D. and Egan, C. (1992), 'Power, conflict and co-operation in brewer–tenant distribution channels', *International Journal of Service Industry Management*, 3, 4, 44–62

Slack, N. (1991), *The Manufacturing Advantage: Achieving Competitive Manufacturing Operations*, London: Mercury

Slywotzky, A. J. and Shapiro, B. P. (1993), 'Leveraging to beat the odds: the new marking mindset', *Harvard Business Review*, September–October, 97–107

Smith, A. (1776), *The Wealth of Nations*, Harmondsworth: Penguin

Smith, S., Tranfield, D., Foster, M. and Whittle, S. (1994), 'Strategies for managing the TQ agenda', *International Journal of Production and Operations Management*, 14, 1, 75–88

Stacey, R. D. (1993), *Strategic Management and Organisational Dynamics*, London: Pitman

Stalk, G., Jr, (1988), 'Time – the next source of competitive advantage', *Harvard Business Review*, July–August, 41–51

Stalk, G., Evans, P. and Shulman, L. E. (1992), 'Competing on capabilities: the new rules of corporate strategy', *Harvard Business Review*, March–April, 57–69

Stern, L. W. and El-Ansary, A. J. (1988), *Marketing Channels*, Englewood Cliffs, NJ: Prentice-Hall

Stewart, I. (1989), *Does God Play Dice? – The New Mathematics of Chaos*, Harmondsworth: Penguin

Taylor, W. (1991), 'The logic of global business: an interview with ABB's Percy Barnevik', *Harvard Business Review*, March–April, 91–105

Thackray, J. (1993), 'Fads, fixes and fictions', *Management Today*, June, 40

The Economist (1991a), 'Economics Focus: the wolf at the door', 3 August

The Economist (1991b), 'It's in the mail: Dell Computer marketing', 2 March

The Economist (1991c), 'Spare the rod and spoil the child: Pampered by governments and protected from the full discipline of the market, Europe's indigenous computer makers are in a mess. It is time they grew up', 20 April

The Economist (1992a), 'Sorting out Russia: World Bank/IMF', 26 September

The Economist (1992b), 'Silicon Valley's revenge: Japan's computer makers are facing a hard time at home as foreign companies hit their market with snazzier products', 17 October

The Economist (1992c), 'Toy joy: Retailing in Japan', 4 January

The Economist (1992d), 'Europe's insurers stride out: Corner-shop insurance is giving ground to supermarkets and telesales, as insurers look for ways to cut distribution costs', 2 February

The Economist (1992e), 'An American tragedy/The Rise and Fall of Wang Labs', 22 August

The Economist (1992f), 'The Elusive Euro-manager', 7 November

The Economist (1992g), 'The lure of leisure', 2 May

The Economist (1994), 'Re-engineering reviewed', 2 July, 80

Thorelli, H. B. (1986), 'Networks: between markets and hierarchies', *Strategic Management Journal*, 7, 37–51

Tushman, M. L., Newman, W. H. and Romanelli, E. (1986), 'Convergence and upheaval: managing the unsteady pace of organisational evolution', *California Management Review*, Fall

Van de Ven, A. H. (1988), 'Control problems in the management of innovation' in Tushman, M. L. and Moore, W. L. (eds), *Readings in the Management of Innovation*, New York: Ballinger

Vanderbroeck, P. (1992), 'Long-term human resource deployment in multinational organisations', *Sloan Management Review*, Fall

Vandermerwe, S. (1993), *From Tin Soldiers to Russian Dolls: Creating added value through services*, Oxford: Butterworth-Heinemann

Vicere, A. A. (1991), 'The changing paradigm for executive development', *Journal of Management Development*, 10, 3, 44–47

Whittington, R. (1993), *What is Strategy – and does it matter?*, London: Routledge

Wikstrom, S. and Normann, R. (1994), *Knowledge and Value: a new perspective on corporate transformation*, London: Routledge

Williamson, O. E. (1975), *Markets and Hierarchies: Analysis and Antitrust Implications*, New York: The Free Press

Williamson, O. E. (1985), *The Economic Institutions of Capitalism*, New York: The Free Press

Wilson, D. C. (1992), *A Strategy of Change: Concepts and Controversies in the Management of Change*, London: Routledge

Wilson, D. C. and Rosenfeld, R. H. (1990), *Managing Organisations*, Maidenhead: McGraw-Hill

Womack, J. P., Jones, D. T. and Roos, D. (1990), *The Machine That Changed the World*, New York: Rawson Associates

Woodcock, A. and Davis, M. (1978), *Catastrophe Theory: A Revolutionary New Way of Understanding How Things Change*, Harmondsworth: Penguin

Woodward, J. (1965), *Industrial Organisation: Theory and Practice*, Oxford: Oxford University Press

Index